Smuggling of Migrants by Sea

I would like to dedicate my book to my mum
for her support and positive attitude
which made me successfully complete this book

SMUGGLING OF MIGRANTS BY SEA

EU Legal Framework and Future Perspective

MATILDE VENTRELLA

Senior Lecturer in Law, Liverpool John Moores University.

SMUGGLING OF MIGRANTS BY SEA: EU LEGAL FRAMEWORK AND FUTURE PERSPECTIVE

Matilde Ventrella

Published by:

Vandeplas Publishing, LLC – October 2018

801 International Parkway, 5th Floor
Lake Mary, FL. 32746
USA

www.vandeplaspublishing.com

ISBN 978-1-60042-300-0

Table of content

CHAPTER 3: EU SHORT-TERM LEGAL MEASURES AGAINST SMUGGLING OF MIGRANTS AND HUMAN TRAFFICKING

CHAPTER 4: EUROPOL, EUROJUST AND THE EUROPEAN PUBLIC PROSECUTOR ROLES' IN THE FIGHT AGAINST SMUGGLING OF MIGRANTS AND HUMAN TRAFFICKING

TABLE OF ABBREVIATIONS

ACHPR	African Commission of Human and People's Rights
ACP	African, Caribbean and Pacific Group of States
AFIC	Frontex Intelligence Community
AFSJ	Area of Freedom Security and Justice
AQIM	Al-Qaida in Maghreb
AU	African Union
AUBP	African Union Border Programme
CEPOL	European Union Agency for Law Enforcement Training
CJEU	Court of Justice of the European Union
CFSP	Common Foreign and Security Policy
CSDP	Common Security and Defence Policy
EASO	European Asylum Support Office
EAW	European Arrest Warrant
EC	European Communities
EDPP	European Director of Public Prosecution
EDelPPS	European delegated Public Prosecutors
ECHR	European Convention on Human Rights
ECOWAS	Economic Community of West African States
ECtHR	European Court of Human Rights
EEAS	European Union External Action
EJN	European Judicial Network
EMSC	European Smuggling Centre
ENP	European Neighbourhood Policy
EP	European Parliament
EPP	European Public Prosecutor
EPPO	European Public Prosecutor Office
EU	European Union
EUBAM	EU Border Assistance Mission
EUNAVFOR	European Union-led naval force
EU Op Cen	EU Operation Centre
Eurosur	European Border Surveillance System
EUTM Mali	EU-Training Mission in Mali
GNA	Government of National Accord
GRETA	Group of experts on action against trafficking in human beings
HRVP	High Representative Vice President

IBM	Integrated Border Management
IGAD	Intergovernmental Authority and Development
IOM	International Organization for Migration
JHA	Justice and Home Affairs
JITs	Joint Investigation Teams
JOT	Joined Operational team
PNR	Passenger Name Records
RAP	Sahel Regional Action Plan
SC	Security Council
TEU	Treaty of the European Union
UN	United Nations
UNCLOS	United Nations Convention on the Law of the Sea
UNCHR	United Nations Refugee Agency
UNCTOC	United Nations Convention against Transnational Organized Crime
THB	Trafficking in Human Beings
TFEU	Treaty on the Functioning of the European Union
WAPIS	West African police information system

Chapter 1: Introduction

1. Possible overlapping between smuggling of migrants and human trafficking

This book analyses the EU legal framework on smuggling of migrants committed by sea and its connections with human trafficking. The book will use the expression smuggling of migrants by sea when referring to people smuggled by criminal organisations from as far as Sub-Saharan Africa to Europe. They are migrants who leave their countries of origin or of residence to travel to Europe by the support of criminals. If they successfully reach Northern Africa, they will cross the Mediterranean Sea by the use of poor boats. Many of them will dies in the Sea and others will become victims of human trafficking.

The European Commission (Commission) has recently reported that 67% of trafficked people, can be classified as victims of human trafficking for sexual exploitation and 95% of these victims are women and girls.[1] Victims of labour exploitation concern 21% of registered victims and other forms of exploitation amount to 12% of the total of victims. The European Commission requires that global action in the EU and externally is taken against criminal organisations which commit human trafficking.[2] The European Parliament (EP) in the Report on the fight against trafficking in human beings in the EU's external relations[3] pointed that trafficking and smuggling are two different crimes because migrants have consented to be smuggled,[4] instead victims of human trafficking have not expressed any consent to the illicit activity, as they have been victims of coercion, abuse and deception. However, the Report highlighted that smuggling and trafficking can overlap because there is the risk that smugglers force

1 See COM (2017) 728 final, 4/12/2017, p. 1.

2 See COM (2017)...*op. cit.* note 1, p. 3.

3 P8_TA(2016)0300), 13/6/2016 on http://www.europarl.europa.eu/sides/getDoc.do?pubRef=-//EP//NONSGML+TA+P8-TA-2016-0300+0+DOC+PDF+V0//EN, accessed on 15/9/2016.

4 See P8_TA(2016)0300),...*op. cit.* note 3, p. 10.

migrants and refugees into exploitation and as a consequence, they become victims of human trafficking. This risk is particularly high in between unaccompanied minors and women travelling alone. Therefore, the EP emphasised that it is very important that competent authorities of EU Member States concentrate on the possible to the possible crossover between smuggling and trafficking during their investigations and law enforcement activities. The EP also stressed that trafficking and the connected crime of smuggling must be fought by enhancing police and judicial cooperation between EU Member States and third countries. The cooperation with third countries should focus on eradicating the root causes of migration, by increasing public education and by eradicating corruption of public officials. 5 Finally, the EP urges that Frontex, Europol and the European Asylum Support Office (EASO) and other officials identify victims and potential victims of trafficking and that for this purpose, they receive adequate training.

Migrants at sea are forced migrants and, thus, exploited by their smugglers and, for this reason, they should be considered presumed victims. According to Eurostat, presumed victims are those people who have met the criteria to be identified as victims on the basis of Directive 2011/36/EU but who have not been formally identified by relevant authorities or who have refused to be identified as such.[6] Migrants at sea could be considered presumed victims as, they are forced to leave their countries of origin because of extreme poverty and eventually, they are abused and exploited by smugglers. These criminals take an advantage of their conditions of extreme poverty for a financial gain, by endangering the lives of migrants in the desert and during their journeys to the EU. It has been reported that often migrants die long before they reach the Mediterranean Sea and in the Sahara. Deaths are caused by accidents or because there are breakdowns or the fuel runs out.[7] In some cases migrants are abandoned by smugglers in the desert because they fear to be arrested by authorities.[8] It is important to reiterate that smuggling and trafficking are two distinct crimes because people smuggled take the decision to trust smugglers and travel by them.[9] Therefore,

5 See P8_TA(2016)0300),...*op. cit.* note 3, p. 21.

6 See Eurostat Statistical Working Papers 'Trafficking in Human Beings', 2014 available on http://epp.eurostat.ec.europa.eu/cache/ITY_OFFPUB/KS-TC-14-008/EN/KS-TC-14-008-EN.PDF accessed on 18/10/2014.

7 See Brachet, J., 'Manufacturing Smugglers: From Irregular to Clandestine Mobility in the Sahara'. On ANNALS, AAPSS, 676, March 2018, p. 28.

8 Ibid

9 See Brachet, J.,...*op. cit.* note 7, p. 28.

the two terms of smuggling and trafficking cannot be used as synonymous as the two crimes are distinct. However, they can overlap as investigations conducted by public prosecutors from Africa to Italy have shown.[10] If from one side, the connections between smuggling and trafficking should not be used by the EU and its Member States to impose restrictions on migration. Restrictions can facilitate the smuggling of people as migrants would feel compelled 'to put themselves under the protection of "criminal networks" and pay the extra-price-financially, and in terms of their own independence-that comes with this'.[11] From the other side, it is important to investigate connections between smuggling and trafficking as smugglers can become traffickers and exploit many vulnerable people. The book argues that investigations should be undertaken in cooperation with countries of origin and transit by the EU. In the meantime, the book argues that long terms policies should be adopted as a priority to prevent people from looking for smugglers and pay for very dangerous journey in the desert and by sea and risk eventually to become victims of human trafficking. Long terms policies should be adopted by the EU in cooperation with African countries and should concentrate on addressing the root causes for migration to prevent the death of many migrants at sea.

Migrants at sea are not recognised as victims by relevant authorities of EU Member States because those authorities consider them irregular migrants with no rights of residence, apart from the right not to be collectively expelled and the right to be rescued at the sea. However, Directive 2011/36/EU (from now on Trafficking Directive)[12] does not expressly include smuggling of migrants at sea in its scope. It should be noted that the Trafficking Directive has provided a wide definition of trafficking, which includes slavery and other forms of exploitation. However, it has not provided adequate provisions for the identification and protection of victims of human trafficking. Article 11 (2) leaves wide discretion to the competent authorities of Member States by requiring them to give assistance and support to people on the basis of the 'reasonable-ground indication'. If from one side, the 'reasonable-grounds indication' criteria can permit them to identify as many victims as possible at an early stage and identification is very important, in order to grant victims the residence permit and to prevent

10 See section 3 p. 20, chapter 2 of this book.

11 See Brachet, J.,...*op. cit.* note 7, p. 29.

12 See Directive 2011/36/EU 5 April 2011. OJ L. 101/1, 15/4/2011. (Trafficking Directive)

re-victimization.[13] This is because victims would not be left in detention centers with other migrants or deported unidentified. Indeed, if they are left in detention centers, they will be at high risk of re-victimization.[14] From the other side, leaving wide discretion to Member States can lower the standard of protection of the Council of Europe Trafficking Convention.[15] This is because the Trafficking Directive does not establish a specific procedure that can permit the identification of victims and prevent their immediate deportation on the basis of the reasonable grounds to believe that they could be victims of trafficking rather than only irregular migrants that should be deported.[16] The specific procedure is left entirely to the discretion of EU Member States. Some of them may apply legislation aimed to identify as many victims of human trafficking as possible, other Member States may decide to give a strict interpretation to the Trafficking Directive and as a result they can leave many victims unidentified. There is also a factor to consider. Migrants at sea who travel from as far as the Sub-Saharan Africa are vulnerable and they are potential victims of exploitation because of their status of vulnerability.

2. POSITION OF VULNERABILITY

Smuggled migrants who cannot claim asylum can be in a position of vulnerability. According to the International Organization for Migration (IOM), migrants can be in a position of vulnerability because they are in a diminished capacity of ensuring their rights are respected and they have difficulties to deal with exploitation and abuses.[17] There are migrants who may be escaping severe food insecurity, conflicts and people who may become victims of human trafficking. These people may need protection even if they do not fall within the category

13 See Craggs. S., and Martens, R. "Rights, Residence, Rehabilitation: A Comparative Study Assessing Residence Options for Traffickers Persons. (2010). < http://publications.iom.int/system/files/pdf/iml24.pdf> p.55 *at* 56, accessed on 14/7/2017.

14 See Craggs. S., and Martens, R....*op. cit.* note 13, p. 56.

15 See Stoyanova, V., *Human Trafficking and Slavery Reconsidered.* (Cambridge University Press), 2017, p. 448.

16 See Stoyanova, V.,...*op. cit.* note 15, p. 449.

17 See Galos, E., Bartolini, L., Cook, H., and Grant, N., *Migrant Vulnerability to Human Trafficking and Exploitation: Evidence from the Central and Eastern Mediterranean Migration Routes.* International Organization for Migration (IOM), 2017, p. 3.

of individuals covered by the Refugee Convention.[18] Irregular migration involving smuggling can make people very vulnerable as 'Such situations frequently involve transactions between people in a vulnerable situation and those who might prey upon them, with overreaching formal and informal institutions affecting the dynamics of interaction between potential victims and perpetrators of exploitation and abuse'. [19] Vulnerable migrants may be unable to seek the help and support of law enforcement authorities because they are at the mercy of smugglers and very vulnerable to exploitation and human trafficking.[20] Article 2 (1) of the Trafficking Directive states that trafficking in human beings is

> "the recruitment, transportation, transfer, harbouring or reception of persons,... by means of the threat or use of force or other forms of coercion,...of a position of vulnerability...for the purpose of exploitation".

Forms of coercion include the abuse of a position of vulnerability which, according to Article 2(2) "means a situation in which the person concerned has no real or acceptable alternative but to submit to the abuse involved". This is the position of people smuggled at sea as they do not have other alternatives than accepting to be recruited by smugglers. It is desirable Article 2(1) specifies that the concept of vulnerability shall include vulnerable people recruited in the desert for the purpose of smuggling at sea. In this way the scope of the human trafficking's definition will be widened without any misinterpretation and Member States will be legally obliged to consider people smuggled by sea at the same level of victims of human trafficking.

Human trafficking also includes the recruitment for the purpose of exploitation. Article 2(3) states that:

> "Exploitation shall include, as a minimum, the exploitation of prostitution of others or other forms of sexual exploitation, forced labour or services, including begging, slavery or practices similar to slavery, servitude, or the exploitation of criminal activities, or the removal of organs".

18 See Galos, E., Bartolini, L., Cook, H., and Grant, N.,...*op. cit.* note 17, p. 4. See also Crisp, J., 'Beyond the Nexus: UNHCR's evolving perspective on refugee protection and international migration'. Research paper no. 155, April, 2008.

19 See Galos, E., Bartolini, L., Cook, H., and Grant, N.,...*op. cit.* note 17, p. 5.

20 Ibid

Smuggled migrants by sea should be considered exploited migrants when they suffer serious abuses of human rights, after having been recruited by smugglers in the desert.[21] They are victims of abuse, torture and rape perpetrate by smugglers in order to keep them under their control and ensure that they repay the price for their journey.[22] These abuses can be compared to slavery or practices similar to slavery which are contemplated by Article 2 (3) of the Directive on human trafficking. According to the International Criminal Tribunal for the former Yugoslavia (ICTY), indications of enslavements could be the vulnerable position of a victim and other elements such as "psychological oppression or socio-economic conditions".[23] The ICTY was referring to the crime committed during a war.[24] However, the same concepts could be extended to people smuggled by sea because of their vulnerable socio-economic conditions. They are forced to suffer abuses of their human rights such as rape and torture which smugglers might practise. Is smugglers commit these atrocities, from one side, migrants at sea cannot avoid these abuses as they depend on smugglers' support without which, they would not be able to travel to the EU by sea. From the other side, smugglers exploit the vulnerability of migrants at sea and reduce them to a condition similar to slavery, in order to ensure they obtain a financial gain from the victims. This practice could be considered a form of slavery and within the scope of Article 2 (3) of the Trafficking Directive.

3. PEOPLE SMUGGLED BY SEA AS POTENTIAL VICTIMS OF HUMAN TRAFFICKING

On the basis of the mid-term report on the EU strategy towards the eradication of human trafficking published by the Commission, people smuggled by sea could also be considered potential victims (and not only presumed victims) of human trafficking and deserving the same legal protection of these victims. The Commission has highlighted that the defeat of human trafficking requires

21 See section 3 p. 20, chapter 2 of this book.

22 See Section 3 p. 20, chapter 2.

23 See Case No IT-96-23-T *Prosecutor v. Kunarac, Kovac and Vukovic*, para 542.

24 See Piotrowicz, R., ' States' Obligations under Human Rights towards Victims of Trafficking in Human Beings: Positive Developments in Positive Obligations'. In *International Journal of Refugee Law* Vol. 24/2, p. 184.

early identification of victims who "cannot be effectively assisted and protected if they are not properly identified".[25] For this purpose, the Commission called on Member States to establish appropriate mechanisms to ensure that victims are identified at an earlier stage and that they are provided with adequate protection, assistance including legal assistance in criminal proceedings. The Commission published Guidelines for the identification of victims which are particularly addressed to border guards and consular services.[26] The Guidelines emphasize that the early identification of victims should be a priority. In order to achieve this outcome, not only victims but also potential victims of human trafficking should be identified at an early stage. In this way, victims will be protected and supported and police and prosecution authorities will be in a better position to investigate and detect traffickers. There are two elements to be considered in these reports. The first one is that the crime can be better detected if victims are identified as they might start a programme of recovery and eventually report traffickers. The second element is that the Commission also considers as priorities the identification of potential victims and their legal protection. The Commission in its mid-term report states that once victims, including potential victims as indicated by the Guidelines, are identified, they shall be entitled to residence permits, labour rights, access to justice and compensation on the basis of Directive 2011/36/EU and of Directive 2012/29/EU. Consequently, the Commission is widening the scope of the human trafficking legal framework as it states that victims are not only those people who have been identified as such, but also those people who can become victims because of their circumstances. People smuggled by sea can be considered potential victims of human trafficking when, for instance, they cannot repay the price for their journey they become victims of human trafficking. The legal protection that should be granted to migrants at sea is a residence permit as established by Directive 2004/81/EC.[27] At the moment, the Directive does not make it compulsory but it leaves the choice to Member States' discretion and it is difficult to identify potential victims and the crime of human trafficking will not be defeated. Instead, it is important to

25 See SWD (2014) 318 final, 17/10/2014.

26 See http://ec.europa.eu/dgs/home-affairs/e-library/docs/thb-victims-identification/thb_identification_en.pdf accessed on 18/10/2014.

27 See Council Directive 2004/81/EC of 29 April 2004 on the residence permit issued to third-country nationals who are victims of trafficking in human beings or who have been the subject of an action to facilitate illegal immigration, who cooperate with the competent authorities. OJ L 261/19, 6/8/2004.

address the problem of trafficking and its roots because its eradication can be successfully achieved by defeating the connected crime of people smuggling by sea. Widening the concept of vulnerability and exploitation, granting compulsory legal protection to migrants at sea, on the basis of Directive 2004/81/EC, are essential to make the global fight against trafficking in human beings, effective.

The Commission seems determined to address smuggling of migrants at sea. Indeed, in one of its Communications, it identified the strict links between smuggling of migrants by sea and human trafficking.[28] The Commission stated that it intends to implement "the actions identified by the Task Force Mediterranean, set up in October 2013 with the aim of preventing the loss of migrants' lives at sea by, inter alia, stepping up the fight against migrants trafficking and smuggling". Therefore, the Commission calls for a Global Approach to Migration and Mobility (GAMM) by concentrating on different actions.[29] One action consists of cooperating with countries of transit and origin of migrants at sea in order to prevent them from attempting to enter the EU irregularly and by the support of criminal organizations. Another action should focus on resettlement as it is "an important mean by which persons in need of protection can arrive safely to the European Union without going on hazardous journeys over the Mediterranean".[30] The Commission supports resettlement through the Union Resettlement Programme which will be supported by the EU funding available under the Asylum and Migration Fund and it could publish guidelines on a common approach to humanitarian permits/visas.[31]

The Commission reports are full of good intentions. However, an effective policy on the protection of migrants at sea can be adopted only if Member States will collectively tackle the problem with responsibility. Unfortunately, the Commission has reported that Member States are issuing low numbers of residence permits in exchange for cooperation and, only in exceptional circumstances, the residence permit is issued beyond the willingness of victims to cooperate.[32] The Commission is also concerned because it is unclear how Member States identify victims and potential victims and inform them of their rights "to initiate a recovery process and to reflect before deciding whether to

28 See COM (2014) 635 final, 17/10/2014.

29 See COM (2013) 869 final, 4/12/2013.

30 ibid

31 ibid

32 See above note 28.

cooperate with the authorities".[33] Indeed, in the legislation of Member States, it is not specified whether the information is provided to officially identified victims or also to presumed victims. It is thought that presumed victims should be given the information as it could be a way to give them the opportunity to escape from the traffickers and smugglers by starting a programme of recovery.

4. SCOPE OF THE BOOK

The book analyses all the problems identified by the Commission and the EP and it proposes to fight against human trafficking by focusing on the identification and protection of victims and potential victims. It shows that actual law permits to protect victims and potential victims by applying the law on legal migration.

Chapter 2 focuses on smuggled migrants by sea and it highlights the connections with trafficking. The chapter focuses on international and EU legal framework on smuggling of migrants because one is of the opinion that victims of human trafficking should be identified in between smuggled migrants. Therefore, smuggled migrants should be protected against collective expulsion which prevent competent authorities to expel irregular migrants without investigating whether they may be entitled to stay in the country of arrival. By undertaking these investigations, it could be possible to identify victims of human trafficking and provide them legal protection. Chapter 2 highlights that immigration control prevents the identification of victims of human trafficking in between people smuggled by sea and it proposes to protect irregular migrants when there is an indication that they could be victims of human trafficking, by applying the Temporary Protection Directive. The application of this Directive can give law enforcement authorities the opportunity to undertake investigations and to ascertain whether an irregular migrant is a victim of human trafficking. However, chapter 2 also highlights that the EU and Member States are too focused on applying immigration controls and on returning as many migrants as possible to their countries of origin and this is the reason why it is very difficult to protect victims of human trafficking which is increasing. The chapter moves to focus on other ways to protect smuggled migrants by applying EU migration law and policies and it proposes reforms which could extend more

33 See above note 28.

protection to smuggled migrants by sea which otherwise remain vulnerable to human trafficking.

Chapter 3 focuses on the fight against smuggling and trafficking and in particular on short-term measures adopted to fight against smuggling and trafficking. EUNAVFOR Med is fully analysed and it is argued that this mission is a failure because not able to fight against criminal organisations committing smuggling and trafficking. Subsequently, the chapter focuses on the external relations between the EU and the coastal country of Libya which has seen a surge in migrants' arrivals from Africa. The chapter highlights that the EU intends to fight against smuggling and trafficking by negotiating agreements with Libya. This policy is criticised as there have been reports proving that migrants detained in Libya are being tortured and suffering many other abuses of human rights. Therefore, an agreement with this country is not feasible. It is also emphasised that a similar agreement will not defeat smuggling and trafficking in the long term but it will only create obstacles for migrants to enter the EU in the short term. This is because it has been reported that criminal organisations are able to adapt their routes on the basis of EU policies. They will always find a way to smuggle migrants to Europe and short term measures will not be a deterrent to irregular migration and smuggling of migrants. If legal routes are banned, people will always find alternative ways even if unlawful to leave their countries of origin and ravel in desperate conditions in Europe.

Chapter 4 proposes to fight against smuggling and trafficking by EU agencies which are Europol Eurojust, Frontex and the European Public Prosecutor Office (EPPO). These agencies should coordinate the efforts between EU Member States and their cooperation with third countries' law enforcement authorities. The legal instruments which established these agencies are examined and it is highlighted that although the EU has improved the Europol's scope, the EPPO's project is not feasible because it creates issues related to national sovereignty. Chapter 4 emphasises that the fight against smuggling and trafficking remains mainly of single EU Member States' responsibility.

Chapter 5 focuses on the external relations of the EU in the fight against smuggling and trafficking. The European institutions have highlighted that smuggling and trafficking can be defeated by addressing the root causes of migration and by creating socio-economic development in origin and transit countries. For this purpose, chapter 5 analyses all initiatives undertaken by the EU to address these causes and to create opportunities in origin and transit countries so that people will not be willing to leave these countries anymore to improve their economic situations. Chapter 5 highlights that the EU external cooperation should be accountable before the EP because decisions related to external cooperation in criminal matters with countries whose human rights standards may be very low, requires the approval of the representatives of EU citizens. Chapter 5 also highlights the importance of involving the African Union (AU) in the fight against trafficking and smuggling in in addressing root causes of migration. The AU institutions' are analysed as external agreements already concluded by the EU with some African countries.

Chapter 2: EU legal protection on smuggled migrants

1. Introduction

This chapter will focus on smuggled migrants and it will analyse when legal protection can be granted to this category of migrants. The chapter will analyse the extent of smuggling of migrants, legal protection established by international law and by the ECHR. It will also examine how granting legal protection to smuggled migrants within the EU is challenging because EU law and policies are too focused on immigration controls and thus, on returning as many migrants as possible to their countries of origin or of residence. EU migration law could support the protection of smuggled migrants and prevent them from being returned to their countries of origin or transit. Nevertheless, these laws are applied very strictly by EU Member States.

Smuggling of migrants can take place by air, by land and by sea. Smuggling of migrants by sea is a crime which is causing the death of many migrants.[1] Migrants smuggled at sea are either genuine asylum seekers or unauthorized labour migrants.[2] Asylum seekers are eligible refugees whilst unauthorized labour migrants or economic migrants are not entitled to asylum unless they are victims of human trafficking. This chapter analyses international legislation and EU law on smuggling of migrants by sea and the legal protection granted to them. The chapter will argue that smuggled people by sea may be vulnerable migrants who leave their countries of origin to avoid death because of famine, disease and poverty and they are not granted appropriate legal protection unless they fall in the scope of other EU legal instruments. Although they are not forced by criminals to leave their countries of origin, they do this because the alternative would be living in extreme poor conditions in their countries of origin.

1 See COM (2015) 285 final, 27/5/2015.

2 See Fargues, P., 'Is what we hear about migration really true?'. 2014, available on http://cadmus.eui.eu/bitstream/handle/1814/31731/MPC_2014_FARGUES.pdf?sequence=1, accessed on 11/8/2014.

Their exact number is unknown because there is no reliable data on the reasons why they leave their countries of origin.[3] Identifying exactly how many people are refugees and how many are economic migrants looking for a better life in Europe, requires information about the cause of migration which is lacking.[4] Statistics on migrants at sea stop when they land and no one really knows what they do once they land and what is their fate.[5] Hence, it is important to focus on the root causes of migration to identify the categories of migrants who leave their countries of origin, in order to implement adequate global actions to prevent them from leaving in poor conditions and by risking their lives. The need of global actions is confirmed by the High Representative Vice President (HRVP) Federica Mogherini, who stated that the EU is dealing with a migration and refugee crisis that should be tackled by a global action because 'It is a regional crisis: it's not only a European crisis, it is a regional crisis... and a global crisis, too...'.[6]

EU Member States are adopting very restrictive policies on immigration such as reintroducing checks at internal border due to an unprecedented influx of migrants in the past months.[7] The Council has clarified in a leaked document, that these measures cannot be adopted for more than six months. When migrant and refugee crisis persists for longer, the Council can adopt a recommendation on Commission's proposal, in accordance with Article 26 of the Schengen Borders Code.[8] The Recommendation on the reintroduction of internal border, can be adopted in exceptional circumstances and when there are continuous and serious deficiencies on the external border controls.[9] As Peers emphasised, it is not clear which Member States have serious deficiencies in external border controls as the Commission has recently adopted a Schengen evaluation system but it is not

---

3 Ibid

4 See Fargues, P., and Bonfanti, S., *When the best option is a leaky boat: why migrants risk their life crossing the Mediterranean and what Europe is doing about it'. European University Institute, Migration policy Centre. Available at* http://cadmus.eui.eu/bitstream/handle/1814/33271/MPC_PB_2014-05.pdf?sequence=1, accessed on 27/10/2014.

5 Ibid

6 See Remarks by High Representative/Vice-President Federica Mogherini following the informal meeting of the EU Foreign Ministers, Gymnich, 5/9/2015, available on http://eeas.europa.eu/statements-eeas/2015/150905_01_en.htm, accessed on 7/9/2015.

7 See Doc 14300/15, 1/12/2015. On http://data.consilium.europa.eu/doc/document/ST-14300-2015-INIT/en/pdf accessed on 28/1/2016.

8 ibid. See Article 23 of the Schengen Border Code, Regulation (EC) No 562/2006 of the European Parliament and of the Council of 15/3/2006. OJ L 105/1, 13/4/2006.

9 Above note 1.

public.[10] Certainly, Schengen cannot be abolished completely without amending EU Treaties.[11] It can be suspended in the short-term for no more than three months and in the long term for up to two years with the procedure indicated by the leaked Council document.[12] There are also EU Member States which are charging asylum seekers by seizing their belongings. The Danish Parliament, for instance, has amended the Aliens Act (Bill no. 87) by establishing that police can search and confiscate asylum seekers' goods to ensure they contribute to the payment of their expenses associated to their stay in Denmark.[13] The Bill has become law since 26 January 2016. The new Act is very controversial because it gives police the power to search and seize property and, thus, it is contrary to the Refugee Convention.[14] The Convention imposes nations to respect refugees' properties as the properties of any other foreign citizen. [15] The Danish government argued that refugees are considered as unemployed Danes who have to sell their properties in order to be entitled to social benefits. [16] According to EU law, Member States can withdraw properties from asylum seekers as a contribution to their sustainment.[17] The right of Member States to require for contribution, was already part of Directive 2003/9/EC where Article 13(4) stated that

> 'Member States may require applicants to cover or contribute to the cost of the material reception conditions and of the health care provided for in this Directive,... if the applicants have sufficient resources, for example if they have been working for a reasonable period of time'.

Nevertheless, on the basis of the principle of proportionality, it is doubtful Member States could refuse access to social benefits to asylum seekers, just

10 See 'Can Schengen be suspended because of Greece?. Should it be?'. On http://eulawanalysis.blogspot.co.uk/2015/12/can-schengen-be-suspended-because-of.html, accessed on 28/1/2016.

11 Ibid

12 Ibid

13 See Hartmann, J., and Tan, N.F, 'The Danish Law on Seizing Asylum Seekers' Assets'. On http://www.ejiltalk.org/the-danish-law-on-seizing-asylum-seekers-assets/#more-13995, accessed on 28/1/2016.

14 Ibid

15 Ibid

16 Ibid

17 See Article 17 (3) and (4) of Directive 2013/33/EU of 26 June 2013. OJ L 180/96, 29/6/2013.

because they have a small amount of money with them. They should be refused access to benefits only when it is ascertained that they are wealth.[18] Decisions must be taken on a case-by case basis and reasons for the decision must be given, otherwise they will be incompatible with EU law. Denmark is not bound by this Directive but other Member States have to comply with it.[19] The other point to make is that these measures taken by States not bound by the Directive (Ireland and Denmark are not bound by this Directive), will contribute to create a fragmented policy on migration and asylum which will aggravate the situation of asylum seekers and by making future possible migrant and refugee crises very difficult to overcome. It must be added that other Member States are planning to return asylum seekers whose claim was rejected. This is the case of Sweden where it has been decided that 80.000 rejected asylum seekers, will be returned in their countries of origin in the next years.[20] These strict measures do not support the protection of asylum seekers and other categories of vulnerable migrants. In between these categories there are smuggled people and other undocumented migrants such as minor who, because of these restrictions, risk to become victims of THB. This chapter examines the categories of irregular migrants who cannot claim asylum and who remain unprotected within the EU. The chapter will focus on people smuggled by sea and who live undocumented within the EU territory. What is their fate and how the EU is going to address this issue? The EU legal framework on return policies, family reunion, legal migration and other important legal instruments will be analysed.

The next section will introduce the topic by explaining who smuggled people by sea are. Subsequently, it will be analysed the legal protection that can be recognised to them, by international law and the ECHR. The chapter will argue that migrants at sea are vulnerable because they do not enjoy the same legal protection granted to other categories of people recognised as asylum seekers and refugees. Subsequently, it will be argued that policy and law on legal migration should be expanded to ensure that people smuggled by sea, are not returned to their countries of origin as they will end up in the same situation of poverty they left in their countries of origin and they will try to escape by the same

18 See Groenendijk, K., and Peers, S., 'Can Member States seize asylum seekers' assets?'. On http://eulawanalysis.blogspot.co.uk/2016/01/can-member-states-seize-asylum-seekers.html, accessed on 29/1/2016.

19 Ibid

20 See http://www.bbc.co.uk/news/world-europe-35425735, accessed on 29/1/2016.

poor means again. By doing this, they will be smuggled again and they will put at risk their life and the life of their family members.[21] The more EU policies on legal migration are restrictive, the more people will seek the support of criminal organisations to enter the EU territories. Consequently, smuggling and the connected crime of trafficking will only increase.

2. THE EXTENT OF SMUGGLING OF MIGRANTS IN BETWEEN SOPHISTICATED CRIMINAL GROUPS AND RUDIMENTAL HIERARCHIES

International law and EU law have distinguished smuggling of migrants from human trafficking and, by doing this, they have allowed nations to prioritize border security rather than victims' protection. Consequently, all law addressing smuggling of migrants by sea at international, EU and national level, have concentrated on border controls when people smuggled by sea should have been legally protected as victims of human trafficking. This is because they are exposed to risk of death.

Many migrants coming from Africa, especially from the Horn of Africa are drowning while they are trying to reach the EU through Italy. The accident of October 2013 beside the Italian island of Lampedusa where 366 migrants died, and the accident of April 2015 when 700 migrants died, have both shown the extent of the problem. Frontex has published data on the number of people crossing the Mediterranean by sea. In 2012, the number of migrants arriving in Europe irregularly across the Mediterranean has dramatically decreased from 141051 in 2011 to 72437.[22] However, in 2013, the number of irregular migrants crossing the Mediterranean Sea from Africa, increased sharply and reached the number of 107365,[23] because of the war in Syria, Iraq and the destabilizing

21 See on these points Ventrella, M., *The control of people smuggling and trafficking in the EU: Experiences from the UK and Italy Routledge, 2010. See also Triandafyllidou, A., and Maroukis, T., Migrant Smuggling. Irregular Migration from Asia and Africa to Europe, Palgrave Macmillian, 2012.*

22 See Frontex Annual Risk Analysis 2013 available at http://frontex.europa.eu/assets/Publications/Risk_Analysis/Annual_Risk_Analysis_2013.pdf accessed on 1/7/2014. See also Manrique, M., G, Barna J., Pekka Hakala, P., Rey, B., Claros, E., Mediterranean Flows into Europe: Migration and the EU's Foreign Policy, March 2014, p. 4. Available on http://www.europarl.europa.eu/RegData/etudes/briefing_note/join/2014/522330/EXPO-JOIN_SP(2014)522330_EN.pdf accessed on 1/7/2014.

23 See Frontex Annual Risk Analysis 2014 available at http://frontex.europa.eu/assets/Publications/Risk_Analysis/Annual_Risk_Analysis_2014.pdf accessed on 1/7/2014.

situation in the Horn of Africa.[24] The Frontex Annual Report published in 2015, has indicated that migration flows from the Horn of Africa and Western Africa, are increasing rather than falling.[25] In December 2017, Frontex reported that the number of arrivals from Eastern Mediterranean has decreased compared to 2015 and 2016 and this is due to the EU-Turkey agreement concluded in 2016.[26] Conversely, pressure on the Central and Western Mediterranean routes have both seen a surge in arrivals of migrants mainly from Africa which number had continued to increase apart from nationals from Gambia (-22%) and Guinea (-39%).[27] Most of migrants are supported by facilitators committing smuggling who mainly operate from Turkey and Libya.[28]

When migrants at sea were interviewed, they stressed that they left their countries of origin because of insecurity and economic concerns.[29] In addition, Somalis and Eritreans stated they used the route from Sudan and Ethiopia to reach the EU through the Central Mediterranean route, specifically Italy and Malta.[30] In between migrants detected in the Central Mediterranean route, there were also Syrians who were leaving their country because of war.[31] According to Frontex, the Central Mediterranean route particularly from North Africa to Italy, has accounted for 38% of all detection of irregular migrants at EU level.[32] People from Horn of Africa have used the route from Libya and Tunisia to reach Italy and this route has seen episodic surges in migrant flows during the past ten years.[33] These data have been confirmed by the UNHCR which stated, in their most recent report, that the Central Mediterranean route received the majority

24 Above note 1.

25 See Frontex Annual Report Quarter 1. January-March 2015, available on http://frontex.europa.eu/assets/Publications/Risk_Analysis/FRAN_Q1_2015.pdf, accessed on 8/9/2015.

26 See FRAN Quarterly. Quarter 2, April-June 2017 available on http://frontex.europa.eu/assets/Publications/Risk_Analysis/FRAN_Q2_2017.pdf, accessed on 5/2/2018.

27 Ibid.

28 See Frontex Risk Analysis for 2018, p. 35. On https://frontex.europa.eu/assets/Publications/Risk_Analysis/Risk_Analysis/Risk_Analysis_for_2018.pdf, accessed on 31/5/2018.

29 Ibid note 26.

30 See in particular Table 6 of the Frontex Annual Risk Report 2014, p. 31.

31 Ibid note 26.

32 See http://frontex.europa.eu/news/frontex-publishes-annual-risk-analysis-2014-wc71Jn accessed on 1/7/2014.

33 See also Mediterranean flows into Europe...*op. cit.* note 22, p.6.

of sea arrivals in 2013 with a dramatic increase compared to the previous year.[34] In addition, Frontex has reported that most people coming from the Horn of Africa use dangerous routes across the Sahara to reach Libya, prior to embarkation to Italy.[35] They cross the Saharan desert[36] and many of them die in the desert and the survivors often report that they have to cross the borders of different countries at night time and, during these journeys, they spend much time without food, water or a shelter.

Subsequently, criminal organizations recruit migrants in the desert and support them in their difficult journeys. These organizations are usually hierarchically structured. In the organizations, there are intermediaries and brokers and the latter might be the only contacts migrants have with smugglers. This fact makes migrants very vulnerable as they have no other choice than trusting brokers. [37] Brokers and other intermediaries might be of the same ethno-linguistic background of migrants or they can be people who have become affiliated to smugglers after an unsuccessful sea-crossing they want to attempt again by earning money to pay smugglers for their journeys. Therefore, they have to work for smugglers until they gain enough money to try crossing the Mediterranean Sea again.[38] Brokers can also be nationals of migrants who have developed a very profitable business and may have no interest in crossing the sea. They liaise with middlemen who subsequently create a contact between migrants and smugglers and may be guarantors of payments by keeping the money until the journeys have been completed. Smugglers might also promote their services to migrants through people who act as recruiters. Usually, recruiters work independently as they are not stranded to smugglers. They come from countries of origin of migrants or from transit countries. Other people involved with smuggling at sea are transporters who accompany migrants from one country to another until the point of embarkation. There are then, people who pilot the boat who might not be aware of migration or people smuggling issues, including the involvement of criminal organisations.[39] They are usually fishermen who, because of

34 See http://www.unhcr.org/539809e10.html accessed on 1/7/2014.

35 Above note 26.

36 Above note 26.

37 See 'Smuggling of Migrants: the harsh search for a better life'. On http://www.unodc.org/toc/en/crimes/migrant-smuggling.html accessed on 15/9/2014.

38 Ibid

39 Above note 37.

their skills, are recruited by smugglers to transport migrants from one coast to another. Spotters provide specific information on controls at the borders and, in some occasions, sailors of commercial boats in the world, have informed smugglers about possible surveillance at the borders.[40] Research has suggested that corrupted officials in States, even of very high level such as border officials, police, immigration officials, soldiers and employees of embassies can participate in the smuggling of migrants at sea. They can be involved as organizers or facilitators.[41] Migrants take weeks, months and even years to reach the Italian coast as their money run out and they cannot pay the price for their trips to the smugglers to reach Italy or other EU Mediterranean countries. Therefore, whilst waiting for embarkation, migrants can be threatened by enforcers who use violence in order to keep them under control or to make sure they pay the price for their journey. Many smuggled migrants have testified in Lampedusa that in Libya they are abused, tortured and raped.[42] Testimonies of migrants have also reported that they work in Libya for sometimes in order to pay smugglers for their embarkation. Migrants at sea can pay their smugglers in different ways. One way is up front before departure; the second way is *en route* to the different smugglers involved or by credit. This latter method of payment often leads to human trafficking as the trip by boat is paid in advance by a third party but when migrants reach the countries of destination, they become victims of human trafficking because they are unable to repay the price for their trip.[43] These facts have also been confirmed by Interpol, which has published

40 Ibid

41 See 'Issue paper: Smuggling of Migrants by Sea'. Available on http://www.unodc.org/documents/human-trafficking/Migrant-Smuggling/Issue-Papers/Issue_Paper_-_Smuggling_of_Migrants_by_Sea.pdf accessed on 15/9/2014.

42 See also De Bruycker, P., Di Bartolomeo, A., Fargues, P., 'Migrants smuggled by sea to the EU: facts, laws and policy options'. Migration Policy Centre (MPC) Report 2013/09 on http://www.migrationpolicycentre.eu/docs/MPC-RR-2013-009.pdf accessed on 7/8/2014.

43 Ibid note 40. See also the document presented by the United Nations Department of Economic and Social Affairs "International Migration Policies: Government Views and Priorities" available on http://www.un.org/en/development/desa/population/publications/pdf/policy/InternationalMigrationPolicies2013/Report%20PDFs/k_Ch_5.pdf accessed on 10/7/2014. See The International Organization for Migration and People Smuggling available at http://www.iom.int/jahia/webdav/shared/shared/mainsite/activities/ibm/10-IOM-IBM-FACT-SHEET-People-smuggling.pdf accessed on 10/7/2014. See also "Smuggled futures: the dangerous path of a migrant from Africa to Europe. On http://www.globalinitiative.net/smuggled-futures/ accessed on 16/7/2014. See The International Organization for Migration and People Smuggling on http://www.iom.int/jahia/webdav/shared/shared/mainsite/activities/ibm/10-IOM-IBM-FACT-SHEET-People-smuggling.pdf accessed on 27/6/2014.

the result of evidence showing that smugglers continue to exploit migrants in the country of destination in order to obtain additional fees for their journeys.[44] Furthermore, recent research undertaken by Italian journalists has found out that people smuggled by sea are often victims of traffic of organs since, when they cannot repay the price for their journey, they are left with no choice other than selling their kidneys and even corneas to smugglers.[45] Do migrants at sea make a free choice to leave their countries of origin and accept to be recruited by smugglers? They may be tortured, raped and eventually become victims of human trafficking and of removal of organs. Would they travel by the support of criminal organizations if they had other alternatives? It is thought that no people would travel in these conditions if they had other alternatives. In addition, how do many migrants become victims of trafficking once recruited by smugglers? It is important to understand the connections between these two crimes because the response towards smuggled migrants who have become victims of trafficking and others who have not become victims of this crime, may differ.

Smuggling by land can take place from Turkey to Bulgaria, from Ethiopia to Libya through Sudan, from Pakistan to Turkey through Iran.[46] Migrants who are awaiting in Greece, are smuggled through Macedonia to Serbia and Hungary.[47] Usually migrants wait in small villages for some days before being recruited by smugglers. In the central Saharan, there is transportation managed by "Afrod" system which is controlled by Tuareg transport entrepreneurs which connect Northern Niger, Algeria and parts of Libya and which are able to carry two or three dozens of individuals. [48] There are then other criminal groups controlled by Tebu, Hausa and Arab criminal groups involving large trucks able to transport up to 120 migrants. Smuggling of migrants by land and in the desert can take several weeks because of the unstable situation in countries which are crossed

44 See http://www.interpol.int/Crime-areas/Trafficking-in-human-beings/People-smuggling accessed on 27/6/2014.

45 See http://www.ansa.it/sito/notizie/magazine/numeri/2014/10/10/africa-take-away_9037661f -41a5-4e68-9ebf-686a1486678c.html accessed on 21/10/2014.

46 See European Commission, DG Migration & Home Affairs 'A Study on Smuggling of Migrants, Characteristics, responses and cooperation with third countries, p. 38. On https://ec.europa.eu/home-affairs/sites/homeaffairs/files/case_study_5_greece_-_former_yugoslav_republic_of_macedonia_-_serbia_hungary.pdf, accessed on 15/10/2015.

47 Ibid

48 Ibid

by smugglers which makes the travel impossible to undertake. [49] There have been evidence showing that often migrants are abandoned in the desert when trucks encounter difficulties in the different transit countries. [50] Many incidents have been reported in 2015 and 48 migrants have died in the Sahara desert in Niger whilst they were travelling to reach Europe. [51]. The sea routes consists of transporting migrants from their place of accommodation in Hub cities to places of embarkation.[52] Smugglers are able to adapt their routes on the basis of where the international search and rescue operations take place and weather conditions. [53] There evidence that in Libya, criminal organisations have been supported by Libyan security officials and migrants had been shipped to Europe in prearranged times in order to avoid controls that could have been carried out by officials undertaking search and rescue operations.[54] Before commencing their trips, migrants are provided with a satellite phone and GPS and a list of contacts which allow them to contact Maltese or Italian authorities in order to be rescued. If they are not rescued by these authorities, they are rescued by private ships and merchant vessels. Smuggling can be carried out by air through falsification of documents as reported by Frontex in 2015.[55] Furthermore, migrants entering the EU are not only refugees from Syria. Frontex has reported that in the second half of 2015, people entering the EU are mainly from Nigeria, Somalia, Sudan, Eritrea, Morocco and Cameroon and they crossed the EU borders irregularly not only from Mediterranean routes but also from other routes such as Eastern European and Western Balkan routes.[56] Incidents have been reported in the Eastern Mediterranean route and particularly between migrants who crossed the Turkish coast, the Greek Islands and the Evros River. [57] Fatalities have also

49 Ibid

50 Ibid

51 Ibid

52 Above note 46, p. 39.

53 ibid

54 ibid

55 See Frontex Risk Analysis Quarter 2. April-June 2015, p. 14. On http://frontex.europa.eu/assets/Publications/Risk_Analysis/FRAN_Q2_2015_final.pdf, accessed on 16/2/2016.

56 See Frontex Risk Analysis Quarter 3. July September 2015 pp. 6 and 7. On http://frontex.europa.eu/assets/Publications/Risk_Analysis/FRAN_Q3_2015.pdf, accessed on 16/2/2016.

57 See Frontex Risk Analysis for 2016, (March 2016), p. 46. On https://frontex.europa.eu/assets/Publications/Risk_Analysis/Annula_Risk_Analysis_2016.pdf, accessed on 12/4/2018.

been reported in the Western Mediterranean route in between Morocco and Spain.[58]

Smuggling can be carried out by air through falsification of documents as reported by Frontex in 2015.[59] This agency has also reported that in the second half of 2015, people entering the EU were mainly from Nigeria, Somalia, Sudan, Eritrea, Morocco and Cameroon and they crossed the EU borders irregularly not only from Mediterranean routes but also from other routes such as Eastern European and Western Balkan routes.[60]

Most recently, Frontex has reported that people from Sub-Saharan Africa are 'the single largest group being detected/rescued'[61] in the central Mediterranean route. In April 2016, Frontex reported that most people crossing the EU borders irregularly, were from Syria, Afghanistan, Iraq, Iran, Pakistan, Morocco, Somalia, Nigeria and Palestine.[62] Certainly, according to Frontex, the Mediterranean route is still the most crossed route.[63] The EU sought to reduce the number of people smuggled from Africa by establishing the EUNAVFOR Med. which is a military operations which may only touch the tip of the iceberg but they will not contribute to fight against the crime as it requires police and judicial cooperation with third countries of origin and transit rather than a military operation. [64]

There are many reports show that smuggling of migrants is very well organised and all members of the organisations have different roles. There are coordinators, organisers, recruiters, transporters, spotters, drivers, messengers, enforcers, service providers and suppliers.[65] In the last few years, smuggling of

58 Ibid.

59 See Frontex Risk Analysis Quarter 2. April-June 2015, p. 14. On http://frontex.europa.eu/assets/Publications/Risk_Analysis/FRAN_Q2_2015_final.pdf, accessed on 16/2/2016.

60 See Frontex Risk Analysis Quarter 3. July September 2015 pp. *6 at 7. On http://frontex.europa.eu/assets/Publications/Risk_Analysis/FRAN_Q3_2015.pdf, accessed on 16/2/2016.*

61 See Africa-Frontex Intelligence Community Joint Report, 2015, p. 12. On http://frontex.europa.eu/assets/Publications/Risk_Analysis/AFIC/AFIC_report_2015.pdf, accessed on 16/2/2016.

62 See Frontex Risk Analysis Quarter 4. October-December 2015, p. 10. On http://frontex.europa.eu/assets/Publications/Risk_Analysis/FRAN_Q4_2015.pdf, accessed on 6/6/2016.

63 See Frontex Risk Analysis Report...*op. cit. note 28, pp. 18 at 19.*

64 See section 3, p. 66 of chapter 3 for an analysis of the EUNAV for Med.

65 See Issue Paper: A short introduction to migrant smuggling, 2010, pp. 14 at 16. *On https://www.unodc.org/documents/human-trafficking/Migrant-Smuggling/Issue-Papers/Issue_Paper_-_A_short_introduction_to_migrant_smuggling.pdf, accessed on 16/2/2016.*

migrants has become more organised and professional.[66] Smugglers networks rely on social media and it is almost impossible for migrants to travel on their own initiative, without the support of these criminal networks.[67] In addition, migrants have to pay prices and fees for their journey. [68] On this aspect smugglers are very well organised because they 'tailor their prices to the economic means of their clients'. [69] In other terms, migrants pay what they can afford and usually Syrian refugees pay more than migrants coming from Sub-Saharan Africa as the former are healthier than the latter. [70] Often migrants have to pay several times for each journey they will and the payment modalities have become more organised compared to some years ago. [71] Migrants are requested to pay for their journey on the Southern Mediterranean route before they start travelling.[72] If the journey is interrupted or the departure is halted, migrants do not have the right to a reimbursement.[73] Instead, for travels from Pakistan to Greece through Greece, migrants can repay the price of their trip after safely arrived at a certain and agreed destination. [74] The nationality of a number of smugglers within the EU has been identified. [75] The nationality of smugglers committing the crime outside the EU may be difficult to identify and this is the reason why JHA agencies should be reinforced and conduct investigations in cooperation with law enforcement authorities of origin and transit countries of migrants.

Smuggling of migrants committed by organised criminal networks have also been described by further research which highlights that these networks 'are made up of actors with specialized, often highly localized knowledge and experience'.[76] Smugglers networks are organised as a pyramid where at the

66 See European Commission, DG Migration & Home Affairs 'A Study on Smuggling of Migrants...*op. cit. note 46, p. 48.*

67 See note 46, pp. 47 at 48.

68 See note 46, p. 45.

69 ibid.

70 ibid.

71 See note 46, pp. 45 at 46.

72 See note 46, p. 46.

73 Ibid

74 Ibid

75 Above note 46, p. 46.

76 See Tinti, P., and Reitano, T., *Migrant Refugee Smuggler Saviour. OUP 2017, p. 47.*

bottom of it there are brokers and recruiters. They will have the most interaction with migrants.[77] There are then the logisticians who are in charge of transporting migrants and the corruptors who are in the position of authority and who are able to secure final destinations by adopting corrupting practices.[78] Criminal groups can be very violent as the level of enforcement and controls are very strict in a State. In this context, it has been observed that the higher is the State's control on borders, the more vulnerable smuggled migrants will be as they will be victims of exploitation and violence.[79]

However, recent research has shown different ways smugglers operate compared to the way described above in this section. It has been analysed a group of smugglers who facilitated irregular migration from the Horn of Africa to Europe, especially Northern Europe.[80] These criminal groups analysed were based in Libya and in Sudan. Those operating in Libya included corrupt officials responsible to manage detention centres, organisers and aides.[81] Organisers give orders but do not receive them and aides receive order and are dependent on organisers in their activities. The group in Sudan was specialised in selling smuggling service.[82] What emerged from this research is that smuggling activities are very fragmented geographically and in the organisation and these features of smugglers go 'against narratives that conflate these separate sets of activities under the same 'smuggling' label.'[83] There are hierarchies but they are very rudimental and local with no evidence that there is a single centralised organisation which controls the activities of single groups perpetrating smuggling of migrants.[84] It could be that this research only concentrating on specific criminal investigations conducted in Italy have these features, whilst other organisations might have different characteristics and may be centralised. Cooperation between the different police forces of nations involved in smuggling should cooperate with each other especially, if the crime is not perpetrated by a centralised criminal

77 See Tinti, P., and Reitano, T.,...*op. cit. note 76, p. 59.*

78 See Tinti, P., and Reitano, T.,...*op. cit. note 76, p. 65.*

79 See Tinti, P., and Reitano, T.,...*op. cit. note 76, p. 64.*

80 See Campana, P., 'Out of Africa: The Organization of migrant smuggling across the Mediterranean'. On *European Journal of Criminology 2017, p. 7.*

81 See Campana, P.,...*op. cit. note 80, p.8.*

82 See Campana, P.,...*op. cit. note 80, p.9.*

83 See Campana, P.,...*op. cit. note 80, p.11.*

84 Ibid

organisation. Campana highlights that criminal justice response should aim to coordination between police located in all countries where smuggling is perpetrated. [85] Coordination should also involve non-EU countries.[86]

3. CONNECTIONS BETWEEN SMUGGLING AND HUMAN TRAFFICKING

Understanding connections between smuggling and trafficking can reduce the latter crime by reducing the chances of people smuggled to become victims during their trips and after they reach Europe. It has been reported that there are three ways by which a smuggled migrant becomes victim of THB.[87] One way is when the migrant has reached his or her final destination as the tie with smugglers does not end upon the end of his or her trip. At this point migrants can become victims of trafficking as they have to repay the price for their trip.[88] Nevertheless, this practice seems not to be in use anymore on the southern Mediterranean route, as migrants have to pay the price of their journey before they travel from Egypt and from Libya.[89] Another way by which smuggling can become trafficking is when the migrant is still travelling to reach his or her final destination and is trafficked either for the purpose of sexual exploitation or forced labour or drug smuggling. [90] There are also reports which show that women become victims of torture and rape whilst travelling from the Sub-Saharan Africa.[91] These reports have been confirmed by recent investigations

85 See Campana, P.,...*op. cit. note 80, p.17.*

86 Ibid The topic is analysed in chapter 5.

87 See Triandafyllidou, A., and Maroukis, T., *Migrant Smuggling. Irregular Migration from Asia and Africa to Europe, Palgrave Macmillian, 2012, p. 191.*

88 Ibid.

89 See European Commission, DG Migration & Home Affairs 'A Study on Smuggling of Migrants. Characteristics, responses and cooperation with third countries'...*op. cit. note 46, p. 46.*

90 See Triandafyllidou, A., and Maroukis, T., ...*op. cit. note 87, p. 192.*

91 Ibid. See also European Commission, DG Migration & Home Affairs 'A Study on Smuggling of Migrants. Characteristics, responses and cooperation with third countries'... *op. cit. note 46, p. 20.*

conducted by Italian public prosecutors in Palermo (Italy) in the Glauco case I [92] who have successfully detected a criminal network which smuggled migrants from Libya, Eritrea, Ethiopia, Sudan and Israel to Sicily.[93] Subsequently, the same organisation smuggled migrants to Northern Italy and eventually to Sweden, Germany, Norway, the Netherlands, France, Austria, Australia and Canada.[94] During the investigations, public prosecutors have found out that migrants have been kidnapped, tortured and raped.[95] In addition, kidnapped migrants have been kept in detention in Libya until their families, contacted by the organisations, have paid the ransom for their release. [96] One of the migrants from Eritrea witnessed that the criminal network was able to contact his mother in Eritrea and ask the payment of 3300 US dollars in exchange for his release. [97] In prison, migrants have been forced to assist to the torture of other migrants and they have been forced to stand on their feet while they were beaten and tortured by electric discharge. [98] Public prosecutors stated that these cases fall within the scope of human trafficking as the consent initially given, has lost its validity since it is not more free, unconditional and reversible. [99] Finally, it has been identified another way by which smuggling can become trafficking and it is enslavement which may occur through employment opportunities during the migrant's trip.[100] Usually, migrants start to work in sweatshops or in the construction sector and soon realise they are trapped. In other cases, migrants whilst *en route*, become involved with the smuggling business to be able to pay

92 See Statement of UNODC Executive Director Yury Fedotov on Italian criminal investigation known as "Glauco 1". On https://www.unodc.org/unodc/en/press/releases/2016/February/statement-of-unodc-executive-director-yury-fedotov-on-italian-criminal-investigation-known-as-glauco-1.html, accessed on 15/6/2016.

93 See Decreto di Fermo disposto dal P.M.-art 384 c.p.p. *Procura della Repubblica presso il Tribunale di Palermo, Direzione Distrettuale Antimafia, 30/5/2014, p. 16 (Arrest warrant issued by the Prosecutor's Office at the Court of Palermo, District Antimafia Directorate). Document received by Public Prosecutor Dr Gery Ferrara by e mail on 23/3/2016.*

94 Ibid, p. 2.

95 Above note 93, p. 41 *et seq.*

96 Above, note 93 page 41 *et seq.*

97 Above note 22, p. 43.

98 Ibid

99 Above note 93, p. 13.

100 Ibid

part of their journey.[101] These cases should be clearly investigated and distinguished by cases of smuggling where these violations of human rights do not occur. Research conducted from 1990 to 2015, in a particular Italian region called Apulia, has revealed that not always smuggling of migrants is connected to trafficking and that not always there are centralised and highly organised criminal networks which smuggle people.[102] Smuggling groups analysed by this particular research, are characterised by heterogeneity and, in the Eastern Mediterranean, they mainly consist of family-based businesses.[103] It has also been reported that for many irregular migrants, smugglers are the only way to escape from poverty and other dangerous situations. [104] In other terms, smugglers may be providing the service without being exploiting migrants and asylum seekers who, conversely, may work for smugglers as recruiters, intermediaries and in other positions. [105] Hence, investigating whether migrants have been victimised by smugglers and traffickers is very important to understand links between smuggling and trafficking and address these serious criminal activities. Certainly, as public prosecutors in Palermo have highlighted, smuggling and trafficking can be defeated by EU policy on legal migration as this policy would reduce demand by people who otherwise would not be able to leave their countries of origin when they are in a situation of danger or poverty.[106] In the meantime, migrants who risk to become victims of trafficking should be protected, by adopting a policy which is addressed specifically to them. The European Commission has published the European Agenda for Migration and has identified as a priority the fight against migrant smuggling and trafficking in human beings.[107] For this purpose, it has highlighted how important is to address the root causes of irregular migration and cooperate with third countries to fight against criminal networks.[108] It has also emphasised that EU agencies can support Member States to

101 Ibid

102 See L. Achilli, *The smugglers: hero or felon? Migration Policy Centre, European University Institute, June 2015, page 4. On http://cadmus.eui.eu/bitstream/handle/1814/36296/MPC_2015_10_PB.pdf?sequence=1, accessed on 15/12/2015.*

103 Ibid, p. 5.

104 Above, p. 6.

105 Above, p. 7.

106 Above, p. 10.

107 See COM (2015) 240 final, 13/5/2015, p. 9.

108 Ibid pp. *7 at 8.*

identify smugglers, investigate and prosecute them, freeze and confiscate their assets.[109] However, the Agenda seems too concentrate on security rather than on the protection of victims of trafficking.[110]

Identifying victims and obtaining their support in investigations, can also make the difference in the fight against these two crimes as they can witness against smugglers who become eventually traffickers.[111] Certainly, identified victims should not be legally bound to give their support in investigations as the priority should be to protect them. However, it is thought that the victims' testimony should also be a priority. The next sections will analyse the legal framework on trafficking and smuggling and evaluate whether they can support the identification of victims of trafficking who have been previously smuggled.

4. LEGAL FRAMEWORK ON PEOPLE SMUGGLING AND THE RECOGNITION OF SOME FORMS OF PROTECTION TO SMUGGLED MIGRANTS

4.1 Legal framework on people smuggling in international law and in the EU law

International level.

At International level, in 2000, the UN has adopted the United Nations Convention on Transnational Organised Crime (UNCTOC).[112] The UNCTOC

109 Above note 107.

110 See section 4 of this chapter. For an in depth analysis of EU policies concentrated on securitisation of borders rather than on adequate protection of asylum seekers and migrants see Basilien-Gainche, M.L., "The EU immigration and asylum policy in the post-Lisbon institutional context", in Rubini, L., and Robertson, D., (ed.), *The Treaty of Lisbon and the Future of European Law, London, Edward Elgar Publishing, 2012, pp. 355-378.*

111 It has already been demonstrated by semi-structured interviews that the support of witnesses is very important in investigations against smuggling and trafficking. See Ventrella, M., *The control of people smuggling and trafficking in the EU: Experiences from the UK and Italy' Routledge, 2010, chapter 5.*

112 See General Assembly Resolution 55/25 of 15 November 2000. Available on https://www.unodc.org/documents/treaties/UNTOC/Publications/TOC%20Convention/TOCebook-e.pdf, accessed on 27/5/2016.

includes the Convention on the fight against trans-national crime and different Protocols. In between these Protocols, there is one on Human Trafficking and another one on Smuggling of Migrants. The Trafficking Protocol has different provisions which define the crime and provide all the measures that have to be taken to prevent human trafficking. Human trafficking is 'the recruitment, transportation and transfer...by means of the threat or use of force or other forms of coercion, of abduction, of fraud, of deception, of the abuse of power or of a position of vulnerability'.[113] Human trafficking is characterised by exploitation which according 'shall include, at a minimum, the exploitation of the prostitution of others..., forced labour or services, slavery or practices similar to slavery, servitude or the removal of organs'[114] and the victims' consent is irrelevant.[115] Victims shall be protected by State Parties which shall ensure they are provided with appropriate information, assistance to permit them to be heard in criminal proceedings. [116] Furthermore, victims shall be provided with housing, counselling and information, medical assistance, psychological support, material assistance, employment, education and training opportunities. [117] State Parties shall also guarantee victims a shelter, in order to protect their physical safety and the possibility of obtaining compensation for damage suffered. [118] The UNCTOC Protocol also establishes that victims should be given the opportunity to remain on the territory of each State Party temporarily or permanently.[119] If State Parties decide to return victims to their countries of nationality or of permanent residence, they have to do this 'with due regard for the safety of that person and for the status of any legal proceedings related to the fact that the person is a victim of trafficking and shall preferably be voluntary'.[120] Thus, the UNCTOC Trafficking Protocol does not encourage the immediate return of victims as the priority shall be their safety.

113 See Article 3 UNCTOC Trafficking Protocol.

114 See Article 3 (a) UNCTOC Trafficking Protocol.

115 See Article 3 (b) UNCTOC Trafficking Protocol.

116 See Article 6 (2) UNCTOC Trafficking Protocol.

117 See Article 6 (3) UNCTOC Trafficking Protocol.

118 See Article 6 (5) and (6) UNCTOC Trafficking Protocol.

119 See Article 7 UNCTOC Trafficking Protocol.

120 See Article 8(2) UNCTOC Trafficking Protocol.

The UNCTOC Smuggling Protocol defines smuggling of migrants as 'the procurement, in order to obtain directly or indirectly, a financial or other material benefit, if the illegal entry of a person into State Party of which the person is not national or a permanent resident'. [121] The Smuggling Protocol requires State Parties to criminalise smuggling and then it focuses on smuggling of migrants by sea.[122] State Parties shall take measures against vessels suspected to smuggle migrants, they must 'Ensure the safety and human treatment of the persons on board'.[123] The Smuggling Protocol never refers to smuggled migrants as victims as Article 16 (1) states that 'each State Party shall take...all appropriate measures...to preserve the rights of persons' who have been smuggled. Legal protection recognised by the Smuggling Protocol is of high standard as it requires State Parties to preserve 'the right to life and the right not to be subjected to torture or other cruel, inhuman or degrading treatment or punishment'. State Parties shall take all the appropriate measures to protect migrants who have been smuggled from the violence of their smugglers.[124] Certainly, Article 18 states that smuggled migrants should be returned to their countries of nationality or of permanent residence. Nevertheless, State Parties have to ensure that the life of migrants is preserved as their right not to be tortured and subject to inhuman and degrading treatment. As shown above, [125] this may be the case of many migrants who trust smugglers who eventually turn into traffickers. Hence, UNCTOC Smuggling Protocol provisions, support investigations on trafficking by linking this crime to smuggling of migrants.

In 2005 it was adopted the Council of Europe Convention on Action against Trafficking in Human Beings. The definition given by Article 4 of the Convention is identical to the definition that can be found in the Trafficking Protocol. However, the Council of Europe Convention is more focused on the protection and assistance of victims.[126] Victims shall be identified by competent authorities

121 See Article 3 UNCTOC Smuggling Protocol.

122 See Articles 6 and 7 UNCTOC Smuggling Protocol.

123 See Article 9 (1) (a) UNCTOC Smuggling Protocol.

124 See Article 16 (2) UNCTOC Smuggling Protocol.

125 See section 2.

126 Available on http://www.coe.int/en/web/conventions/full-list/-/conventions/rms/090000168008371d, accessed on 27/5/2016.

of State Parties and protected.[127] Furthermore, 'if the competent authorities have reasonable grounds to believe that a person has been victim of trafficking in human beings, that person shall not be removed from its territory until the identification process as victim'[128] of trafficking has been completed. The Council of Europe Convention has also more specific provisions on the assistance of victims and on the residence permit. 'Each Party shall issue a renewable residence permit to victims'[129] when it 'is necessary owing to their personal situation'[130] or when their presence 'is necessary for the purpose of their co-operation'[131] with law investigative and judicial authorities. Further attention is given to the victims when the Convention states that when victims are returned to their countries of origin or permanent residence, the receiving State has to accept them, 'with due regard for the rights, safety and dignity of that person and for the status of any legal proceedings related to the fact that the person is a victim, and shall preferably be voluntary'.[132] State Parties shall ensure that victims of human trafficking are protected 'from potential retaliation or intimidation in particular during and after investigations'.[133] This provision applies to victims of human trafficking and to all people who witness against traffickers.[134] Nevertheless, the Convention does not establish the possible links that may occur with smuggling of migrants by providing an identification system which may include smuggled migrants who might have become victims of trafficking during their journey.

127 See Article 10 (1) of the Council of Europe Convention on Action against Trafficking in Human Beings, 2005.

128 See Article 10 (2) of the Trafficking in Human Beings Convention.

129 See Article 14(1) of the Trafficking in Human Beings Convention.

130 See Article 14(1) (a) of the Trafficking in Human Beings Convention.

131 See Article 14(1) (b) of the Trafficking in Human Beings Convention.

132 See Article 16 (2) of the Trafficking in Human Beings Convention.

133 See Article 28 (1) of the Trafficking in Human Beings Convention.

134 See Article 28(1) (a), (b) and (c) of the Trafficking in Human Beings Convention.

EU legal framework.

At EU level, Framework Decision 2002/629/JHA has been adopted in 2002[135] and replaced in 2011 by the Trafficking Directive.[136] The Trafficking Directive defines the crime and it establishes a very detailed programme for the protection of human trafficking victims'[137] The Directive is more specific in the definition of trafficking and in providing protection, compared to the previous Framework Decision. It defines the concept of vulnerability as 'a situation in which the person concerned has no real or acceptable alternative but to submit to the abuse involved'.[138] The Trafficking Directive also recalls two very important legal sources which are Framework Decision 2001/220/JHA[139] and Directive 2004/81/EC (Residence Permit Directive).[140] Paragraph 17 of the Trafficking Directive identifies the difference with the Residence Permit Directive and clarifies that whilst the latter deals with third-country nationals who are victims of trafficking, the Trafficking Directive deals with 'specific protective measures for any victim of trafficking in human beings'. Article 1 of the Residence Permit Directive states that the aim of this Directive 'is to define the conditions for granting residence permits of limited duration...to third-country nationals who cooperate' against trafficking and smuggling. Article 3 (1) states that the provisions of this Directive shall be applied 'to the third-country nationals who are, or who have been victims of offences related to the trafficking in human beings, even if they have illegally entered the territory of the Member State'.

The Trafficking Directive includes additional forms of sexual and labour exploitation which were outside the scope of Framework Decision 2002/629/JHA and which are 'begging, slavery or practices similar to slavery, servitude or the exploitation of criminal activities, or the removal of organs'. [141] The Trafficking Directive complies fully with the requirements of the European Court of Human Right (ECtHR) which considers human trafficking a form of

135 See Council Framework Decision 2002/629/JHA of 19 July 2002. OJ L 203/1, 1/8/2002.

136 See Directive 2011/36/EU 5 April 2011. OJ L. 101/1, 15/4/2011. (Trafficking Directive)

137 See Articles 1 and 11-16 of the Trafficking Directive.

138 See Article 2 (2) of the Trafficking Directive.

139 See Framework Decision 2001/220/JHA. OJ L 82/1, 22 March 2001.

140 See Council Directive 2004/81/EC of 29 April 2004. On OJ L 261 p. 19, 6 August 2004. (Residence Permit Directive).

141 See para. 1 and Article 2(3) of the Trafficking Directive.

slavery prohibited by Article 4 ECHR.[142] The Trafficking Directive also complies with the Strasbourg Courts' case-law which has recognised that State Parties have the positive obligation to protect victims of trafficking. The Strasbourg Court has been very strict on this point and has sanctioned Greece because they did not protect a victim of human trafficking as they did not undertake investigations on trafficking and did not prosecute criminals in a reasonable time.[143] The Trafficking Directive states that Member States shall impose appropriate penalties and shall use effective investigations instruments to ensure that perpetrators of trafficking are arrested and prosecuted.[144] The Directive requires that Member States impose jurisdiction over human trafficking when the crime 'is committed in whole or in part within their territory; or the offender is one of their nationals'. [145] Member States can impose extraterritorial jurisdiction by informing the Commission when the crime has been committed against one of its national or against a person who has the habitual residence on their territory; when the offence is committed for the interests of a legal person established on its territory or the perpetrator has his or her habitual residence on its territory.[146] Extraterritorial jurisdiction cannot be subject to the condition that the act is a criminal offence in the place where it is committed and that the prosecution can be initiated following a statement made by the victim or the State of the place where the crime was committed.[147] The Directive pays particular attention to the protection of victims by imposing Member States not to criminalise victims and not to bind investigation and prosecution to the report of the victim. [148] There are specific Articles in the Trafficking Directive establishing the form of protection victims of human trafficking are entitled to and there is a particular attention given to children. Conversely, the Framework Decision had only one

142 See Case *Rantsev v. Cyprus and Russia, Application no. 25965/04, judgement of 7 January 2010, paragraphs 282 at 283. See Case Siliadin v. France, Application no. 73316/01, Para 112. See Chowdury and others. V. Greece, Application No. 21884/15, 20/3/2017. For an in-depth analysis of trafficking as a form of slavery see* Piotrowicz, R., (2012) "States' Obligations under Human Rights towards Victims of Trafficking in Human Beings: Positive Developments in Positive Obligations'. In *International Journal of Refugee Law*, Vol. 24/2, pp. 181-201.

143 See Case *L.E. v. Greece, Application no. 71545/12, Judgement of 21 January 2016.*

144 See Articles 4 and 9 of the Trafficking Directive.

145 See Article 10(1) of the Trafficking Directive.

146 See Article 10(2) of the Trafficking Directive.

147 See Article 10(3) (a) (b) of the Trafficking Directive.

148 See Articles 8 and 9(1) of the Trafficking Directive.

provision on the protection of victims as it prioritized the fight against trafficking rather than protection of victims.[149] The victim centered approach can also be found in other provisions of the Trafficking Directive which establish that victims shall receive assistance and support before, during and after the conclusion of criminal proceedings for an appropriate period of time.[150] The Directive has a provision very wide in the scope which supports the identification of victims. The provision states that victims shall be provided support as soon as 'the competent authorities have a reasonable-grounds indication for believing that the person might have been subjected' to human trafficking (Article 11 Para 2 of the Trafficking Directive).[151] Article 12(1) of the Trafficking Directive states that provisions on the protection of victims of trafficking in criminal investigations, 'shall apply to the rights set out in Framework Decision 2001/220/JHA'. This Framework Decision provided protection of victims of crimes in criminal proceedings and has been replaced by Directive 2012/29/EU.[152] By linking the legal framework on the protection of victims in general to victims of human trafficking, these provisions prioritize the protection of victims and the prevention of re-victimization. This is because victims of human trafficking can be protected under the specific provisions established by the Residence Permit Directive or by the Trafficking Directive in connection with Directive 2012/29/EU on protection of victims of crime. Article 1(1) of this latter Directive states that 'The purpose of this Directive is to ensure that victims of crime receive appropriate information, support and protection and are able to participate in criminal proceedings'. Article 2 (1) (a) (i) states that "victim' means a natural person who has suffered harm, including physical, mental or emotional harm or economic loss which was directly caused by a criminal offence'. Victims of human trafficking can fall into this category and receive the appropriate protection.

It can be noted that the Human Trafficking Directive has provided a wide definition of trafficking, which includes slavery and other forms of exploitation. However, it has not provided adequate provisions for the identification and protection of victims of human trafficking. Article 11 (2) leaves wide discretion to the competent authorities of Member States by requiring them to give assistance and support to people on the basis of the 'reasonable-ground indication'.

149 See Article 7 of Framework Decision 2002/629/JHA...op. cit. note 135.

150 See Article 11(1) of the Trafficking Directive.

151 See Article 11(2) of the Trafficking Directive.

152 See Directive 2012/29/EU of 25 October 2012. On OJ L. 315/57, 14 November 2012.

If from one side, the 'reasonable-grounds indication' criteria can permit them to identify as many victims as possible at an early stage and identification is very important, in order to grant victims the residence permit and to prevent re-victimization.[153] This is because victims would not be left in detention centres with other migrants or deported unidentified. Indeed, if they are left in detention centres, they will be at high risk of re-victimization. From the other side, leaving wide discretion to Member States can lower the standard of protection of the Council of Europe Trafficking Convention (CoE Trafficking Convention).[154] This is because the Trafficking Directive does not establish a specific procedure that can permit the identification of victims and prevent their immediate deportation on the basis of the reasonable grounds to believe that they could be victims of trafficking rather than only irregular migrants that should be deported.

EU legal framework on smuggling of migrants.

The crime of smuggling of migrants, at EU level, has been established by Council Directive 2002/90/EC (from now on Smuggling Directive).[155] The Directive defines assisting irregular migration with or without the purpose of a financial gain.[156] The latter criminal activity can be classified as smuggling of migrants because its definition is the same given by the UNCTOC Smuggling Protocol. The EU has also set up a Council Framework Decision which requires Member States to adopt 'effective, proportionate and dissuasive criminal penalties' against assisting irregular migration with or without the purpose of a financial gain.[157] In terms of protection of victims and as emphasized above, Article 3 (2) of the Residence Permit Directive states that 'Member States may apply this Directive to the third country nationals who have been the subject of an action to facilitate illegal immigration'. Hence, the issue of a resident permit to people who have been smuggled is optional and not compulsory as it is in the case of victims of trafficking. The issue of a residence permit becomes compulsory

153 See Craggs. S., and Martens, R. "Rights, Residence, Rehabilitation: A Comparative Study Assessing Residence Options for Traffickers Persons. (2010). Available on http://publications.iom.int/system/files/pdf/iml24.pdf p.55 *at 56. 14 July 2017.*

154 See Stoyanova, V., (2017) *Human Trafficking and Slavery Reconsidered (Cambridge University Press), p. 448.*

155 See Council Directive 2002/90/EC of 28 November 2002. On L 328/17, 5/12/2002.

156 See Article 1 of Directive 2002/90/EC.

157 See Article 1 of Council Framework Decision of 28 November 2002. On OJ L 328/1, 3/12/2002.

only if smuggled persons are identified as victims of human trafficking as only trafficked people can be referred as victims.[158]

There are different considerations to be made on legislation concerning smuggling and trafficking. First of all, international and European law grant legal protection to people smuggled. The UNCTOC Smuggling Protocol states that the right to life of smuggled people and the right not to be tortured or not to suffer inhuman and degrading treatment, shall be protected by State Parties. Secondly, even if people smuggled are not considered victims by legislation examined, they can be granted a resident permit on Member States' discretion. Legal protection can be granted, on the basis of the Residence Permit Directive, when people smuggled decide to testify against traffickers as clearly established by the European Convention against Trafficking and the Trafficking Directive. Nevertheless, international and EU law do not support the identification if victims of human trafficking in between smuggled migrants. This is because the two crimes are considered separate and no law indicates that they can overlap. Legislation which makes optional the protection of smuggled migrants confirmed that links between smuggling and trafficking are not clearly defined and identified by international and EU law. Certainly, The EU and the UNCTOC consider a priority to detect connections between smuggling and trafficking as they have launched a global action not only to prevent and address trafficking but also to prevent and address smuggling for the years 2015-2019.[159] However, these actions should be supported by specific law indicating connections between smuggling and trafficking which at the moment is lacking. Furthermore, the European Commission (Commission) has reported that Member States do not even apply the Residence Permit Directive to victims of human trafficking.[160] Many Member States only grant protection to victims who decide to cooperate with law enforcement authorities.[161] Conversely, they have to ensure that investigations and prosecutions do not depend on the victims' willingness to testify

158 See Stoyanova, V., 'Complementary Protection for Victims of Human Trafficking under the European Convention on Human Rights'. On *Goettingen Journal of International Law, 3 (2011) 2, p. 782. See also* Bett, A., 'Towards a 'Soft 'Law framework for the Protection of Vulnerable Irregular Migrants'. On *International Journal of Refugee Law*, (2010) 22/2, p. 233 at 234.

159 See https://www.unodc.org/unodc/en/human-trafficking/index.html?ref=menuside, accessed on 10/6/2016. See also Global Action against Trafficking in Persons and the Smuggling of Migrants (2015-2019) on https://www.unodc.org/unodc/en/human-trafficking/glo_act.html, accessed on 10/6/2016.

160 See COM (2014) 635 final, 17/4/2014, p. 10.

161 Ibid

or to withdraw their statements previously given.[162] This problem has also been highlighted by the Group of Experts on Action against Trafficking in Human Beings (GRETA) established by the Council of Europe to monitor how State Parties of the European Convention on human trafficking apply it.[163] GRETA have highlighted that often the grant of a residence permit is bound to the victims' willingness to cooperate with law enforcement authorities and that the identification of victims is excessively based on a criminal law approach, with the consequence that many victims of trafficking are left without protection. [164] Instead, Member States have the legal obligation to protect victims of trafficking and provide them assistance as soon as the competent authorities have evidence showing that individuals have been victims of trafficking.[165] Assistance shall not be given only if victims decide to cooperate with law enforcement authorities in investigations,[166] otherwise many victims will remain unprotected and links between smuggling and trafficking will not be detected. In order, to protect victims of trafficking, it is essential to identify them in between smuggled migrants. This is because if it is true that not all smuggled migrants, become victims of trafficking as shown above,[167] there are people smuggled who become victims of trafficking. They have to be protected either by the law on trafficking or by other legal instruments such as the ECHR. The first step in this direction should be to identify them. This is a very difficult task as victims of trafficking may not claim their state. Research has shown that victims of human trafficking usually do not make claims, unless police and non-governmental organisations adopt specific

162 See Article 9(1) of Directive 2011/36/EU.

163 See Rules of procedure for evaluating implementation of the Council of Europe Convention on Action against Trafficking in Human Beings by the parties. THB-GRETA (2014)52, November 2014. Available on https://rm.coe.int/CoERMPublicCommonSearchServices/DisplayDCTMContent?documentId=09000016805a983c, accessed on 10/6/2016.

164 See Report concerning the implementation of the Council of Europe Convention on Action against Trafficking in Human Beings by Ireland, 26 Sept 2013, GRETA (2013)15, p.43. Available on https://rm.coe.int/CoERMPublicCommonSearchServices/DisplayDCTMContent?documentId=0900001680631cbe, accessed on 10/6/2016.

See also Report concerning the implementation of the Council of Europe Convention on Action against Trafficking in Human Beings by Sweden, 27 May 2014, GRETA (2014)11, page 38. Available on https://rm.coe.int/CoERMPublicCommonSearchServices/DisplayDCTMContent?documentId=090000168063c456, accessed on 10/6/2016. https://rm.coe.int/CoERMPublicCommonSearchServices/DisplayDCTMContent?documentId=090000168063c456, accessed on 10/6/2016.

165 See Article 11(2) of the Trafficking Directive.

166 See Article 11(3) of the Trafficking Directive.

167 See section 3, p. 20 of this chapter.

programmes of protection for them.[168] It has also been reported that victims of trafficking might not make claims because they may suffer from post-traumatic stress which can cause loss of memory and thus, they may forget the names of their traffickers. [169] Another reason they may not claim is because they fear juju ritual common in between victims coming from West Africa and Sub-Saharan Africa and which prohibits victims from revealing what happened during their journey.[170] It must be added that victims of human trafficking for sexual exploitation, for example, may not make any claims because they feel guilty for having been exploited. [171] When victims decide to testify, they and their families who live in their countries of origin, receive threats which demonstrate that there are strong connections between criminal networks in different countries.[172] Hence, it is important that Member States take their responsibility in identifying victims beyond the fact that they may not claim their status. There is also another problem to consider. Many smuggled migrants may not make claims because they may be blamed for having been smuggled and eventually trafficked. This may be the case of many smuggled migrants who are only culpable of having left their countries of origin irregularly because of the desperate situation they were experiencing. Investigations on smuggling of migrants undertaken in Palermo, for example, have revealed that public opinion and some stakeholders working in the field of smuggling and trafficking, mistakenly emphasise that the consent initially given by migrants, should be the reason to blame victims of human trafficking for having ended up in a situation of exploitation. [173] The public opinion and some stakeholders working in the field of trafficking and smuggling, use to distinguish between culpable consent and innocent consent by shifting the burden of proof to the victim and by considering an innocent victim only the person who can demonstrate that he or she has been forced to become a victim of trafficking for the purpose of sexual exploitation, forced labour or other forms of trafficking.[174] The victim is culpable when he or she has

---

168 See Ventrella, M., *The control of people smuggling and trafficking in the EU: Experiences from the UK and Italy. Routledge, 2010, pp. 196-201 and pp. 208-213.*

169 See Triandafyllidou, A., and Maroukis, T.,... *op. cit., note 87 pp. 183 et 186.*

170 Ibid.

171 Ibid.

172 Above note 169.

173 Ibid

174 Above note 93, pp. 12 *at 13.*

chosen to emigrate irregularly.[175] In other terms, having decided to leave irregularly his or her country of origin is the reason why the victim is not innocent but culpable and the public opinion and some stakeholders do not consider the fact that exploiters have misled migrants with the aim to obtain the consent to be smuggled and eventually, the smugglers have become traffickers by exploiting, torturing, raping and using other forms of coercion against migrants who are in a vulnerable position. [176] Victims must be identified beyond biases otherwise they will be re-victimised by criminal organisations. A recent report issued by the Commission revealed that victims are not identified as 'Trafficking remains 'an invisible crime' as the number of identified victims remains low'.[177]

The identification of victims of trafficking, can be done by respecting law on the prohibition of collective expulsion expressly recognized by Article 4, Protocol 4 of the ECHR. [178] By respecting this provision, immigration authorities will have the opportunity to question migrants and obtain indications, as stablished by Article 11(2) of the Trafficking Directive, on whether they can be victims of human trafficking.

4.2 Prohibition of collective expulsion

On the basis of Article 4, the ECtHR has ruled in *Becker v. Denmark*[179] that aliens cannot be pushed back without a "reasonable and objective examination of the particular cases of each individual alien of the group". This ruling has been confirmed by other cases such as *Conka v. Belgium* [180] where the ECtHR ruled that there was a violation of Article 4 Protocol 4 of the ECHR[181] because

175 Above note 93, p. 13.

176 Above note 93, p. 12.

177 See Report from the European Commission to the European Parliament and the Council. Report on the progress made in the fight against trafficking in human beings (2016) as required under Article 20 of Directive 2011/36/EU on preventing and combating trafficking in human beings and protecting its victims {SWD(2016) 159 final}. COM (2016) 267 final, 19/5/2016, p.11

178 See Article 4 Protocol no. 4 to the Convention for the Protection of Human Rights and Fundamental freedoms, securing certain rights and freedoms other than those already included in the Convention and in the first Protocol thereto as amended by protocol no. 11 on http://conventions.coe.int/Treaty/en/Treaties/Html/046.htm accessed on 20/7/2014.

179 Application no. 7011/75.

180 See *Conka v. Belgium* ECHR 2002I.

181 Ibid.

the personal situation and circumstances of individuals concerned had not been fully examined. Migrants were all requested to attend the police station at the same time and they were all requested to leave the Belgian territory at the same time. These facts were considered by the ECtHR as collective expulsion because the individual situations had not been considered separately and on a case by case basis. In *Hirsi Jamaa and others v. Italy,*[182] the ECtHR ruled that irregular migrants rescued in the extraterritorial sea, are under the control of the rescuing State and for this reason the prohibition of collective expulsion, applies also in this situation.[183] In this case, Italian authorities pushed back to Libya a group of Eritreans and Somali. The Italian government stated that the push-back was the result of an agreement with Libya on return policy of irregular migrants intercepted at the sea.[184] They also argued that migrants were intercepted in the high sea and not in the national jurisdiction.[185] Hence, the Italian government argued that they did not have the full and exclusive control of migrants and this is the reason why there was not collective expulsion.[186] However, the ECtHR ruled that the applicants had fallen within the jurisdiction of the Italian State because in between the period of boarding the ship with migrants rescued at the high sea and the period of handing them over the Libyan authorities, migrants had been under the continuous and exclusive control of the Italian authorities.[187] The ECtHR ruled that the notions of expulsion and jurisdiction are territorial and therefore, Article 4 only prohibits collective expulsion committed on the national territory. Nevertheless, in this particular situation, the Italian government had exceptionally exercised extraterritorial jurisdiction and, thus, extraterritorial expulsion by sending migrants back to Libya whilst rescuing them at the high sea. Certainly, the ECtHR stated that States have the right to adopt a restrictive immigration policy, with the aim to prevent irregular migration.[188]

182 See *Hirsi Jamaa and Others v. Italy, judgement of 23/2/2012, Application no. 27765/09.* For an in-depth analysis of the case see M. Den Heijer 'Reflections on Refoulement and Collective Expulsion in the Hirsi Case. On *International Journal of Refugee Law* 2013, 25/2, pp. 265-290. See also Giuffre', M., 'State Responsibility Beyond Borders: What legal basis for Italy's Push-Back to Libya?' On *International Journal of Refugee Law*, 2012 24/4, pp. 692-734.

183 See *Hirsi Jamaa and Others v. Italy...op. cit. note 182, para. 178.*

184 Para. 93.

185 See para. 64-66.

186 See para. 160 *et 172.*

187 See para. 178.

188 See para. 179.

However, this policy can be exercised only in respect of the Convention by not allowing collective expulsion and by giving migrants the right to appeal against the expulsion decision.[189] Since, the Italian government did not examine the individual situation and neither proceeded to the identification of migrants as they just embarked them on an Italian military ship, to return to Libya without conducting appropriate individual inteviews with trained personnel supported by interpreters or legal advisers.[190] Migrants were not even recognised an effective remedy as established by Article 13 ECHR because their situation had not been examined singularly.[191] These actions amounted to collective expulsion as per Article 4 Protocol 4 of the ECHR to the breach of Article 13 ECHR.

In *Khlaifia and Others v. Italy*,[192] the ECtHR ruled that the Italian government had acted in breach of Article 4 Protocol 4 because it did not produce documents capable of proving that migrants had been interviewed and that their individual circumstances had been taken into consideration.[193] In addition, all applicants were given the same outcomes and the external agreement concluded between Italy and Tunisia and not made public, provided for the possibility of returning migrants after their identification.[194] For these reasons the ECtHR ruled that there was a violation of Article 4 Protocol 4. The Court also found that the Italian government acted in breach of Article 13 because the justice of peace did not suspend the expulsion decision whilst ascertaining whether Article 3 ECHR (prohibition of torture and inhuman and degrading treatment) had been violated in hosting centres, as the applicants were alleging.[195]

These cases can be the legal bases to protect victims of trafficking who have been smuggled because they impose on Member States to examine the situation of all migrants who land in Europe no matter whether they are migrants and not 'genuine' asylum seekers. These cases clearly impose on Member States the

189 See para. 180 *at 181.*

190 See para. 185.

191 See para. 196.

192 See *Khlaifia and others v. Italy*, judgement of 1/9/2015, Application no. 16483/12.

193 See para. 156.

194 Ibid.

195 See *Khlaifia and others v. Italy...op. cit.* note 192, para. 172. See also *De Souza Ribeiro v. France, judgement of 18 December 2012 Application no. 22689/07, para 82. See Hirsi Jamaa and Others v. Italy... op. cit. note 129, para 200. See Jabari v. Turkey, Judgement of 11 July 2000, Application no. 40035/98, para 50. See Gebremedhin [Gaberamadhien] v. France*, judgement of 26 April 2007, Application no. 25389/05, para 66.

legal obligation to disembark all migrants, interview them by the support of trained personnel to understand whether they may make claims and be entitled to asylum either because they are escaping from conflicts or violation of their human rights or because they have been smuggled and eventually trafficked.

At EU level, following the ECtHR case-law, particularly *Hirsi v. Italy*, the EU Council and the Parliament have adopted a Regulation (Regulation 656/2014) which establishes new rules on maritime surveillance and rescue operations coordinated by Frontex.[196] The new Regulation clearly prohibits collective expulsion.[197] It is based on the principle of solidarity established by Article 80 of the Treaty on the Functioning of the European Union (TFEU).[198] Principle of solidarity means that all Member States shall share responsibility in order to implement the EU policies, including policies on asylum and immigration. This is a very positive element of the Regulation as it prioritizes cooperation between EU Member States when facing smuggling of migrants by sea. The Regulation introduces new interception and rescuing rules in order to protect migrants at sea more effectively and gives them the opportunity to disembark while waiting on a decision on their particular case. The Regulation addresses smuggling of migrants by establishing specific rules when one Member State suspects that one vessel is engaged in the smuggling of migrants by sea. [199] For this purpose, the Regulation introduces new rules on the interception of migrants in the territorial sea, on the high seas and in the contiguous zone.[200] These legal measures strengthen rules on rescue operations and the prohibition of collective expulsion because they guarantee that smuggled migrants will be rescued and disembarked. In addition, these legal instruments will guarantee that the situation of each smuggled migrant will be examined on a case by case basis as collective expulsion is prohibited. By this assessment, it can be possible to identify victims of trafficking in between smuggled migrants.

196 See Regulation (EU) no 656/2014 of the European Parliament and the Council of 15 May 2014 establishing rules for the surveillance of the external sea borders in the context of operational cooperation coordinated by the European Agency for the Management of Operational Cooperation at the External Borders of the Member States of the European Union, L 189/93, 27/6/2014. The UK and Ireland are not bound by this Regulation (paragraphs 25 and 26).

197 See Article 4 (3) which states that the personal circumstances of people rescued in the sea, must be assessed.

198 See paragraph 2 of Regulation 656/2014.

199 See Articles 6 and 7 of Regulation 656/2014...*op. cit.* note 196.

200 See Articles 6-10 of Regulation 656/2014...op. cit. note 197.

There are other provisions which can ensure smuggled migrants are protected against smugglers and traffickers. These provisions are Article 3 and Article 4 of the ECHR. Article 3 prohibits torture and inhuman and degrading treatment. As shown above,[201] many smuggled migrants could be victims of torture and if this is the case, they should be protected. Article 4 prohibits slavery and forced labour. Many smuggled migrants can become victims of these two crimes as shown above.[202]

4.3 Protection of smuggled migrants by applying Articles 3 and 4 of the ECHR

International law and the ECHR require that smuggled migrants are protected by the violence of their smugglers and that their right to life and not to be subject to torture or inhuman and degrading treatment, are protected. The UNCTOC Protocol clearly states that the right to life and not to suffer torture and inhuman and degrading treatment of smuggled migrants, shall be protected and that smuggled migrants should also be protected against the violence of smugglers.[203] These provisions can be read in combination with the rulings of the ECtHR.

The ECtHR has clarified when Article 3 ECHR can be claimed. In *Soering v. United Kingdom,* where the ECtHR stated that a violation of Article 3, can be claimed when there are 'substantial grounds for believing' that if the person will be returned, he or she will suffer torture or inhuman and degrading treatment.[204] In *Chahal v. United Kingdom,* The ECtHR confirmed that a person cannot be returned if he or she will suffer torture or inhuman and degrading treatment. On this occasion, the Court was very rigorous and ruled that in order to assess whether there is a real risk, the actual situation the individual is experiencing, must be taken into account and it must be evaluated rigorously.[205] The real risk shall be assessed on the basis of the personal circumstances and it must be shown that if the person is returned, he or she would face a worse position compared

201 See section 4.1, p. 22 of this chapter.

202 See section 3, p. 20 of this chapter.

203 See Article 16(1) and (2) of the UNCTOC Smuggling Protocol.

204 See ECtHR *Soering v. UK, Application no. 14038/88, judgement of 7/7/1989, para. 88.*

205 See ECtHR *Chahal v. United Kingdom, Application no. 22414/93, judgement of 15/1//1996, para. 86 et 96.*

to most people in the same situation.[206] Demonstrating a potential risk is not sufficient as the situation of risk has to be concrete and actual.[207] In other cases the court distinguished between inhuman and degrading treatment. The breach could be considered inhuman treatment when the treatment is 'premeditated... applied for hours at a stretch and caused either actually bodily injury or intense physical or mental suffering'.[208] The treatment is degrading when 'it humiliates or debases an individual, showing a lack of respect for, or diminishing, his or her human dignity, or arouses feelings of fear, anguish or inferiority capable of breaking an individual's moral and physical resistance'.[209] For the purpose of degrading treatment, it suffices that the humiliation is felt solely by the victim as it is not necessary that it is perceived in that way by other persons.[210] From the study of these cases, it could be asserted that smuggled people can be granted a visa and thus, can remain on the hosting territory, when they may face the risk to suffer torture or inhuman treatment. Smuggled migrants may face this ill-treatment, if they are smuggled by people who eventually turn in traffickers as shown above.[211] If returned to their countries of origin, they may fall into a vicious circle by being smuggled and trafficked again.

The ECtHR has expressly recognised that State Parties have the positive obligation to protect victims of trafficking which is considered a form of slavery and prohibited by Article 4 ECHR and to criminalise perpetrators.[212] As shown above,[213] most people who reach Europe, are supported by criminal networks. These criminal networks can become traffickers or cover traffickers who will eventually exploit migrants.[214] Investigations should evaluate whether migrants have become victims of trafficking during their journeys to reach Europe. The

---

206 Para. 96.

207 ibid

208 See ECtHR *Kudla v. Poland [GC], Application no. 30210/96, para. 92.*

209 ibid. See also ECtHR *Pretty v. United Kingdom, Application no. 2346/02, para. 52.*

210 See ECtHR *Tyrer v. United Kingdom, Application no. 5856/72, judgement of 25/4/1978, para. 32.*

211 See section 3.

212 See Case *Rantsev v. Cyprus and Russia, Application no. 25965/04, judgement of 7 January 2010, paragraphs 282 at 283. See Case Siliadin v. France, Application no. 73316/01, para 112. For an in-depth analysis of trafficking as a form of slavery see* Piotrowicz, R., ' States' Obligations under Human Rights towards Victims of Trafficking in Human Beings: Positive Developments in Positive Obligations', 2012. In *International Journal of Refugee Law*, Vol. 24/2, pp. 181-201.

213 See section 2, p. 13, of this chapter.

214 See section 3, p. 20 of this chapter.

ECtHR has been very strict on this point and has sanctioned Greece because they did not protect a victim of human trafficking as they did not undertake investigations on trafficking and did not prosecute criminals in a reasonable time.[215] The applicant was L.E. a Nigerian national who claimed to have been become victim of human trafficking and that Greek authorities did not take the necessary steps to investigate the crime and prosecute perpetrators.[216] The ECtHR ruled that Greece acted in violation of Articles 4 (prohibition of slavery and forced labour), Article 6 (1) (right to fair trial) and Article 13 (right to an effective remedy) of the ECHR. [217] Specifically, the ECtHR ruled that Article 4 had been violated by the public prosecutor because witnesses' statements had not been included within the evidence gathered and the public prosecutor did not initiate criminal procedures on the basis of statements made by the applicant on 26 January 2007, until 1 June 2007. [218] The Court also ruled that no tangible steps had been taken by the police in order to arrest and prosecute the perpetrator, as the police simply added his name in the police criminal record research files.[219] Hence, there was also a violation of Article 6(1) and Article 13 because the length of criminal procedure had been unreasonable and no effective remedy had been granted to the claimant. [220]

Articles 3 and 4 of the ECHR can permit legal protection of smuggled migrants. However, these legal provisions can only be applied when smuggled migrants claim to have been tortured during their journey or to have been trafficked. If they do not claim, they will remain with no protection.

The Human Trafficking Directive, as shown above,[221] make it clear that domestic law enforcement authorities of Member States have to undertake investigations and criminal proceedings when victims make claims. If people do not make claims, they will remain unprotected.

GRETA have emphasised that a priority, in order to identify victims in between irregular migrants, should be to train adequately border police officers,

215 See Case *L.E. v.Greece, Application no. 71545/12, Judgement of 21/1/2016.*

216 Para. 50, 60-63.

217 Para. 64-86.

218 Para. 79-82.

219 Para. 85.

220 Para. 96-100.

221 See section 3, p. 20 of this chapter.

asylum officials, members of staff in reception centres for asylum seekers and irregular migrants and judicial bodies in charge for issuing expulsion.[222] GRETA reported that in some Member States training as such does not take place.[223] At EU level, legislation does not support identification of victims of trafficking and of torture in between smuggled migrants. The recast Directive on the reception of applicants for international protection, for example, does not support this identification.[224] Article 21 (1) of the recast Directive states that victims of human trafficking can be considered vulnerable persons. However, Article 22(1) and (2) of the same Directive states that after the individual has made an application for international protection, Member States shall assess it within a reasonable time. The recast Directive assumes that victims of human trafficking will make a claim when often this will not be the case.

It has to be added that the EU Return Directive and relevant case-law, are only focusing on returning illegal staying to their countries of origin or residence without facilitating the identification of trafficked people in between smuggled migrants and the protection of smuggled migrants from the violence of smugglers as requested by the UNCTOC Smuggling Protocol. The EU Return Directive is characterized by inconsistencies as whilst from one side requires that migrants who should be returned are not kept in prison without valid reasons, from the other side, restricts the right of migrants to be heard prior deportation.

222 See 5th General report on GRETA's Activities covering period 1 October 2014 to 31 December 2015, p. 31. Available on https://rm.coe.int/CoERMPublicCommonSearchServices/DisplayDCTMContent?documentId=090000168063093c, accessed on 10/6/2016.

223 See GRETA's report on Spain, GRETA (2103), 27 September 2013, p. 31. Available on https://rm.coe.int/CoERMPublicCommonSearchServices/DisplayDCTMContent?documentId=090000168063c3dc, accessed on 10/6/2016.

224 See Directive 2013/33/EU of 26 June 2013 (recast). On OJ L 180/96, 29/6/2013. For an analysis of this Directive in relation to the protection of victims of human trafficking see Stoyanova, V., 'Victims of Human Trafficking. A Legal Analysis of the Guarantees for 'Vulnerable Persons' under the Second Phase of EU Asylum Legislation'. In *Seeking Asylum in the European Union: Selected Protection Issued Raised by the Second Phase of the Common European Asylum System. Martinus Nijhoff Publishers, 2015, chapter 3.*

5. ANALYSIS OF THE EU RETURN DIRECTIVE IN RELATION TO THE SITUATION OF SMUGGLED MIGRANTS

By analyzing the case-law on the right to be heard and the EU Return Directive, it will be noticed that if from one side, the ECHR and the Strasbourg Court recognize human trafficking as a form of slavery and impose State Parties to identify and protect victims. From the other side, the CJEU case-law states that the principle of prohibition of collective expulsion will be respected as soon as law enforcement authorities of Member States will have ascertained that the individual does not have the right to stay on their territory. On the basis of this case-law, no identification of victims of human trafficking in between smuggled migrants will be possible unless migrants claim to be victims which is very unlikely on the basis of what it has been highlighted above.[225]

Migrants who have been smuggled and who are not asylum seekers, refugees or victims of human trafficking, have to be returned to their countries of origin or permanent residence. The return of irregular migrants is established by the EU Return Directive 2008.[226] Migrants, before being returned, have the right to be heard otherwise Member States competent authorities, would be in breach of Article 4 Protocol 4 ECHR and subsequent ECtHR case-law.

The CJEU has ruled on the right of migrants to be heard prior returning to their countries of nationality or of residence.[227] Settled case-law has established that the respect of the right of defence and of the right to be heard can be restricted if this is in compliance with the general interests pursued by an adopted law measure, unless the objectives of the measure are 'a disproportionate and intolerable interference which infringes upon the very substance of the rights guaranteed.[228] The objective of the Return Directive is 'the effective return

225 See section 4.1 p. 22 of this chapter.

226 See Directive 2008/115/EC of 16/12/2008. On OJ L 348/98, 24/12/2008. (Return Directive). For recent developments of the EU Return Directive, see S. Peers, 'Irregular Migrants: Can human treatment be balanced against efficient removal?' On *European Journal of Migration and Law pp. 289-304. See D. Acosta Arcarazo 'The Charter, detention and possible regularization of migrants in an irregular situation under the Return Directive: Mahdi'. On Common Market Law Review 52, 2015, pp. 1361-1378.*

227 See Case C-129/13 *Kamino International Logistics EU:C:2014:2041, para. 29 and Case C-166/13 Mukarubega, EU:C:2014:2336, para. 13.*

228 See Case C-249/13 *Boudjlida EU:C:2014:2431,, para. 43. See also Case C-317/08 to C-320/08 Alassini and Others, EU:C:2010:146, paragraph 63. Case C-383/13 PPU, G. and R., EU:C2013:533, para. 33 and case C-418/11 Texdata Software, EU:C:2013:588, para. 84.*

of illegal-staying third-country nationals to their countries of origin'.[229] For this purpose, the return decision must be adopted as soon as domestic authorities determine that the stay is illegal.[230]

The return decision must be taken in compliance with Article 5 of the Return Directive and thus, 'the best interest of the child', 'family life' 'the state of health of the third-country national concerned'; 'and the respect of *non-refoulement'* have to be respected and, for this purpose, persons concerned must be heard.[231] Domestic competent authorities shall provide all information related to their particular situation in order to justify why a return decision cannot be issued in their case.[232] Victims of trafficking can be protected under Article 5 if they make claims and, if, after investigations based on the Trafficking Directive and the Council of Europe Convention against human trafficking, it is concluded that their return would be a violation of the principle of *non-refoulement.* In all cases not contemplating the exceptions of Article 5, the competent authorities do not have the legal obligation to disclose evidence in advance prior interview to the illegal stayers or to grant them a reflection period.[233] The right to be heard prior the adoption of a return decision, shall permit the domestic competent authority, to undertake an investigation only on the matter concerning return of the illegal stayer and to give a decision where reasons are adequately stated so that the person concerned will be able to bring a legal action against the decision.[234] The CJEU neglects victims of trafficking who do not make claims, as it does not permit to smuggled migrants who might have become victims of trafficking during their journey, to be recognised a reflection period. The CJEU is in compliance with Article 5 as this provision does not recall legal instruments on human trafficking and on people smuggling. Early identification mechanisms established by law on human trafficking, are not recalled by Article 5. The problem is that the Return Directive leaves too much discretion to Member States in identifying the categories of migrants who can fall within the scope of this Article. Such discretion is allowed because the EU Return Directive is only concentrated

229 See *Boudjlida, para. 45.*

230 See *Boudjlida, para. 46. See also Case C-61/11 PPU, El Dridi, EU:C:2011:268, paragraph 35 and case C C-329/11 Achughbabian EU:C:2011:807, paragraph 31 and Mukarubega, para. 57.*

231 See *Boudjlida , para. 49.*

232 Para. 50.

233 Para. 53-55.

234 Para. 59.

on returning migrants and in order to achieve this purpose, the Directive risks to contribute to neglect trafficked people who do not make claims. The return of irregular stayers should be adopted only when police authorities and humanitarian organisations are satisfied that there are not victims of trafficking in between the illegal stayers to be returned. Unfortunately, a new Draft Regulation is aiming to facilitate even more the return of irregular migrants and the adoption of this legal measure may be even more detrimental for victims of human trafficking.[235] Conversely, identification of trafficking victims in hotspots could be achieved by reforming the Facilitation Directive which should give specific tasks to humanitarian organisations in hotspots and in reception centres, in order to permit identification of trafficking victims in between smuggled people.

The right to be heard is a fundamental right expressly recognised by Articles 47 and 48 of the Charter of Fundamental Rights which recognise respectively the right to an effective remedy and to a fair trial and the right to be presumed innocent and the right of defence. The right to be heard is also guaranteed by Article 41 of the Charter of Fundamental Rights.[236] However, settled case-law has established that by reading Article 41, it is clear that the provisions are addressed to European institutions and not to Member States.[237] It discerns that an applicant for a residence permit cannot acquire on the basis of Article 42 of the Charter, the right to be heard in all proceedings concerning his or her application.[238] This right can be derived, instead, from the right of defence as it is a fundamental principle of EU law.[239] The right to be heard allows a person to explain his or her personal situation in an administrative decision and to correct an error.[240] Furthermore, this right requires that domestic authorities examine carefully and impartially all the aspects of the case and that they reach a decision where reasons are clearly stated.[241] Settled case law has established that the respect of the

235 See Draft Regulation of the European Parliament and of the Council on a European travel document for the return of illegally third-country nationals (first reading). Doc 10638/16, 28 June 2016.

236 See Article 41(2) (a) of the Charter of Fundamental Rights. See case C-129/13 *Kamino International Logistics EU:C:2014:2041, para 29 and Case C-166/13 Mukarubega, EU:C:2014:2336, para. 43.*

237 See Case C-482/10 *Cicala, EU:C:2011:868, para. 28. See also Cases C-141/12 and C-372/12 YS and Others, EU:C:2014:2081, para 67.*

238 See *Mukarubega, para 45. See also Case C-249/13 Boudjlida, EU:C:2014:2431, para 33.*

239 See *Boudjlida, para 34. See also Mukarubega para. 43.*

240 See *Mukarubega, para 47. See C-349/07 Sopropé* EU:C:2008:746, para 49. See *Boudjlida, para 37.*

241 See Case C-269/90 *Technische Universitat Munchen, EU:C:1991:438, para 14 and C-349/07 Sopropé* para 50.

right of defence and of the right to be heard can be restricted if this is in compliance with the general interests pursued by an adopted law measure, unless the objectives of the measure are 'a disproportionate and intolerable interference which infringes upon the very substance of the rights guaranteed.[242] The objective of the Return Directive is 'the effective return of illegal-staying third-country nationals to their countries of origin'.[243] For this purpose, the return decision must be adopted as soon as domestic authorities determine that the stay is illegal.[244] The return decision must be taken in compliance with Article 5 of the Return Directive and thus, 'the best interest of the child', 'family life' 'the state of health of the third-country national concerned'; 'and the respect of *non-refoulement*' have to be respected and, for this purpose, persons concerned must be heard.[245] They shall provide all information related to their particular situation in order to justify why a return decision cannot be issued in their case.[246] In all cases not contemplating the exceptions of Article 5, the competent authorities do not have the legal obligation to disclose evidence in advance prior interview to the illegal stayers or to grant him or her a reflection period.[247] According to the CJEU, the right to be heard prior the adoption of a return decision, shall permit the domestic competent authority, to undertake an investigation on the matter and to give a decision where reasons are adequately stated so that the person concerned will be able to bring a legal action against the decision.[248]

It can be asserted that if from one side the CJEU case-law permits vulnerable migrants to be heard in order to ensure that the principle of *non-refoulement* is respected by domestic law enforcement authorities. From the other side, it permits to neglect smuggled migrants without investigating whether they have been victims of human trafficking as the principle of *non refoulement* can include victims of human trafficking but not smuggled people. CJEU case-law in

242 See *Boudjlida para. 43. See also Case C-317/08 to C-320/08 Alassini and Others, EU:C:2010:146, para 63. Case C-383/13 PPU, G. and R., EU:C2013:533, para 33 and Case C-418/11 Texdata Software, EU:C:2013:588, para 84.*

243 See *Boudjlida, para 45.*

244 See *Boudjlida, para 46. See also Case C-61/11 PPU, El Dridi, EU:C:2011:268, paragraph 35 and case C C-329/11 Achughbabian EU:C:2011:807, para. 31 and Mukarubega para 57.*

245 See *Boudjlida para 49.*

246 Para. 50.

247 Para. 53-55.

248 Para. 59.

compliance with the Return Directive, rules that if the person concerned cannot fall within the categories indicated by Article 5 of the same Directive, they have to be returned to their countries of origin or residence as soon as possible and the right to be heard shall only guarantee that the case is examined in detail and the decision is clearly reasoned so to permit the illegal stayer to appeal against it. This law and subsequent case-law do not permit to identify victims of trafficking in between smuggled migrants. There is a gap in between the EU Return Directive and the protection of victims of human trafficking as early identification mechanisms such as interviews to smuggled migrants, which may support the identification of victims of human trafficking in between smuggled people, are made difficult by restrictive legal measures on the return of irregular migrants. This situation may leave many victims unidentified and subjected to smugglers and trafficked when they are returned to their countries of origin or if they escape by hosting centres and are eventually recruited by traffickers within EU Member States. It must be taken into account that irregular migrants are not only those people who are waiting for removal and thus, people who can be monitored by public authorities within Member States. There are also undocumented migrants who reach the EU border and do not make any claims. Subsequently, they disappear and their fate remains unknown. The European Commission has reported on the basis of the Eurostat data that on 386,230 irregular migrants apprehended in 2013, only 166,470 had been returned to their countries of origin.[249] When migrants cannot be detained anymore because the CJEU ruled that detention is only allowed pending the return of irregular migrants and for no more than 18 months from the apprehension of migrants,[250] they disappear and become undocumented. In the UK, for example, there is a high rate of human trafficking for the purpose of labour exploitation.[251] Research has revealed that forced labour is linked to trafficking and that many undocumented migrants entered to the UK via smuggling or trafficking routes, have become victims of trafficking

249 See Communication from the European Commission to the European Parliament and the Council. 5th Annual Report on Immigration and Asylum (2013) {SWD (2014) 165 final}. COM (2014), 288 final, p. 4.

250 See section 3.2. See, for instance, also Case C-61/11 *PPU El Dridi [2011] ECR I-3015; Case C-329/11 Achughbabian [2011] ECR I-11189; Case C-430/11 Sagor ECLI:EU:C:2012:777 and Case PPU G and R ECLI:EU:C:2013:533.*

251 See Annison, R., *In the dock. Examining the UK's criminal Justice Response to Trafficking, Anti-Trafficking Monitoring Group, June 2013, p. 18. For an overview on the extent of human trafficking in EU Member States see Perez Cepeda A.I., & Benito Sanchez, D.,Trafficking in Human Beings. A Comparative Study of the International Legal Documents. 2014 Europa Law Publishing.*

for the purpose of sexual exploitation and forced labour.[252] Qualitative research undertaken in two Italian cities which are Rimini and Siracusa, ascertained that in between 2006 and 2008 many undocumented migrants, have been trafficked for the purpose of sexual exploitation.[253] It has also been reported that many migrants, become victims of human trafficking after they have been smuggled.[254] Protecting people from trafficking is a legal obligation as shown in this chapter.[255] However, EU Member States and the EU are not focusing on them as they are too concentrated to return as many migrants as possible to their countries of origin or transit. Instead, the priority should be to identify victims of trafficking in between smuggled migrants to grant them legal protection. The identification of victims should be done in hotspots because the Commission stressed that the first step to protect victims and prevent trafficking is to identify actual or potential victims in the hotspots.[256] Thus, the repatriation of smuggled migrants and the application of the EU Return Directive should be delayed until the identification of victims in hotspots.

6. THE HOTSPOT APPROACH

The EU has then adopted the hotspot approach in 2015, to ensure that the European Asylum Support Office (EASO), Frontex and Europol will work with frontline Member States to identify, resister and fingerprint migrants.[257] Individuals who will claim asylum will undergo the asylum procedures and will be assisted by the EASO, the others will be assisted by Frontex which will support Member

252 See Forced Labour in the United Kingdom. On https://www.jrf.org.uk/report/forced-labour-united-kingdom, accessed on 8/6/2016. See also Clark, N. (2013) Detecting and tackling forced labour in Europe, p. 62 on https://www.jrf.org.uk/sites/default/files/jrf/migrated/files/forced-labour-europe-full.pdf, accessed on 8/6/2016. See Dwyer, P. Lewis, H., Scullion, L. and Waite, L. (2011) Forced labour and UK immigration policy: Status matters? p. 16. On https://www.jrf.org.uk/file/41487/download?token=DsgZ8vrL, accessed on 8/6/2016.

253 See Ventrella, M.,...*op. cit. note 168, chapter 5.*

254 See 'How are the war in Syria and the Refugee Crisis affecting Human Trafficking?'. *International Centre for Migration Policy Development on http://www.icmpd.org/news-centre/news-detail/news-detail/new_research_how_are_the_war_in_syria_and_the_refugee_crisis_affecting_human_trafficking/ accessed on 27/1/2016. The report focuses on Syrian refugees who become victims of human trafficking.*

255 See sections 4.1, 4.2, 4.3 of this chapter.

256 See COM (2016) 85 final, 10/2/2016, p. 16.

257 Ibid

States to return all irregular migrants. [258] In addition, the Commission stated that 'Europol and Eurojust will assist the host Member State with investigations to dismantle the smuggling and trafficking networks'. [259] The Commission highlighted that hotspots shall 'ensure screening, identification and fingerprinting'[260] of irregular migrants reaching the EU from its external border. Registration has the aim to control and manage the in-flows and irregular migrants fingerprinted and registered will be channelled either in 'the national asylum system' or in 'the European relocation system' or in 'the return system'.[261] The system will be automatic and aimed to return as many irregular migrants as possible in a situation which is considered an emergency. [262] Hotspots have been established in Greece and Italy.[263] In Greece, 5 hotspot areas have been identified which are Lesvos, Leros, Kos, Chios and Samos but only Lesvos is operating identification, fingerprint and registration of migrants and asylum seekers.[264] In Italy, 6 hotspot areas have been identified which are Lampedusa, Pozzallo, Porto Empedocle/ Villa Sikania, Trapani, Augusta and Taranto but only the hotspot of Lampedusa is fully operating as requested by the European Commission. [265]

The problem with the hotspots approach is that not only they are not fully operating but they also do not seem to address human trafficking and smuggling, by the identification of victims and by giving them adequate support. People who do not claim asylum will be automatically returned to their countries of origin as they will be considered not genuine asylum seekers. Member States law enforcement authorities' will not investigate human trafficking by interviewing people who might be victims of this crime who are vulnerable and who may not make claims.[266] This approach is against international and EU law

258 Ibid

259 Ibid

260 See COM (2016) 85 final...*op. cit. note 256, p. 5.*

261 Ibid

262 See COM (2016) 85 final...*op. cit. note 256, p. 8. See Ippolito, F., La 'Tragedia' delle Frontiere Europee. European Papers, European Forum, 9/5/2016 p. 3 available on www.europeanpapers.eu accessed on 13/6/2016.*

263 See Communication from the Commission to the European Parliament and the Council Progress Report on the Implementation of the hotspots in Greece COM (2015) 678 final and COM (2015) 679 final, 15/12/2015.

264 See Com (2015) 678 final...*op. cit. note 263, p. 5.*

265 See Com (2015) 679 final...*op. cit. note 263, p. 3.*

266 See section 3.

on the protection of victims of human trafficking examined above.[267] Hotspots have been established to facilitate the return of irregular migrants who do not claim asylum without investigating whether there are victims of human trafficking. EU policies on smuggling and trafficking are too focused on securitisation of borders rather than on protection of victims. All Communications published by the Commission on smuggling and trafficking stressed that these two crimes should be fought by cooperation with transit countries 'to prevent and detect smuggling activities as early as possible'[268] and by maximising cooperation with Europol and Eurojust in detecting trafficking.[269] The EU Action Plan against migrants smuggling was also focused on securitisation as it highlighted that joint investigation teams and strong cooperation with third countries should be established to fight against smuggling.[270] The EU Select Committee of the House of Lords stated that 'It is very disappointing that no meaningful proposals have been made to address assistance to vulnerable smuggled migrants'.[271]

Hotspots should be improved, in order to protect vulnerable smuggled migrants. Early identification systems should be launched to give assistance to smuggled migrants who have been trafficked or who can be trafficked. These vulnerable individuals should initially be given temporary protection to ensure that victims of trafficking are identified in between smuggled migrants. Subsequently, the Trafficking Directive and the protection indicated in this Directive should be applied to victims identified.

There is EU legislation which could permit the protection of smuggled migrants. This legislation is the Temporary Protection Directive.[272] The next section focuses on this Directive and on whether it can be applied to smuggled migrants, especially those migrants smuggled by sea, who otherwise would remain vulnerable to trafficking.

---

267 See section 3.

268 See COM (2015) 185 final, 28/4/2015, p. 18.

269 Ibid

270 Above note 268, p. 4 and pp. 8-10.

271 See House of Lords European Union Committee 'EU action plan against migrant smuggling' 4th Report of Session 2015-16 HL Paper 46, p. 31.

272 See Council Directive 2001/55/EC of 20 July 2001 on minimum standard for giving temporary protection in the event of a mass influx of displaced persons and on measures promoting a balance of efforts between Member States in receiving such persons and bearing the consequences thereof. OJ L 212/12, 7/8/2001.

7. APPLYING THE TEMPORARY PROTECTION DIRECTIVE TO SMUGGLED MIGRANTS NOT ENTITLED TO ASYLUM, TO REMAIN WITHIN THE EU TERRITORY

The Temporary Protection Directive has the aim to give temporary protection to displaced people in the case of a mass influx of people who cannot be returned to their countries of origin.[273] This situation could be the case of many smuggled migrants, especially the migrants smuggled by sea who risk their life when they travel by boat from North Africa to Italy and Greece. Peers stated that 'the grounds in the Temporary Protection Directive are clearly non exhaustive'.[274] This is because Article 2 (c) states that displaced persons are third country nationals or stateless persons who may fall within the scope of the Geneva Convention 'or other international or national instruments giving international protection'. Peers asserted that, on the basis of this provision, temporary protection could be recognised to persons fleeing environmental disasters.[275] What about victims of human trafficking initially smuggled? Victims of human trafficking can be protected under the UNTOC Trafficking Protocol, the Council of Europe Convention on human trafficking and different Directives adopted at EU level.[276] Conversely, smuggled people do not have the same form of protection and if they cannot be protected either by the Trafficking legal framework or by Article 3 ECHR or by Article 4 because they do not make any claims, they should be protected by applying the Directive on temporary protection. By applying the Directive on temporary protection and extending the protection to other vulnerable persons protected by 'other international or national instruments

273 See Article 1 Council Directive 2001/55/EC.

274 See Peers, S., 'Temporary Protection'. On Peers, S., Moreno-Lax, V., Garlick, M., and Guild, E., *EU Immigration and Asylum Law (Text and Commentary): Second Revised Edition, Volume 3 EU Asylum Law, p. 573.*

275 Ibid.

276 See Protocol to Prevent, Suppress and Punish trafficking in Persons, Especially Women and Children, supplementing the United Nations Convention against Transnational Organized Crime. A/RES/55/25, 8.1.2001. Document A/55/383. See Council of Europe Convention on Action against Trafficking in Human Beings, http://conventions.coe.int/Treaty/EN/Treaties/Html/197.htm accessed on 26/6/2014. See Council and European Parliament Directive 2011/36/EU of 5 April 2011 on preventing and combating trafficking in human beings and protecting its victims, and replacing Council Framework Decision 2002/629/JHA, OJ 101, p.1, 15/4/2011. See Council Directive 2004/81/EC of 29 April 2004 on the residence permit issued to third-country nationals who are victims of trafficking in human beings or who have been the subjects of an action to facilitate illegal immigration, who cooperate with the competent authorities, OJ L 261 p. 19, 6/8/2004.

giving international protection' as indicated by Article 2 (c) of the Directive on temporary protection, Member States should host many smuggled people who might have been victims of trafficking who do not make claims or who have been smuggled by sea. This is because they are more likely to be re-victimised or they are more likely to risk their life if they embark in dangerous journeys by sea. Smuggled people should be included in the scope of this Directive as the decision to travel irregularly from their countries of origins and by very poor means, is not a free decision as it has been influenced by their desperate situation.[277]

The Temporary Protection Directives should be applied on the basis of the spirit of solidarity as established by Article 25 of the Directive on temporary protection. Member States in a spirit of solidarity 'shall receive persons who are eligible for temporary protection'.[278] It is thought that Article 25 should be interpreted widely because if, as Peers suggested, the list of grounds of temporary protection is not exhaustive,[279] then the meaning of spirit of solidarity in the Temporary Protection Directive, should embrace the migrants who cannot be returned to their countries of origin because they would face extreme poverty and who cannot be protected otherwise, thus, at least people smuggled at sea should be included. This is because they will attempt to leave these countries again by trusting smugglers and by risking to die in the sea. It is thought that the Temporary Protection Directive should be applied mainly to these people as other displaced persons are protected by the Refugee Convention. There is who argues that the Directive on temporary protection has not been activated because Member States fear that it could create a pull factor.[280] However, it is thought that restricting protection to people who are vulnerable, although not asylum seekers or refugees, is not the adequate policy to prevent people to come to Europe. The recent tragedies have demonstrated that even if the law on migration is strict, people who are desperate will always try to come to Europe by all means they can possibly use. It is unfortunate that according to EU law,

277 See Ventrella, M., Recognising Effective Legal Protection to People Smuggled at Sea, by Reviewing the EU Legal Framework on Human Trafficking and Solidarity between Member States. *Social Inclusion Vol 3, 1, 2015, pp. 80-82.*

278 See Article 25 of Council Directive 2001/55/EC, OJ L. 212/12, 7/8/2001.

279 Above note 274.

280 See Ineli-Ciger, M., 'The Missing Piece in the European Agenda on Migration: the Temporary Protection Directive'. On http://eulawanalysis.blogspot.co.uk/2015/07/the-missing-piece-in-european-agenda-on.html accessed on 7/10/2015.

migrants who cannot be categorized either as asylum seekers or refugees or victims of human trafficking, or who cannot be reunited to their families who live on the EU territory, should eventually be returned to their countries of origin. Smuggled migrants especially those smuggled by sea, should be protected under the Temporary Protection Directive.

External policy only consisting of returning migrants to their countries of origin is not adequate. EU external policies do not take into consideration that migrants are in a state of necessity.[281] The EU has built fences and extremist political parties have stereotyped them as invaders, clandestine, illegals, cheats and opportunists. [282] The reality is that these people escape from war, persecution and poverty and they risk their life when they attempt to cross the Mediterranean Sea.[283] Many people who do not die in the sea, become victims of human trafficking and the crime is caused by authorities who want to create more security in Europe.[284] This is because

> 'each obstacle placed in the path of the exiles increases the price as well as the risks, because the immigrants have no other solutions. For many of them, the dangers of a sea crossing are the only alternatives to a life of violence or death in countries of conflicts'.[285]

There are many people expose to vulnerability in the migration's context. Migrants who escape from famine, for example, may not be covered by the Refugee Convention but they may be as vulnerable as refugees because they are using the same route, means and transport.[286] Migrants may be exposed to trafficking and if irregular migration involves smuggling, migrants can be vulnerable because at the mercy of criminal organisations.[287] The priority should be to

281 See 'Human Rights on the Southern Border'. Editing APDHA Immigration Section, April 2015 p. 6.

282 See 'Human Rights on the Southern Border'...*op. cit. note 281 p. 7.*

283 Ibid

284 Ibid

285 Ibid

286 See Migrant Vulnerability to Human Trafficking and Exploitation: Evidence from the Central and Eastern Mediterranean Migration Routes. International Organization for Migration 15/3/2017, p. 4 on https://publications.iom.int/system/files/pdf/migrant_vulnerability_to_human_trafficking_and_exploitation.pdf, accessed on 24/1/2018.

287 Above p. 5.

protect these people by fulfilling the obligations of Directives and other EU law adopted for this purpose. Subsequently, the EU external policy should concentrate on fighting the phenomenon by long term policies. Research has shown that no effective external action has been taken to prevent people leaving their poor countries of origin. The Ministry of Foreign Affairs and the Ministry of Public Service and Employment of Senegal in 2011, stated that the EU selective immigration policies are inappropriate because they cause losses of many talented and qualified people in Senegal. [288] The Ministry of Foreign Affairs also added that the EU common approach to migration prioritizes control of external borders. Instead, an effective way to prevent migration could be adopted by creating more wealth in African countries.[289] On the basis of these assertions, one thinks that return policies should be accompanied by more long term policies aimed at fighting against smugglers of migrants and at addressing the root cause of migration. The migrant and refugee crisis could only be resolved by strengthening the principle of solidarity in order to protect people in need and guarantee an area of freedom, security and justice for all people within Europe and outside this region. This objective can be achieved by addressing migration and refugee crisis as a whole problem. In a Communication of 2015, the European Commission highlighted that one of the priority to address the problem is by launching a new policy on legal migration.[290] At the moment, there is not a clear policy on legal migration and migrants at sea who are mostly people smuggled, remain with no rights with the risk to become victims of human trafficking in the EU or if returned to their countries of origin.

Neither the EU Directive on family reunification can be applied to ensure that they are not returned to their countries of origin or residence. The Family Reunion Directive has too many restrictions which make it very difficult to permit migrants at sea to remain in the EU territory.

288 See Reslow, N., ' The Role of Third Countries in EU Migration Policy: The Mobility Partnership'. In *European Journal of Migration and Law*, 14, 2012, p.403.

289 Ibid

290 See COM (2015) 240 final,...*op. cit. note 107, p. 14.*

8. THE FAMILY REUNION DIRECTIVE AND THE PROTECTION OF SMUGGLED MIGRANTS WHO CANNOT CLAIM ASYLUM

Before the entry into force of the Lisbon Treaty, the EC (now EU) adopted two Directives one on long term residence and the other one on family reunions.[291] The Family Reunion Directive was adopted in 2003 and it applies to all third country nationals who have their family members already residing legally on the territories of EU Member States. The aim of the Family Reunion Directive is 'To protect the family and establish or preserve family life, the material conditions for exercising the right to family reunification should be determined on the basis of common criteria'.[292] The Directive also states that 'Family reunification should apply in any case to members of the nuclear family, that is to say the spouse and the minor children'. [293] Hence, it can be noted that the Family Reunion Directive poses significant emphasis on the fact that families shall be protected and their reunification shall be enhanced. In the case of refugees, the Directive states that special attention should be given to them and it shall be taken into account the reasons why they were forced to leave their countries and prevented to have a normal family.[294] Nevertheless, the Directive on family reunion has been criticised because it discriminated against third country nationals who have an extended family. Indeed, it restricts the access to the EU only to one spouse of the person entitled to family reunion and it prohibits the access to unmarried partners and same sex partners.[295] In addition, the Directive has been criticised because it can permit an indefinite delay in receiving a reply on admission and this delay could lead to discrimination concerning accommodation and requirements on sick insurance.[296] For this reason, the Directive has

291 See Council Directive 2003/109/EC of 25 November 2003 concerning the status of third-country nationals who are long term residents (Family Reunion Directive). On OJ L 16/44, 23/1/2004 and Council Directive 2003/86/EC of 22 September 2003 on the right to family reunification. On OJ 251/12, 3/10/2003.

292 See Council Directive 2003/86/EC, para. 6.

293 See Council Directive 2003/86/EC, para. 9.

294 See Family Reunion Directive, para. 8.

295 See Article 4 of Directive 2003/86/EC. For a commentary, see S. Peers, N. Rogers *EU Immigration and Asylum Law: Text and Commentary. Martinus Nijhoff, 2006, chapter 19.*

296 See Peers, S. EU Justice and Home Affairs Law OUP2012, p. 472. See Cholewinski, R., 'Family Reunification and Conditions Placed on Family Members: Dismantling a Fundamental Right'. On *European Journal of Migration and Law Vol 4, 2002, p. 271 et seq.*

been seen as being 'another example where the notion of rights in the sensitive field of immigration is effectively reversed and regarded as belonging more to States than individuals'.[297]

In 2008, the first report on the implementation of the Directive showed that it had a low impact on harmonisation in the area of family reunification, mainly due to the fact that the Directive left too much discretion to Member States in implementing it.[298] The report showed that in 2008, although most Member States had implemented the Directive, 19 Member States had not communicated the transposition of the Directive, one was still in the process to transpose it and one had not started the transposition procedure at all.[299] The Commission emphasised that policies on family reunion 'are the key to successful immigration'[300] and for this reason it launched a broader consultation on the topic which was published in 2011.[301] Finally, in 2014, the Commission adopted a Communication on guidance for application of Directive 2003/86 on the right to family reunification.[302] The Communication provided a guide to Member States in order to apply the Directive correctly and in compliance with the rulings of the CJEU which ruled that the Directive has imposed the obligation for Member States 'since it requires them, in the cases determined by the Directive, to authorise family reunification of certain members of the sponsor's family, without being left a margin of appreciation'.[303] In the Guide, the Commission explained in detail how the margin of appreciation should be applied by Member States. Member States have the margin of appreciation to evaluate whether the right of family reunification, can be extended to members of the family other than the spouse and minors. In addition, Member States can assess whether requirements of the Directive are fulfilled and balance the competing interests of the individuals and of the entire community in the single situation.[304] Member States can make these verifications with the limitations imposed by the general rule that

297 See Cholewinski...*op.cit. note 296, p. 288.*

298 See COM (2008) 610 final, 8/10/2008.

299 ibid

300 Ibid p. 15.

301 See COM (2011) 735 final, 15/11.2011.

302 See COM (2014) 210 final, 3/4/2014.

303 See Case C-540/03 *Parliament v. Council*, ECLI:EU:C:2006:429, *para 60.*

304 See Case C-540/03...op.cit. note 303, para 61 *et 62.*

family reunification must be authorised and that derogations must be applied strictly. This rule is confirmed by the CJEU which stated that all measures concerning family reunification shall comply with Article 8 ECHR and Article 7 (1) (c) of the Charter of Fundamental Rights concerning the right to respect for family life.[305]

In the case of refugees, the Guidance for application of Directive 2003/86 on the right to family reunification,[306] the Commission emphasised that the margin of appreciation shall be applied very strictly.[307] Article 10 (2) states that Member States can authorise the reunification of members that normally would not be considered as part of the family as per Article 4, if they are dependent of refugees. In addition, Article 12 states that Member States shall not require refugees or family of refugees to show that they have sufficient resources, accommodation, sickness insurance and integration measures in compliance with their national law. The Commission stated that Member States when facing refugees or their families, have to use the margin of appreciation in a way which does not jeopardise the effectiveness of the Directive, because in the situations of emergencies, it is very difficult to trace family members, documents and dealing with authorities of their countries of origin in very short times.[308] The Commission added that when there are serious doubts that the person belongs to a family living on their territories, DNA tests can be allowed but these tests have to comply with UNHCR procedures on DNA testing.[309]

Smuggled migrants who have relatives within EU Member States, are outside the scope of the Family Reunion Directive. This is because they are irregular migrants and thus, they do not possess a residence permit. However, smuggled people may be included in this Directive either if they have a sponsor living on the EU territory in possess of a valid residence permit, as requested by Article 3 or in compliance with Article 5(b) of the Return Directive, which states that return policies should take into consideration the family life. The CJEU has ruled that the right to family reunification derives from Article 8 ECHR which

305 See Case C-578/08 *Chakroun, ECR I-1839, 2010, para. 44.*

306 See COM (2014) 210 final, 3/4/2014.

307 Above p. 20.

308 See COM (2008) 610 final,...*op. cit. note 298, p. 9.*

309 See UN High Commissioner for Refugees (UNHCR), UNHCR Note on DNA Testing to Establish Family Relationships in the Refugee Context, June 2008, available at http://www.refworld.org/docid/48620c2d2.html accessed on 21/9/2015.

guarantees the right to respect for family and private life and which includes the right to family reunification in its scope.[310] The principle has also been established by Article 7 of the EU Charter of Fundamental Rights (Charter) which states that 'Everyone has the right to respect for his or her private or family life, home and communication'. Subsequently, the CJEU ruled that even though Article 8 ECHR does not guarantee the right of a foreigner to enter and reside in a specific country, removing the foreigner 'from a country where close members of his family are living may amount to an infringement of the right to respect for family life as guaranteed by Article 8(1) of the ECHR'.[311] However, case-law of the ECtHR has emphasised that in the immigration area, State Parties enjoy a margin of appreciation as they have to balance the general interest of the community with the individual's right protected by Article 8(1).[312] States Parties have the right to control immigration by limiting family reunification.[313] Hence, EU Member States may impose strict requirements such as a condition of integration for children above 12 years old who arrive independently from the rest of the family, before reuniting them to their close members of their family, within their territories.[314] In addition, since EU Member States enjoy a margin of appreciation superior than that recognised in the case of refugees, they have the discretion to restrict the scope of the Family Reunion Directive to smuggled migrants who cannot claim asylum.

Article 6 authorises the use of discretion as it states that derogations to the family reunion Directives can be applied by Member States on the basis of public policy, public security or public health. The Commission pointed that, although the context, purpose and legal regime of the Directive on EU citizens' family reunion are different, case-law of the CJEU is an important background for Member States and national courts to interpret the concept of public policy,

310 See Case C-60/00 *Carpenter [2002] ECR I-6279 paragraph 42. See Case C-109/01 Akrich [2003] ECR I-9607, para. 59.*

311 ibid note 310. See also Case C-540/03 *Parliament v. Council...op. cit. note 251, paragraph 53. See Moustaquim v. Belgium, judgment of 18 February 1991, Application No. 12313/86, para. 16.*

312 See Article 8(2) ECHR. *See Gül v. Switzerland, Application no. 23218/94, judgment of 19 February 1996, para. 38, and Ahmut v. the Netherlands, Application no. 21702/93, judgment of 28 November 1996, para. 63.*

313 See *Ahmut v. the Netherlands, para. 67. See Sen v. the Netherlands, Application no. 31465/96, judgement of 21 December 2001, para. 36.*

314 See Article 4 (1) of the Family Reunion Directive. See Case C-540/03 *Parliament v. Council ECR I-5769, 2006, para 89 et seq. See COM (2008) 610 final, p. 3.*

public security and public health.[315] For this purpose, the Commission emphasised that public security covers internal and external security and has the aim to preserve the integrity of the territory of the Member States and of their institutions.[316] Public policy is understood as the protection of social order.[317] The Commission stated that restrictive measures based on public policy and public security shall be taken on a case-by case basis and thus, by evaluating the personal conduct of the individual without imposing general preventive grounds.[318] The threat must be present in order to be genuine.[319] Past offences are relevant only if there is the likely risk that the individual may reoffend.[320] The Commission also highlighted that if the individual belongs to an organisation, he or she may be considered a threat to public policy or public security only if they participate to the criminal activities of the organisation and they embrace and believe in the aims and designs of the organisation.[321] The Commission concludes that national authorities have to apply the principle of proportionality when assessing whether the individual can be a threat to public policy and public security.[322] In other terms, they have to balance the general interests of the nation with the personal and family situation of the individual.[323] It is clear that the Commission expects that family reunions have to be permitted as much as possible. The UNCHR has stressed that applying EU law on family reunion can be a step forward to solve the situation of refugees in Europe.[324] However, Member States are not keen to host refugees. This is because they are not cooperating with each other in relocating refugees in different EU Member States. This requirement

315 See COM (2014) 210 final,...*op. cit. note 250, p.11.*

316 See COM (2009) 313 final, 2/7/2009, p. 10.

317 Ibid

318 See COM (2009)...*op. cit. note 316, p. 11. See also Case C-67/74 Bonsignore,* ECLI:EU:C:1975:34 *paras 5-7. See Case C-408/03 Commission v Belgium, ECR 2006 I-2647, paras 68-72.*

319 See COM (2009)...*op. cit. note 318.*

320 Ibid note 319. See also Case C-30/77 *Regina v. Bouchereau* ECLI:EU:C:1977:172 *para 25 at 30. See also Cases C-482/01 and 493/01 Orfanopoulos and Oliveri* ECLI:EU:C:2004:262, para. 82 *et 100, and Case C-50/06 Commission v Netherlands* ECLI:EU:C:2007:325 *para. 42 at 45.*

321 See COM (2009)...*op. cit. note 316. See also Case 41/74 Van Duyn* ECLI:EU:C:1974:133 *para 17 et seq.*

322 See COM (2009)...*op. cit. note 316, p. 13.*

323 Ibid

324 See 'UNHCR: 6 steps towards solving the refugee situation in Europe' on http://www.unhcr.org/news/briefing/2016/3/56d96de86/unhcr-6-steps-towards-solving-refugee-situation-europe.html, accessed on 5/7/2016.

was established in September 2015 when, the Council adopted two provisional Decisions,[325] based on Article 78(3) TFEU which states that provisional measures can be adopted by the Council when one or more Member States are confronted by emergencies 'characterised by a sudden inflow of nationals of third countries'. Countries affected by these emergency were Greece and Italy.[326] According to these Decisions, asylum seekers with 75 per cent or more of refugee recognition rate should have been relocated.[327] People relocated were mostly nationals from Syria, Eritrea, Iraq, Central African Republic, Yemen, Bahrain and Swaziland.[328] Nevertheless, the Commission has reported that Member States have offered relocation to only 2000 people and only twelve Member States have relocated them, whilst five Member States have not relocated any individual.[329] It must be added that the Decision adopted on 22 September 2015 has been challenged by Hungary and Slovakia and two cases are pending before the CJEU.[330] If this is the situation of refugees, one can imagine how reluctant Member States can be in hosting migrants who are not refugees. In fact, the Commission has established that whilst individuals who score 75% or more of refugee recognition can be relocated. What is the fate of the other migrants? They are people with no rights. They risk to be returned to their countries of origin even if they may face violations of their human rights.[331] One shares the same concerns of Webber who rightly pointed out that

325 See Council Decision (EU) 2015/1523 of 14 September 2015. On OJ L239/146, 15 September 2015. See Council Decision (EU) 2015/1601 of 22 September 2015. On OJ L 248/80, 24/9/2015.

326 See Council Decision (EU) 2015/1523 of 14 September 2015, para 9.

327 See Council decision (EU) 2015/1523, para 20.

328 See European Commission EMN Inform 'Inform on Migrants' Movements through the Mediterranean', page 2. On http://ec.europa.eu/dgs/home-affairs/what-we-do/networks/european_migration_network/reports/docs/emn-informs/emn_policybrief_movementsmediterranean_final.pdf, accessed on 3/6/2016.

329 See COM (2016) 85 final, 10/2/2016, p. 11. For updated data on relocation see European Commission, Member States' Support to Emergency Relocation Mechanism (Communicated as on 9 June 2016), available on http://ec.europa.eu/dgs/home-affairs/what-we-do/policies/european-agenda-migration/press-material/docs/state_of_play_-_relocation_en.pdf, accessed on 13/6/2016.

330 See Case C-643/15, Slovakia v. Council, ECLI:EU:C:2017:631 *and Case C-647/15, Hungary v. Council,* ECLI:EU:C:2017:618.

331 See Webber, F., ''Hotspots' for asylum applications: some things we urgently need to know'. On http://eulawanalysis.blogspot.co.uk/2015/09/hotspots-for-asylum-applications-some.html, accessed on 6/10/2015.

> 'Without clear and robust safeguards in place, the EU's relocation package could turn out to be a figleaf for a quiet but massive removal operation against, rather than a protection operation for, those arriving on Europe's shores'.[332]

A removal operation which is not even feasible as EU return policies have not worked adequately in the past, as shown above in the book.[333] In addition, what about investigations on smuggling and trafficking? There may be many cases of people victims of trafficking which are from other African countries, who risk to remain without protection and vulnerable to become victims of trafficking again. As clearly emphasized by public prosecutors in Palermo, only an adequate policy on legal migration, can prevent them from being smuggled and trafficked.[334] If migrants could access to legal migration, they would not leave their countries of origin illegally and risking to be smuggled and to become victims of trafficking. It is important to reduce the demand and this could be done by 'the adoption of schemes that resettle refugees directly from conflict zones'[335] and by permitting the other migrants who are not refugees to access Europe legally. For this purpose, the EU should adopt policies facilitating the legal access of its territory.

9. IMMIGRATION POLICIES AND PROPOSALS FOR REFORMS

9.1 The need of skilled and unskilled migrants in the European Union

It has been estimated that in between 2012 and 2025, there will be an increased need for higher educated labour. The increase will be up to 23%.[336] There are significant gaps in areas such as science, technology, engineering and healthcare.

332 Ibid

333 See section 5, p. 36 of this chapter.

334 Above note 93.

335 See Campana, P., 'Out of Africa: The organization of migrant smuggling across the Mediterranean'... *op. cit. note 80.*

336 See COM (2015) 240 final, 13/5/2015, p. 14.

The European Commission emphasised that the EU is facing shortages in jobs where high skilled workers are required.[337] The Commission asserted that

> 'without migration the EU's working age population will decline by 17.5 million in the next decade. Migration will increasingly be an important way to enhance the sustainability of our welfare system to ensure sustainable growth of the EU economy'.[338]

New policy on legal migration should be adopted otherwise it will be difficult to fulfil those gaps. The Commission highlighted that policy on economic migration should be inclusive to ensure that in the medium and long term the gaps are fulfilled, although this is very unlikely.[339] The EU also needs unskilled workers.[340] Europe is living the shortage in population and this is why the whole continent needs skilled and unskilled workers.[341] Low skilled migrants play an important role in Europe as they allow native workers to be recruited in jobs requiring higher skills. [342] In addition, low skilled migrants save industries from collapse or stagnation caused by shortage of native workers.[343] The need of unskilled workers will increase in the next twenty years. [344] Smuggled migrants could be employed as unskilled workers and not returned to their countries of origin. This policy could be done by adopting law on migration which can establish the issue of a short-term visa for smuggled migrants whether they can cover vacancies required in EU States where they finally arrive, after their long journey. The European Commission supports temporary migration because it helps 'EU Member States to address their labour needs while exploiting potential positive impacts of migration on development and responding to the needs of countries of origin in terms of skill transfers and of mitigating the impact of

337 Ibid.

338 Ibid.

339 Ibid

340 See Fargues, P., 'Is what we hear about migration really true?'. 2014, available on http://cadmus.eui.eu/bitstream/handle/1814/31731/MPC_2014_FARGUES.pdf?sequence=1 accessed on 11/8/2014, p. 27.

341 See Fargues, P.,...*op. cit.* note 340, p. 28.

342 See Fargues, P.,...*op. cit.* note 340, p. 25.

343 Ibid

344 See Fargues, P.,...*op. cit.* note 340, p. 27 at 28.

brain drain'.[345] However, the EU has not adopted legal measures 'to promote long-term low-skilled migration'.[346]

The EU could focus on these policies in the future, as it has competence on EU migration policies.

9.2 EU competence on migration policies

Policies on migration should be adopted by the EU and Member States which have shared competence on migration policy.[347] This is established by Article 79 (1) TFEU which states that the EU shall develop a common immigration policy with the aim to ensure

> 'the efficient management of migration flows, fair treatment of third-country nationals residing legally in member States, and the prevention of, and enhanced measures to combat, illegal immigration and trafficking in human beings'.

The Commission highlighted that the decision on the number of visa to admit on the national territory, will remain of Member States' competence.[348] This is because Article 79 (5) TFEU states that the Union competence over a common immigration policy,

> 'shall not affect the right of Member States to determine volumes of admissions of third-country nationals coming from third countries to their territory in order to seek work, whether employed or self-employed'.

However, the EU has competence on migration policy, including smuggling and trafficking.[349] In addition, the EU has 'the power to regulate economic migration of third-country nationals, limited only by the expressed restriction on

345 See COM (2007) 248 final, 16/5/2007, p. 2.

346 Ibid note 340.

347 Se Articles 2(2) and 4(2) j TFEU.

348 ibid note 345.

349 See Article 79 (2) TFEU.

competence in Article 79(5) TFEU'.[350] This is established by Article 79 (2) (a) which states that the Council and the European Parliament can enact legislation on 'the conditions of entry and residence, and standards on the issue by Member States of long-term visas and residence permits'. Hence, it can adopt a common policy allowing smuggled migrants to be included in the immigration policy, with the aim to fight against trafficking in human beings. A similar policy could be adopted as a way to prevent people from being re-victimised, if returned to their countries of origin and to fulfil the gaps of skilled and unskilled workers, existing in the EU job market and which will experience a surge in the future. Short-term legal measures on low-skilled migrants should be adopted. However, at the moment, the EU has only adopted legal measures on long-term migration and on highly qualified migrants.

9.3 Legislation adopted by the EU on migration

The Council within its competence, has adopted the Directive on long-term residence.[351] The long-term residence Directive aims to grant third country nationals who hold a permanent residence permit, rights similar to the rights enjoyed by EU citizens.[352] Integration long-term residents, is essential in order to promote 'economic and social cohesion a fundamental objective of the Community'.[353] A pre-requisite to acquire the status of long-term residence should be the legal and continuous residence in the territory of a Member State. [354] If third country residents have acquired the long-term residence status as per Article 5 of Directive 2003/109/EC, they will enjoy equal treatments with citizens in terms of social rights, employment opportunities' and freedom of association and of membership to trade Unions.[355] If the long-term resident moves to a second Member State, he or she has to apply for a resident permit, within three months from his or her entry.[356] The CJEU has ruled that even if Member States can impose inte-

350 See Article 79(2) (a) TFEU.

351 See Council Directive 2003/109/EC of 25 November 2003, OJ L 16/44, 23/1/2004.

352 Se Recital 2 of Directive 2003/109/EC.

353 Recital 4.

354 Recital 6.

355 Article 11 (1).

356 Article 15 (1).

gration tests to third-country nationals before granting permanent residence, these tests cannot jeopardise the purpose of the Directive which is, 'the integration of third-country nationals who are settled on a long-term basis in the Member States'.[357] The same principle applies when one third-country national moves from one Member State to another. Article 15 (1) of the Directive, states that he or she shall apply for the residence permit within three months from his or her arrival in the second Member State. The CJEU ruled that the Netherlands, by applying excessive and disproportionate charges to acquire the residence permit, failed to comply with the purpose of the Directive.[358] These cases demonstrate that the CJEU has requested cooperation by Member States in integrating third-country nationals. This cooperation has been requested not only by applying correctly the Directive within their territories but also by granting the residence permit to a third-country national coming from another Member State, when there is the prerequisite to acquire it and without imposing heavy burdens which would jeopardise the aim of the Directive.

The EU has also adopted the Directive on highly qualified third-country nationals, the so called Blue Card Directive.[359] However, in two years the blue card was only issued to 16,000 third-country nationals and 13,000 of those 16,000 blue cards, were mainly issued by one single Member State.[360] Hence, the Commission has launched a consultation with the aim to review the blue card in order to make it more effective.[361] The review will focus on entrepreneurs who want to invest in Europe and on improving the opportunities for intra EU mobility for Blue Card holders. [362] New provisions to attract highly skilled workers will be adopted in the area of services which includes third-country nationals who travel for short period in EU Member States to provide services to businesses or governments.[363]

357 See case C-508/10 *Commission v. Netherlands EU:C:2012:243, para 66. See also Case C-579/13 P and S, 4/6/2015* ECLI:EU:C:2015:369. In this latter case, the CJEU stated that the Netherlands could organise a language test as a condition for integration but this test should not have jeopardise the aim of the Directive which is integration of third-country nationals. See paragraph 29 *et seq. of the judgement.*

358 See Case C-508/10 *Commission v. Netherlands , para 56 et seq. See also* Case C61/11 PPU El Dridi [2011] ECR I3015, para 55.

359 See Directive 2009/50 EC of 29/5/2009, OJ L 155, 18/6/2009.

360 See COM (2015) 240 final, 13/5/2015, p. 15.

361 Ibid

362 Ibid

363 Ibid

9.4 EU legislation in order to protect irregular migrants

In terms of legalisation of irregular migrants, the Commission does not have a clear agenda. At the end of their report, the Commission pointed out that a new model of legal migration will be launched which will include the admission of economic migrants.[364] The Commission highlighted their intention to work with Member States in order to develop an 'expression of interest system'. [365] By this new system, an automatic selection of potential migrants will be adopted and it will consist of inviting employers to select the right candidates for the job.[366] After the selection will take place and recruitment will follow, migration of candidates will be enacted. [367] However, this project has the aim to establish an 'EU-wide pool', as the Commission stated, which will target qualified migrants. [368] Instead, there are no programmes for economic irregular migrants who may be not qualified or who, despite are qualified, cannot be identified because of their status of irregularity. The EU agenda on migration focused on strengthening return policy and on targeting irregular migrants to return them to their countries of origin.[369] In the area of irregular migration, the EU has only adopted an Employers Sanctions Directive which prohibits to recruit third-country nationals who are living on the EU territory irregularly.[370] The Directive states that Member States have to take adequate steps to punish employers who recruit irregular migrants. They have to apply not only financial penalties but also criminal penalties.[371] Furthermore, the Directive imposes to Member States to ban companies which have employed irregular migrants, from participating in public contracts and other very strict measures such as temporary or permanent closure.[372] Nevertheless, the Directive protects irregular migrants who are waiting to be returned as it establishes that they have the opportunity to work whist

364 See COM (2015) 240 final, 13/5/2015, p. 17 *at 18.*

365 See COM (2015) 240 final, 13/5/2015, p. 18.

366 Ibid

367 Ibid

368 Ibid

369 See COM (2015) 240 final, 13/5/2015, p. 8 *at 10.*

370 See Council Directive 2009/52/EC, OJ L 168, 30/6/2009.

371 See Articles 5 and 10.

372 See Article 7.

they are waiting for removal. The Directive states that Member States 'may decide not to apply the prohibition...to illegal staying third-country nationals whose removal has been postponed and who are allowed to work in accordance with national law'.[373] This is because if irregular migrants are waiting for their removal, they would be left in a state of absolute vulnerability, if Member States impose a strict law banning them from working which is important to survive. It is unfortunate that the Commission has reported that only some Member States are using this provision.[374] Most Member States not only are not using this provision, and they are also applying the Directive to regular migrants who possess a visa by not allowing them to perform an economic activity.[375] The Directive and the wider scope by which it is applied by Member States, may contribute to make irregular migrants vulnerable to criminal organisations and hence, these provisions may facilitate THB. This is because, irregular migrants are left without the opportunity to survive

10. CONCLUSIONS

This chapter has concentrated on people smuggled and on the legal protection which can be granted to them by international law, the ECHR and EU law. It has been highlighted that whilst international law and the ECHR including case-law of the ECtHR provide legal protection to smuggled migrants, EU law appears very fragmented as it seems to have been shaped to restrict the access of the EU to as many migrants as possible. This chapter has shown that the EU is in need of skilled and unskilled migrants and for this reason, policy on migration should be more open to host migrants. Opening the legal routes is a way to prevent the death of many migrants at sea. Furthermore, it can prevent trafficking of migrants. It has been shown that 90% of migrants reach Europe from Africa through the support of smugglers.[376] This chapter has indicated that not all smuggled migrants become victims of human trafficking. This is because migrants look for smugglers and are fully aware that they have to repay the

373 See Article 3(3).

374 See COM (2014), 286, final, 22/5/2014, p. 3.

375 Ibid.

376 See section 2, p. 13 of this chapter.

price for their journey.[377] However, research has also demonstrated that many smuggled migrants become victims of human trafficking when the smugglers turn into traffickers. These people should be protected by including them in the scope of Articles 3 and 4 of the ECHR. However, the application of these two Articles may not be always possible because smuggled migrants may not make claims. If this happens, EU law states that they will not be entitled to asylum. Consequently, they will be considered illegal stayers and will be returned to their countries of origin or residence.[378] Their return may lead many migrants to become victims of trafficking when returned to their countries of origin or if they abscond and travel irregularly in other EU Member States. In order to avoid, these perils, EU law on temporary protection and on legal migration should be extended to vulnerable smuggled migrants. The Temporary Protection Directive should be initially applied to vulnerable smuggled migrants to make sure that law enforcement authorities with the support of experts, identify victims of trafficking in between them. Subsequently, identified victims should be protected by the application of the EU Trafficking Directive. Chapter 2 has analysed the Directive on Temporary Protection but also EU law on family reunification, EU law on short-term and long term migration because people who cannot be granted the temporary protection, may be given a legal status by the application of other legislation on EU migration.

After having examined these legal instruments, the chapter has concluded that these laws do not provide a way to ensure that smuggled migrants are not victimized by traffickers. The chapter also concluded that EU is only concentrated on returning irregular migrants by adopting policies addressed on that direction. The EU, for example, has signed an agreement with Turkey to facilitate the return of irregular migrants. EU risks to be complicit of Turkey in the violation of human rights.[379] It has been reported that Turkish authorities have transported by bus, hundreds of asylum seekers and refugees to remote and isolated detention centres.[380] The same report showed that many asylum seekers may have been beaten and forcibly returned to countries such as Iraq and Syria.

---

377 See section 3 p. 20 of this chapter.

378 See section 4.1 *et seq. p. 22 et seq. of this chapter.*

379 See' Turkey: EU risks complicity in violations as refugees and asylum seekers locked up and deported. On https://www.amnesty.org/en/latest/news/2015/12/turkey-eu-refugees-detention-deportation/, accessed on 29/1/2016.

380 Ibid

The EU has also made a list of safe countries and is trying to negotiate other relocation schemes with countries such as Niger. There is the fear that initiatives in Niger, for example, may be adopted only because the EU agenda on migration has as aim to create a pilot multi-purpose centre to resettle migrants in need.[381] Humanitarian organization argue that the attempts to relocate migrants in Niger are unacceptable because in this country there are serious breaches of human rights. Therefore, migrants cannot be resettled in a place which would put their human rights at risk.[382] Resettlement can only be put in place if the economic conditions of the country and the standard of the protection of human rights are addressed and improved. These actions require long-term policies which will be examined in chapter 5.

The next chapter will analyse short-term measures which have been adopted by the EU, in order to fight against smuggling and trafficking and reducing the number of irregular migrants in the EU.

381 See COM (2015) 240 final, 13/5/2015, p. 5.

382 See *Associazione per gli Studi Giuridici sull'Immigrazione (Asgi) http://www.asgi.it/wp-content/uploads/2015/06/proposte_ASGI-su-agenda-europea-migrazione.pdf, accessed on 21/7/2015.*

Chapter 3: EU short-term legal measures against smuggling of migrants and human trafficking

1. Introduction

Chapter 3 focuses on EU legal framework to fight against smuggling of migrants. Measures to fight against human trafficking will be analysed because the two crimes are strictly linked with each other. The Commission stressed that it is very difficult to distinguish the two crimes 'as persons who start their journeys in a voluntary manner are also vulnerable to networks of labour or sexual exploitation'.[1] Hence this chapter will focus on short-term measures adopted to fight against these two crimes where smuggling of migrants by sea will be examined with particular attention as short-term measures have mostly concentrated on the fight against this form of people smuggling.

This chapter will be divided in three parts. In the first part, international law measures against smuggling and trafficking will be analysed. In the second part, EU legal framework on the fight against smuggling and trafficking will be focused on. In the third and final part, chapter 3 will focus on the EUNAVFOR Med, a military operation to fight against smuggling of migrants by sea and on the EU/Turkey deal. In particular, this part of the chapter will focus on how the EU intends to fight against smuggling and trafficking by the military operation and by cooperating with Turkey.

The fight against smuggling and trafficking is a priority for the EU which in 2014 stated that Justice and Home Affairs agencies should be coordinated to fight against trafficking and to protect vulnerable people against this crime.[2] The fight against smuggling and trafficking was part of the European Agenda on Migration.[3] The Commission stated that smuggling and trafficking should be

1 See Com (2014) 635 final, 17/10/2014, p. 8.

2 See Com (2014) 635 final, p. 21 *at* 22.

3 See COM (2015) 240 final, p. 8 *et seq.*

addressed by fighting against criminal networks.[4] For this purpose, the EU will address smuggling and trafficking by the European Agenda for Security and the Maritime Security Strategy.[5] The Commission emphasised that smuggling and trafficking are two different crimes as in the case of smuggling, migrants are willing to pay the smugglers' service to leave their countries of origin and transit.[6] In the case of trafficking, instead, people are 'coerced into severe exploitation which may or may not be linked to the crossing of a border'.[7] In order to detect the criminal networks, the Commission highlighted that it is very important to cooperate with third countries as mostly smugglers are not based in Europe.[8] In addition, the boat drivers are only the last link of a chain belonging to local or international criminal groups which control the smuggling routes.[9] The Commission reiterated the commitment in fighting against smuggling in the EU Action Plan against migrants smuggling (2015-2020) where stated that the fight against smuggling of migrants is a priority.[10] The Commission stressed that cooperation within the EU and with third countries should be activated to dismantle 'the activities of smugglers, bringing them to justice and seizing their assets'.[11] The Action Plan reiterated the importance of addressing the root causes of migration as a way to fight against smuggling of migrants.[12] However, the EU Action Plan on smuggling has been criticised because it focuses too much on law enforcement and not on the protection of refugees and vulnerable migrants and the most recent report published by the Commission on the fight against trafficking, has shown a surge in human trafficking whether for the purpose of sexual exploitation or for the purpose of forced labour.[13] The Commission's report has also revealed that trafficking is a crime linked to organised crime and

4 See COM (2015) 240 final, p. 8.

5 Ibid

6 Ibid

7 Ibid

8 Ibid

9 See COM (2015) 240 final, p. 8 *at* 9.

10 See COM (2015) 285 final, 27/5/2015, p. 1.

11 See COM (2015) 285 final, p. 2.

12 Ibid. See COM (2011) 743 final, 18/11/2011 and the House of Lords European Union Committee *The EU's Global Approach to Migration and Mobility* (8th report, Session 2012-13, HL Paper 91).

13 See the House of Lords European Union Committee *EU Action Plan against migrant smuggling* (4th report, Session 2015-16, HL Paper 46), p. 17. See also COM (2016) 267 final, 19/5/2016, p. 6.

that Member States are not making appropriate efforts to prosecute and convict criminals.[14] In the meantime, people are continuing to be smuggled, trafficked and they are continuing to die. The International Organization for Migration (IOM) has reported that 5,386 people have died in 2017 and already 82 people have died from the beginning of 2018.[15] Efforts have to be made by the EU and Member States to prevent the death of migrants at sea and to fight adequately against smuggling and trafficking whose prosecutions and convictions remain low.

International law and EU law have adopted legislation in order to fight against smuggling and trafficking and the next sections focus on this legislation.

2. INTERNATIONAL AND EU LAW MEASURES TO FIGHT AGAINST SMUGGLING OF MIGRANTS AND HUMAN TRAFFICKING

2.1 International law measures against smuggling and trafficking

The UNCTOC Smuggling Protocol establishes specific provisions on smuggling of migrants by sea. It establishes that 'State Parties shall cooperate to the fullest extent possible to prevent and suppress smuggling of migrants by sea'.[16] For this purpose, a State Party which suspects that one vessel may be committing smuggling of migrants by sea 'may request the assistance of other States Parties in suppressing the use of the vessel for that purpose'.[17] The flag State and the requesting State shall cooperate together to detect smuggling of migrants by sea. The flag State shall cooperate by authorising the requesting State to board, search the vessel and, if evidence is found, the flag State shall authorise the requesting State to take the necessary measures against that vessel.[18] The UNCTOC Smuggling Protocol establishes other measures on preven-

14 See COM (2016) 267 final, p. 8 *et* 10. See also Europol Situation Report: Trafficking in human beings in the EU, February 2016, p. 16. Available on https://www.europol.europa.eu/content/trafficking-human-beings-eu, accessed on 8/7/2016.

15 See http://missingmigrants.iom.int/region/mediterranean, accessed on 10/1/2018.

16 See Article 7 of the UNCTOC Smuggling Protocol.

17 See Article 8(1) of the UNCTOC Smuggling Protocol.

18 See Article 8 (2) of the UNCTOC Smuggling Protocol.

tion and cooperation against this crime. The Smuggling Protocol recalls Articles 27 and 28 of the UNCTOC Protocol concerning law enforcement cooperation and collection, exchange and analysis of information related to the criminal organisation. In addition, the Smuggling Protocol states that, among others, State Parties shall exchange information concerning the embarkation, identity and methods used by criminal organisations, the authenticity of identity documents, means by which persons are transported and documents are misused, legislative measures and practices used to prevent smuggling and other technical and scientific information which can be useful for law enforcement authorities.[19] The Smuggling Protocol as the Trafficking Protocol, establishes that State Parties must strengthen border controls 'to prevent and detect smuggling of migrants'.[20] The Smuggling Protocol contains provisions on security and checks of documents and on the legitimacy and validity of documents.[21] It establishes that, in order to fight adequately against smuggling of migrants, 'States Parties shall provide or strengthen specialized training for immigration and other relevant officials'.[22] In addition the fight of smuggling and the protection of migrants who have been smuggled, States Parties are requested to cooperate with each other and with 'other relevant organizations and other elements of civil society as appropriate to ensure that there is adequate personnel training in their territories'.[23] Finally, States Parties shall ensure that the public is aware that smuggling 'is a criminal activity frequently perpetrated by organized criminal groups for profit and that it poses serious risks to the migrants concerned'.[24] The UNCTOC Protocol also emphasises that in order to prevent smuggling, States Parties shall promote cooperation at regional, national and international level 'to combat the root socio-economic causes of the smuggling of migrants, such as poverty and underdevelopment'.[25] Hence, the Protocol considers the identification of root causes of irregular migration as an important deterrent to this

19 See Article 10 of the UNCTOC Smuggling Protocol.

20 See Article 11 (1) of the UNCTOC Smuggling Protocol.

21 See Articles 12 and 13 of the UNCTOC Smuggling Protocol.

22 See Article 14 (1) of the UNCTOC Smuggling Protocol.

23 See Article 14(2) of the UNCTOC Smuggling Protocol.

24 See Article 15 (1) of the UNCTOC Smuggling Protocol.

25 See Article 15 (3) of the UNCTOC Smuggling Protocol.

criminal activity and particularly, to prevent migrants to rely on their service to leave their countries of origin irregularly.[26]

The two Protocols on Smuggling and Trafficking, including the UNCTOC Convention, promote international cooperation against smuggling and trafficking. However, they encounter the limitation of the sovereignty clause expressly established by Article 4 of the UNCTOC which states:

> '1. States Parties shall carry out their obligations under this Convention in a manner consistent with the principles of sovereign equality and territorial integrity of States and that of non-intervention in the domestic affairs of other States.
>
> 2. Nothing in this Convention entitles a State Party to undertake in the territory of another State the exercise of jurisdiction and performance of functions that are reserved exclusively for the authorities of that other State by its domestic law'.

One of the public prosecutors in Palermo highlighted that public prosecutors have issued in several occasions the European Arrest Warrant (EAW) and in this way, criminals could have been interrogated and persecuted. [27] Cooperation between Italian police and judicial authorities with third countries is based on extradition. However, the public prosecutors emphasised that many of them were unwilling to contribute in the investigations. [28]

The UNCTOC Trafficking Protocol states that State Parties shall adopt criminal measures against human trafficking.[29] Law measures shall be applied to criminalise either who attempts to commit human trafficking or who participates as an accomplice or organises or directs other persons to commit human trafficking.[30] The Trafficking Protocol requires that State Parties adopt strict border measures to ensure that commercial carriers do not transport victims of human

26 For a detailed analysis of measures adopted by the EU to combat the root causes of irregular migration, see chapter 5 p. 125 *et seq.* of this book.

27 E mail interview undertaken with Dr Ferrara on 8/4/2016.

28 Ibid

29 See Article 5 UNCTOC Trafficking Protocol.

30 See Article 5 (2) (a), (b), (c) UNCTOC Trafficking Protocol.

trafficking.[31] Carriers should 'ascertain that all passengers are in possession of the travel documents required for entry into the receiving State'.[32] State Parties should impose sanctions on carriers which violates these obligations[33] including 'the denial of entry or revocation of visas of persons implicated in the commission...'[34] of human trafficking. The Trafficking Protocol recalls the UNCTOC Convention which states that each State Parties shall cooperate in investigations and in sharing information concerning the fight against trans-national crime.[35] It adds that State Parties 'shall considering strengthening cooperation among border control agencies by...establishing and maintaining direct channels of communication'.[36] Finally, the Trafficking Protocol states that State Parties shall ensure that travel or identity documents are not misused or falsified.[37]

The Convention has important provisions that States Parties should adopt in order to fight adequately against this crime. They are examined in this section because, as the Commission has emphasised, smuggling and trafficking are strictly linked with each other.[38] Hence, law measures against trafficking could support the fight against smuggling. The Convention dedicates ample space to the protection of victims. There are also provisions which require States Parties to cooperate with each other to fight human trafficking. These provisions are similar to the provisions of the UNCTOC Trafficking and Smuggling Protocols. The Convention requires that States Parties adopt legal measures with the purpose to discourage demand and that they promote research, awareness, information, raising and education campaigns and other initiatives addressed to vulnerable individuals, to prevent them from becoming victims of human trafficking.[39] The Convention requires States Parties to criminalise human trafficking and to cooperate internationally and with the civil society to prevent the crime, to protect victims and to investigate and prosecute the perpetrators of

31 See Article 11 (1) and (2) UNCTOC Trafficking Protocol.

32 See Article 11 (3) UNCTOC Trafficking Protocol.

33 See Article 11(4) UNCTOC Trafficking Protocol.

34 See Article 11(5) UNCTOC Trafficking Protocol.

35 See Article 11(6) UNCTOC Trafficking Protocol. See Article 27 of the UNCTOC.

36 See Article 11(6) UNCTOC Trafficking Protocol.

37 See Article 12 UNCTOC Trafficking Protocol.

38 See section 1, p. 57 of this chapter.

39 See Articles 5 and 6 of the Council of Europe Convention on Action against Trafficking in Human Beings.

trafficking.[40] The Convention establishes the Group of experts on action against trafficking in human beings with the aim 'to monitor the implementation of this Convention by the Parties'.[41] The Convention is an important legal instrument adopted at European level to tackle against human trafficking but it lacks of supremacy. Conversely, at EU level, CJEU case-law have clearly established the EC supremacy, then recalled EU supremacy.[42] This principle has permitted the establishment of other important principles such as mutual judicial recognition and the EAW which can permit efficient fight against cross-border crimes such as smuggling. The next section analyses legal measures on the fight against smuggling and trafficking which have been adopted at EU level.

2.2 EU law measures against smuggling and trafficking

Smuggling of migrants is considered a crime by Directive 2002/90/EC.[43] Article 1 defines the crime of assisting irregular migration and it distinguishes it in two different categories which are assisting irregular migration without the purpose of financial gain and with the purpose of financial gain. The Directive itself is called Directive on 'defining the facilitation of unauthorised entry, transit and residence' to underline that a person can be committing smuggling of migrants not only when he or she smuggles a person for financial gain but also if he or she has other purposes. Article 2 states that'

1. Each Member State shall adopt appropriate sanctions on:
   a) Any person who intentionally assists a person who is not a national of a Member State to enter, or transit across, the territory of a Member State in breach of the laws of the State concerned on the entry or transit of aliens;
   b) Any person who, for financial gain, intentionally assists a person who is not a national of a Member State to reside within the

40 See Article 18 *et seq.* and Article 32 *et seq.* of the Council of Europe Convention.

41 See Article 36 (1) of the Council of Europe Convention on Action against Trafficking in Human Beings.

42 Case 26/62 *Van Gend & Loos v Netherlands Inland Revenue Administration* [1963] ECR 3-Court of Justice. See also Case 6/64 *Costa v E.N.E.L.* [1964] ECR 1194-Court of Justice. For the EU supremacy in the criminal area See Case C-105/03 *Criminal proceedings against Maria Pupino.* [2005] 2 ECR I-5285-Court of Justice. See Case C-176/03 *Commission v. Council* ECR 2005, I-7879.

43 See L 328/17, 5/12/2002.

territory of a Member State in breach of the laws of the State concerned on the residence of aliens.

2. Any Member State may decide not to impose sanctions with regard to the behaviour defined in paragraph 1(a) by applying its national law and practice for cases where the aim of the behaviour is to provide humanitarian assistance to the person concerned'.

Article 3 states that Member States have to impose 'effective, proportionate and dissuasive sanctions' against who perpetrates the crimes established by Article 1. A subsequent Framework Decision adopted in 2002, established the penalties that should be imposed to persons who commit assisting irregular migration.[44] The Framework Decision establishes penalties against individuals and legal persons. Article 1 (2) states that penalties can consist of 'confiscation of the means of transport used to commit the offence', the prohibition of practicing the work activity used to commit the offence and deportation. The EU has adopted the Trafficking Directive to fight against the connected crime of human trafficking.[45] This Directive has been analysed in the part concerning the protection of victims.[46] This section analyses criminal measures against trafficking. The Trafficking Directive states that Member States have to take the necessary measures to fight against trafficking, although investigations and prosecutions shall not depend on whether victims report traffickers and then withdraw their statements.[47] Member States shall use the same investigative instruments they use to investigate organised crime and other serious crimes. [48] The Trafficking Directive states that each Member State shall establish jurisdiction over trafficking when the crime is committed on their territory or the offender is one of its national.[49] If the offence is committed outside the territory of one Member State, they can still claim jurisdiction if 'the offence is committed against one

44 See Council Framework Decision of 28 November 2002 (2002/246/JHA), L328/1, 5/12/2002.

45 See Directive 2011/36/EU (Trafficking Directive), on OJ L 101/1, 15/4/2011.

46 See section 4.1, p. 22 chapter 2, of this book.

47 See Article 9 (1) of the Trafficking Directive.

48 See Article 9 (4) of the Trafficking Directive.

49 See Article 10 (1) of the Trafficking Directive.

of its nationals or a person who is an habitual resident' of that Member State.[50] Jurisdiction can be claimed when 'the offence is committed for the benefit of a legal person established in its territory'[51] or 'the offender is an habitual resident'[52] in the territory of the Member State concerned. If the offence is committed outside the territory of the Member State concerned, the offender can be prosecuted in its territory if the offender is a legal person established on its territory unless the action is considered an offence in the territory where it took place; or prosecution can take place 'only following a report made by the victim in the place where the offence was committed, or a denunciation from the State of the place where the offence was committed'.[53] As in the case of smuggling, Member States can rely on the EAW and on mutual recognition.

2.3. Other legal instruments adopted by the European Union and future developments

Other legal instruments that the EU has adopted to fight against smuggling of migrants are Council Decisions 2006/616/EC and 2006/617/EC by which the EU adhered to the UNTOC Smuggling Protocol adopted in 2000.[54] The EU also implemented the UNTOC Trafficking Protocol by adopting Council Decision 2006/618/EC and 2006/619/EC.[55] The UNTOC Protocol, as indicated above,[56] aims to fight against smuggling of migrants committed by criminal organisations only for the purpose of financial gain. Assisting irregular migration not for financial gain, is outside the scope of the UNCTOC Protocol.

The Council is planning to reform the legal framework on smuggling of migrants and it has invited Member States, the Commission and relevant EU agencies to contribute in the amendments of the legal framework.[57] Particularly, the Council has emphasised that smuggling of migrants is a serious form

50 See Article 10 (2) (a) of the Trafficking Directive.

51 See Article 10 (2) (b) of the Trafficking Directive.

52 See Article 10 (2) (c) of the Trafficking Directive.

53 See Article 10 (3) (a) (b) of the Trafficking Directive.

54 See OJ L 262/24, 22/9/2006 and OJ L 262/34, 22/9/2006.

55 See OJ L 262/44, 22/9/2006 and OJ L 262/51, 22/9/2006.

56 See section 2.1, p. 58 of this chapter.

57 See Draft Council conclusions on migrants smuggling. Doc, 5481/1/16, 26/1/2016.

of organised crime which should be fought against by 'a comprehensive, multidisciplinary and cross-border approach'.[58] It is important to highlight that the Council recognised that although, smuggling and trafficking are two distinct crimes, they can be interlinked and in particular, smuggling of migrants 'has become an increasingly violent form of crime, often involving serious physical or psychological violence and human rights abuse'.[59] Smuggling and trafficking will continue to be considered two different crimes. However, their links shall be fully investigated. This is because people smuggled, could become victims of human trafficking.[60]

The Council has stressed that in order to fight against smuggling effectively, it should be established a 'single operational contact point on migrant smuggling'.[61] However, the points emphasised by the Council will be just rhetoric if the EU will continue to state that smuggling of migrants can be prevented by enhancing return which is perceived 'as a deterrent for irregular migration.[62] As demonstrated in the previous chapter, return policies have been hardly successful as they do not contribute to identify victims of trafficking in between smuggled people. The Return Directive has been applied automatically to all migrants who do not make any claims. CJEU case-law has established that the right to be heard shall only consist on ensuring that domestic decision-makers will give full reasons on the return decision. There is not a mechanism which provides early identification of victims of human trafficking as required by different legal sources and case-law of the ECtHR.[63] Hence, the Smuggling Directive should be amended to permit the identification of victims on between smuggled migrants. As it has been pointed out in chapter 2,[64] not all smuggled migrants become victims of human trafficking. However, there are people who can become victims of trafficking. In order to identify them, the Smuggling Directive should be amended by giving more operative tasks to international organisations who have experts who can interview smuggled migrants, with the

58 ibid

59 ibid

60 See http://www.icmpd.org/news-centre/news-detail/news-detail/new_research_how_are_the_war_in_syria_and_the_refugee_crisis_affecting_human_trafficking/, accessed on 9/2/2016.

61 ibid

62 ibid

63 See section 4.1 *et seq.* p. 22 *et seq.* chapter 2 of this book.

64 See section 3, chapter 2 of this book.

aim to identify victims of trafficking in between them. Increasing humanitarian assistance can contribute to support victims of trafficking because humanitarian organisations can gain trust of victims who will eventually report the violence, exploitation and abuses they may have suffered from traffickers. In order to identify them, the Smuggling Directive should be amended by giving more operative tasks to humanitarian organisations who have experts who can interview smuggled migrants, with the aim to identify victims of trafficking in between them. Increasing humanitarian assistance can contribute to support victims of trafficking because humanitarian organisations can gain trust of victims who will eventually report the violence, exploitation and abuses they may have suffered from traffickers. Previous research has shown as in the Italian city of Rimini, human trafficking has been defeated by the support of humanitarian organisations who in cooperation with domestic police, promoted the issue of visas to suspected victims who later, decided to cooperate with law enforcement authorities by witnessing against traffickers. Law enforcement authorities stated that by giving trafficked victims a visa, they gained the trust of migrants and this was the reason why they made claims against traffickers.[65] This is why it is important to involve actively humanitarian organisations as they can contribute to reduce smuggling and trafficking. For this purpose, the scope of smuggling of migrants should be restricted. In other terms, the EU Smuggling Directive should persecute smuggling of migrants committed for financial gain and make the crime punishable when not committed for financial purpose, in exceptional circumstances. This is because by reading the Directive on assisting irregular migration, it can be noted that assisting irregular migration is not punishable only in exceptional circumstances. The Directive states that Member States have the discretion not to impose sanctions if the conduct is not committed for financial purpose and 'for cases where the aim of the behaviour is to provide humanitarian assistance'.[66] This provision should be amended to avoid that individuals or organisations which provide humanitarian assistance to people rescued in the sea or elsewhere and hosted in hotspots and other hosting centres in Europe, are accused of assisting irregular migration. By avoiding this risk, humanitarian organisations will be able to focus more effectively on smuggled people with

65 See Ventrella, M. 'Protecting victims of trafficking in human beings in the UK. The Italian 'Rimini Method' that could influence the British approach'. (2007) 3/2. *The Journal of Migration and Refugee Issues* pages 64-86.

66 See Article 1(2) of Directive 2002/90/EC.

the aim to identify victims of trafficking in between them without risking to be criminalised because they provide assistance and protection to smuggled migrants. In 2004, a German vessel belonging to the non-governmental organisation (NGOs) called Cap Anamur, rescued 37 migrants at sea in the Channel of Sicily. The vessel was seized and members of the crew were accused of assisting irregular migration by public prosecutors in the city of Agrigento.[67] After five year of trials, they were eventually acquitted by the Court in Agrigento.[68] The Cap Anamur case is not the only case where members of NGOS were accused of assisting irregular migration, simply because they rescued migrants at sea who were in danger to drawn and brought them to a safe place.[69] Frontex has recently reported that (NGO) involvement in search and rescue operations (SAR) in the Central Mediterranean is increased since 2016.[70] Hence, there is the risk that more NGOs will be criminalised. A solution in order to prevent the criminalisation of NGOs rescuing migrants, could be to introduce a narrower definition of smuggling of migrants stating that although humanitarian organisations cannot be exempted from criminal prosecution if they are not fulfilling the legal obligation to rescue migrants in the sea, they cannot be 'construed as blameworthy smugglers warranting criminalisation'. [71] If there are NGOs supporting criminal organisations, they should be investigated, otherwise NGOs activities should be supported not only because they can contribute to reduce the migrants' death toll, but also because they can contribute to identify and protect victims of human trafficking who, at the moment, are being neglected by EU Member States. Article 1 of the Smuggling Directive and the Draft Council conclusions on migrant smuggling do not address this issue.

These amendments of policy and law have not been activated. Conversely, the EU is concentrating on short-term measures to fight against smuggling of

67 See Handling of Cap Anamur asylum claims was flawed, says UNHCR. On http://www.unhcr.org/4101252e4.html, accessed on 10/2/2016. See also 'Criminalising solidarity-Cap Anamur trial underway. On http://www.statewatch.org/news/2007/apr/03italy-cape-anamur.htm, accessed on 10/2/2016.

68 See Umbriano, P., 'Is it a crime to help people to survive (Cap Anamur and other cases)'. On http://www.eldh.eu/fileadmin/user_upload/ejdm/publications/2013/Pierluigi_Umbriano_-_Speech.pdf?PHPSESSID=051a86793dbac1a0c80a6885a9a9cf03, accessed on 10/2/2016.

69 ibid

70 See Frontex Risk Analysis for 2017, February 2017, p. 32.

71 See Landry, R., 'Decriminalising 'Humanitarian Smuggling'. Refugee Studies Centre Research Brief, March 2017, p. 4. On https://www.rsc.ox.ac.uk/publications/research-in-brief-decriminalising-humanitarian-smuggling, accessed on 7/5/2017.

migrants by sea. Actually, there is also too much emphasis on the EU military operation called EUNAVFOR SOPHIA which demonstrates the lack of seriousness of the Draft conclusions. This is because a military operation could only contribute to reinforce the fortress Europe without addressing on investigations against smuggling and human trafficking. In other terms, the Council states that fighting human trafficking and smuggling is a priority but no serious efforts are taken to address these crimes as military operations are a last resort which, show the EU does not know how to tackle against these crimes.

3. THE EUNAVFOR TO FIGHT AGAINST SMUGGLING OF MIGRANTS AT SEA AND OTHER SHORT TERM SOLUTIONS

3.1 Smuggling of migrants and the UN Council Resolution 2240/2015

In the EU, a military operation was launched in May 2015 by Council Decision (CFSP) 2015/778.[72] The aim of the military operation is to detect and destroy vessels suspected of committing smuggling of migrants at sea. Following the Council Decision, the UN launched a Security Council (SC) Resolution authorising Member States to intercept vessels from Libya, suspected to be committing smuggling of migrants and 'disrupt the organised criminal enterprises engaged in migrant smuggling and human trafficking'.[73] This section will examine the SC Resolution to evaluate whether it may contribute to reduce smuggling of migrants. The next section then, will focus on the EU military operation and on its effectiveness in fighting against smuggling of migrants at sea and beyond.

The Resolution was adopted in October 2015 and in a very short time, following the accident of April 2015 when 800 people drowned in the sea.[74] People who died were mixed migrant inflows as there were 350 people from Eritrea and other migrants were from Syria, Somalia, Sierra Leone, Mali, Senegal, Gambia,

72 See L 122/31, 19/5/2015.

73 See Resolution 2240/2015, 9 October 2015, paragraph 12.

74 See Mercone, I., 'Some notes the relations between UNSC Resolution 2240 (2015) fighting smugglers in Mediterranean and EUNAVFOR Med "Sophia" Operation. On http://free-group.eu/2015/10/19/some-notes-on-the-relations-between-unsc-resolution-2240-2015-fighting-smugglers-in-mediterranean-and-the-eunavfor-med-sophia-operation/, accessed on 10/2/2016.

Ivory Coast, Ethiopia and Bangladesh.[75] As it can be noted, many of them came from countries where there are conflicts and others from countries where economic conditions could have pushed people to leave their houses to look for a better future elsewhere. In order to examine the EUNAVFOR initiative, it is essential to explain what the SC Resolution required Member States to do. The Resolution emphasised that human trafficking and smuggling of migrants are related with each other, although they are regulated by two different legal instruments at international level which are the two UNCTOC Protocols on smuggling and trafficking. The response against these crimes have to be tackled by different legal sources, operational instruments and policy responses. The SC Resolution highlighted that the crime of smuggling of migrants at sea is causing many deaths near the Libyan coast and many of people who are losing their life, are people who fall within the protection recognised by the Refugee Convention 1951 and the 1967 Protocol. In the SC Resolution, the UN stated that it is urgent that 'all States...to comply with their obligations under international law, including international human rights law and international refugee law'.[76] Actions in this direction have to be taken by Member States regardless the immigration status of individuals as all of them have human rights to be respected. The SC Resolution concentrated on the issue that in Libya, smuggling and trafficking networks could be providing support to other criminal organisations and terrorist networks. For this reason, it is important that the Libyan government takes responsibility over smuggling of migrants at sea.[77] The SC Resolution also took note of the Council of Europe Decision to establish the EUNAVFOR of 18 May 2015 and highlighted that the fighting against smuggling and trafficking should be tackled by immediate and long-term initiatives. For this purpose, the SC Resolution requires Member States to cooperate with Libya to coordinate actions against smuggling and trafficking. At this point, the SC Resolution requires that Member States take tough measures against unflagged vessels suspected to be committing smuggling and trafficking. Firstly, the SC Resolution requires Member States to inspect unflagged vessels on the high sea

75 See European Commission, DG Migration and Home Affairs 'A Study of Smuggling of Migrants. Characteristics, responses and cooperation with third countries. Final Report, September 2015. On http://ec.europa.eu/dgs/home-affairs/what-we-do/networks/european_migration_network/reports/docs/emn-studies/study_on_smuggling_of_migrants_final_report_master_091115_final_pdf.pdf, accessed on 15/2/2016

76 See The Preamble of the UN Resolution above note 73.

77 Ibid

when there is the suspicion they are perpetrating smuggling of migrants and THB from Libya.[78] Subsequently, the SC Resolution requires that these inspections are carried out for one year and when there is the suspect that vessels have been used to transport migrants irregularly. The SC Resolution also stated that in exceptional circumstances Member States can dispose of the vessel suspected of being committing smuggling of migrants at sea. These actions have to be carried out by taking into account that the aim of the SC Resolution is to disrupt the organised criminal groups which commit smuggling and trafficking and not to threaten the human rights on individuals or prevent them from applying for the status of refugee.[79] The SC Resolution concludes by stating that the situation will be reviewed and the period of one year will be extended if this is necessary.[80] The problem of the SC Resolution is that it states that smuggling and trafficking are two distinct crimes but then it requires Member States to tackle both crimes by the same short term measures, including the disposal of suspected vessels. The SC Resolution underestimate the fact that smuggling can be a form of trafficking and this may occur when migrants are tortured, raped and abused during their journeys. [81] Furthermore, the SC Resolution states that it will not encroach States' national sovereignty and that the priority in the fight against smuggling the trafficking is the protection of individuals' human rights. Tackling seriously smuggling and trafficking requires encroachment of national sovereignty because it would be very difficult to launch cooperation against smugglers without encroachment of national sovereignty. This crime can be defeated by launching police and judicial cooperation between the EU and transit and origin countries because it is trans-national in dimension and the different criminal groups are based in different States. Smuggling of migrants is a very complex crime which can take place from countries of origin to Europe, by land,

78 See paragraph 11.

79 See paragraph 12.

80 See paragraph 19.

81 See European Commission, DG Migration & Home Affairs 'A Study on Smuggling of Migrants. Characteristics, responses and cooperation with third countries'. Final Report, September 2015,... *op. cit.* note 75, p. 19. See also Libya: Horrific abuse driving migrants to risk lives in Mediterranean crossings, Amnesty International, 11 May 2015. On https://www.amnesty.org/en/press-releases/2015/05/libya-horrific-abuse-driving-migrants-to-risk-lives-in-mediterranean-crossings/, accessed on 16/2/2016.

by air and by sea and often committed by rudimental criminal organisations with rudimental hierarchies.[82]

If smuggling and trafficking are mainly committed by rudimental hierarchies, only the police of the place where these hierarchies have been put in place, could be able to dismantle them. Once they have dismantled them, they could exchange data about these organisations with police authorities of other countries where there are other criminal groups which could be linked to those detected groups. Criminal justice responses should focus on this cooperation in order to detect the criminal groups which smuggle people from as far as the Horn of Africa. Operations only concentrating on countries facing the Mediterranean where smuggling of migrants by sea is committed, are insufficient to detect the criminal groups which undertake their activities in other countries which do not face the Mediterranean Sea and which are located far away from the Mediterranean Sea. Nevertheless, the EU has launched a military operation which has obtained the support of the UN through the SC Resolution. This operation has been considered a failing mission as next sections will demonstrate, because they only concentrate on detecting smuggling of migrants by focusing on countries facing the Mediterranean such as Libya.

3.2 The Sophia Operation

In April 2015, following the incident where 800 people lost their life in the Mediterranean Sea, the European Council emphasised that all efforts should be made to prevent the loss of life in the sea, by cooperating with transit and origin countries of migrants.[83] It is unfortunate that the EU has only concentrated on short term measures and in May 2015 has adopted a Council Decision on EU military operation, taking place in the Southern Central Mediterranean Sea and called EUNAVFOR MED (The mission).[84] The mission was launched on 22 June

82 See European Commission, DG Migration & Home Affairs 'A Study on Smuggling of Migrants. Characteristics, responses and cooperation with third countries'...*op. cit.* note 75, p. 38 *et seq.* See also section 2, p. 13, chapter 2 of this book.

83 See European Union Naval Force-Mediterranean Operation Sophia, Update: 12/2/2016, on http://www.eeas.europa.eu/csdp/missions-and-operations/eunavfor-med/pdf/factsheet_eunavfor_med_en.pdf, accessed on 17/2/2016.

84 See Council Decision (CFSP) 2015/778 of 18 May 2015. OJ L 122/31, 19/5/2015.

2015 by the Council Decision (CFSP) 2015/972.[85] Denmark decided not to take part in the military operation.[86]

The Decision was adopted with the aim 'to identify, capture and dispose vessels before they are used by traffickers'.[87] The Decision also states that on May 18th, 2015, 'the Council approved the crisis management concept for a CSDP[88] operation to disrupt the business model of smugglers in the Southern Central Mediterranean'.[89] Article 1 confirms that the military operation will be conducted with the purpose to disrupt the business of smugglers and traffickers illicit activities in the Mediterranean Sea.

The operation has been recalled Sophia, the name of a baby born on a boat of the operation on 22 August 2015.[90] Sophia operation will consist of three phases. In the first phase, EUNAVFOR gathered information and patrolled the high seas in compliance with international law.[91] In the second phase, EUNAVFOR boarded the suspect vessels, searched, seized and diverted in the high seas and in respect of international law, including the Smuggling Protocol and United Nations Convention on the Law of the Sea (UNCLOS). The second phase also consisted of conducting boarding, search, seize and diversion of suspected vessels within the territorial waters of the coastal State concerned. The operation was conducted in respect of UN SC Resolution or with the consent of the State concerned.[92] In 2016 other two supporting tasks were added. Phase 2B by which EUNAVFOR would move into the Libyan territorial waters and, in the third phase, the mission would fully operate in Libyan territory.[93] In the third phase, EUNAVFOR will take the necessary measures to ensure that the vessels are made inoperable by disposing of them and destroying vessels if this is nec-

85 See OJ L. 157/51, 23/6/2015.

86 See paragraph 3.

87 See paragraph 3.

88 Common Security and Defence Policy.

89 See paragraph 5.

90 See 'EU Names Anti-Human-Smuggling Mission 'Operation Sophia'. 28/9/2015 available on http://www.wsj.com/articles/eu-names-anti-human-smuggling-mission-operation-sophia-1443471234, accessed on 18/2/2016.

91 See Article 2(2)(a).

92 See Article 2(b).

93 See Articles 2a and 2b of Council Decision 2016/993 of 20 June 2016 amending Decision 2015/778 on a European Union Military Operation in the Southern Central Mediterranean (EUNAVFOR MED Operation Sophia). OJ L 162/18, 21 June 2016.

essary[94] and EUNAVFOR MED would fully operate in Libyan territory. These operations are conducted by taking into account the SC Council Resolution and prior consent of the coastal States concerned.[95] Furthermore, the new phases 2B and 3 will have to be authorised by a SC Resolution.[96] EUNAVFOR acts under the political control and strategic direction of the Political and Security Committee (PSC).[97] The PSC directs the EUNAVFOR under the responsibility of the Council and of the High representative (HR).[98] Hence EUNAVFOR is accountable before the Council and the HR which exercise their control through the PSC.

In the six monthly report it was highlighted that Sophia operation has been successful because since the start of the operation forty-six suspected smugglers have been arrested and 67 vessels have been disposed. The operation has been effective as 'smugglers can no longer operate with impunity in international waters'. [99] If these boats do not stay in Libya, they will be apprehended by EUNAVFOR MED operation Sophia assets. The other positive impact of the mission was that the Commander of EUNAVFOR MED had the opportunity to meet senior representatives from six countries, nine EU organisations and fourteen international organisations including the UN, the IOM, the African Union and the Arab League.[100] These meetings were positive because gave the commander of the operation the chance to successfully contribute and improve understanding and acceptance of the operation in the international community.[101] However, the commander emphasised that to move from phase 2A to Phase 2B may have political and legal implications as not only it requires the contribution of the Libyan authorities, but also to arrest, detain and prosecute smugglers. [102] The report highlights that it is necessary to conclude a Government of National Accord and this is seen as a priority to ensure the operation is successfully carried out. Nevertheless, the problem will not be resolved by establish-

94 See Article 2(c).

95 See Article 2(3).

96 See Article 1 of Council Decision 2015/778.

97 See paragraph 10 and Article 6 (1).

98 See Article 6(1).

99 See EUNAVFOR MED-Operation Sophia. Six Monthly Report: June, 22nd to December 31st 2015. On https://wikileaks.org/eu-military-refugees/EEAS/EEAS-2016-126.pdf, accessed on 23/2/2016.

100 Ibid

101 Ibid

102 Ibid

ing a government as such because there are issues of sovereignty that might make the operation unsuccessful. Issues related to sovereignty are not resolved by international instruments such as the UNCTOC Protocol or the UN Council Resolution 2240 (2015). These issues are very important to overcome and one is convinced that they can be overcome in the EU by giving more power to JHA's agencies. The EU as a new legal order of international law, can make the difference in the fight against smuggling of migrants and THB by changing the scope of Europol and giving the EPPO a role in the fight against smuggling and trafficking.[103]

It is predicted that the reaction of smugglers to the seizure and disposal of vessels, will be to adapt quickly to the different situation. If the Sophia Operation will remain outside the Libyan territory, smugglers will not be apprehended. [104] The report promotes cooperation with the Italian authorities, international organisations and international non-governmental organisations and finally with Libyan authorities. The cooperation with Italian authorities will be done through the Frontex Liaison Officers from Italy and the National Judiciary Authority against organised crime (DNAA). [105] Subsequently, the Report mentions cooperation with international organisations such as the European Asylum Support Office (EASO), the UNCHR, UNICEF, the International Committee of the Red Cross (ICRC) and IOM. The report also mentions the cooperation with the non-governmental organisation Medicins Sans Frontieres in Brussels and the Libyan Coastguard.

Nevertheless, it has been emphasised that cooperation with Libyan authorities is very difficult because the Libya Government of National Accord (GNA) cannot guarantee to be able to work closely with the EU.[106] It has also been emphasised that the Sophia Operation has not deterred migrant flows.[107] The Operation permitted to apprehend smugglers' boats. However, criminal organisations have adapted to the situation by replacing the apprehended boats with unsafe inflatables boats from China capable of transporting 100 people and not

103 See chapter 4 section 5, p. 92 and section 8 p. 105 for an analysis of these agencies.

104 Above note 99.

105 Ibid

106 See European Union Committee 'Operation Sophia: a failed mission'. (2nd Report, Session 2017-19, HL Paper 5), p. 3.

107 See European Union Committee 'Operation Sophia: a failed mission'...*op. cit.* note 106, p. 9.

500 or 600 as boats seized by the EUNAVFOR MED did.[108] These boats have increased the number of deaths in the Mediterranean. [109] On this point it has been highlighted that smugglers business should be disrupted by targeting smugglers' suppliers.[110] However, these initiatives will not defeat the crime of smuggling if the root causes of migration are not addressed.[111] In the meantime, the EU is aiming to develop cooperation with Libya in order to start Phase three of the Sophia Operation.

3.3 New development on cooperation with Libya

The EU has always been keen to develop cooperation with Libya, in order to detect smuggling and trafficking.[112] However, the unstable situation in Libya where an effective government lacked, caused a failure in the control of smuggling of migrants and human trafficking.[113] It has been reported that smuggling of migrants is considered by Libyan authorities 'as a low priority, and is seen by many Libyans as a "Western" problem. The migrants themselves are often subject to violence and abuse, and arbitrarily held in detention centres'.[114] Migrants who are in Libya aim to cross the Mediterranean to reach Italy. [115] Many of them have died in the past whilst trying to reach Italy.[116]

In 2013, following the serious incident where many migrants crossing the Mediterranean Sea in between Italy and Libya drowned, the Council launched the EU Border Assistance Mission (EUBAM) which had the aim to support Libyan authorities 'in improving and developing the security of the country's

108 See European Union Committee, 'Operation Sophia, the EU's naval mission in the Mediterranean: an impossible challenge' (14th Report, Session 2015-16, HL Paper 144), p. 16.

109 See European Union Committee, 'Operation Sophia, the EU's naval mission in the Mediterranean: an impossible challenge' ...*op. cit.* note 108, p. 14.

110 See JOIN (2017) 4 final, 25/1/2017, p. 9.

111 Ibid

112 See http://eeas.europa.eu/csdp/missions-and-operations/eubam-libya/index_en.htm, accessed on 12/9/2016.

113 See House of Commons Foreign Affairs Committee 'Libya: Examination of intervention and collapse and the UK's future policy options'. 3rd Report Session 2016-17, HC 119, p. 31.

114 Ibid

115 Ibid

116 See House of Commons Foreign Affairs Committee...*op. cit.* note 113, p. 32.

borders'.[117] On August 4th 2016, the Council extended the mandate for the EUBAM until August 2017.[118] The EUBAM Libya can establish in the future a possible EU mission in the area of criminal justice and in the fight against smuggling, trafficking, border-security and counter-terrorism.[119] The EUBAM gives the EU the opportunity to advise, train and mentor Libyan authorities to strengthen their border managing according to international standards and to develop a national Integrated Border Management (IBM) strategy.[120] All these activities will be undertaken if Libyan authorities so request and under their ownership.[121] It has been reported that Libya denied the possibility of undertaking investigations on their territory despite there were migrants waiting to be embarked to Europe with more people arriving from the Sub-Saharan Africa. [122]

The EU is planning cooperation with Libyan authorities to prevent smugglers from committing their criminal activities. Training will be organised with for the Libyan Coast Guard to equip them to fight against smugglers.[123] For this purpose, the EU is working closely with the EUBAM and Operation Sophia. Other actions are focusing on reinforcing the Niger's control over the Libya-Niger border and on to replace the economic sustainment given by the smuggling illicit activities in Niger with alternative economic and legal activities.[124] Dialogue between Libya, Niger and Chad on border management have been promoted by the EU. The management of migration by Libyan authorities is supported by the EU as their dialogue with UNHCR and IOM in order to give protection to vulnerable people.[125] However, Amnesty International has recently reported that migrants and refugees are suffering serious violations of human

117 Ibid

118 See http://www.consilium.europa.eu/en/press/press-releases/2016/08/04-eubam-libya-mission-extended/, accessed on 12/9/2016.

119 Ibid

120 See http://eeas.europa.eu/csdp/missions-and-operations/eubam-libya/pdf/factsheet_eubam_libya_en.pdf, accessed on 12/9/2016.

121 Ibid note 160.

122 Ibid note 141.

123 See Joint Communication...*op. cit.* note 110, p. 6 and European Union Committee, 'Operation Sophia, the EU's naval mission in the Mediterranean: an impossible challenge' ...*op. cit.* note 108, p. 11.

124 See Joint Communication...*op. cit.* note 110, p.13.

125 Ibid

rights in Libya.[126] It has been reported that EU Member States are aware of the situation and are supporting the Libyan authorities to ensure that the migration in-flows towards the EU is preventing. Abuses against migrants and refugees in detention centres have also been reported by the UNHCR which are trying to negotiate alternatives to detention with Libyan authorities.[127]

On the basis of this analysis, it can be affirmed that migrants and refugees should not be exposed to smugglers and abuses of human rights committed by authorities in Libya. The EU should monitor the situation and not to continue cooperation with Libya if abuses are detected. The NGOs reports should be considered seriously. Trafficking in human beings and the identification of victims in between smuggled migrants should be given the priority. However, the identification will not be possible if migrants and refugees will suffer abuses of their human rights in Libya. In addition, agreements with Libya concentrating only on fighting against smuggling of migrants will not resolve this problem. The EU in the Joint Communication has stated:

> '...the fight against the criminal organisations involved migrant smuggling cannot achieve effective and results unless it is accompanied also by measures aimed at addressing the root causes, making it more difficult for these organisations to recruit manpower for running their business'. [128]

The next section focuses on other international agreements concluded by the EU and will show that these agreements cannot be effective as only based on short-term policies.

126 See "Libya: European governments complicit in horrific abuse of refugees and migrants'. On https://www.amnesty.org/en/latest/news/2017/12/libya-european-governments-complicit-in-horrific-abuse-of-refugees-and-migrants/, accessed on 11/1/2018.

127 See 'UNHCR steps up efforts towards alternatives to detention in Libya and solutions for vulnerable refugees'. On https://unsmil.unmissions.org/unhcr-steps-efforts-towards-alternatives-detention-libya-and-solutions-vulnerable-refugees, accessed on 11/1/2018.

128 See Joint Communication...*op. cit.* note 110, p. 9.

4. COOPERATION BETWEEN THE EU, EXTERNAL ORGANISATIONS AND THIRD COUNTRIES IN THE AREA OF SMUGGLING OF MIGRANTS

Cooperation in the area of smuggling of migrants has been agreed between Egypt, Lebanon and Syria under the European Neighbourhood Policy (ENP).[129] The agreement aimed at achieving settlement and peace in the Middle-East, promote the respect of human rights, increasing economic integration and fighting the poverty in order to eradicate it. [130] In order to fight against smuggling of migrants, the agreement promoted judicial cooperation in criminal matters.[131] The agreement also foresees the opportunity to promote law enforcement cooperation between Egyptian investigative authorities and EU agencies such as Europol and Eurojust.[132] The management of borders should be enacted by cooperation in between Frontex and law enforcement authorities in Egypt.[133] Furthermore, the agreement concentrated on managing legal and irregular migration through readmission agreements and other agreements on visa and asylum law.[134] The cooperation against smuggling of migrants and trafficking should be reinforced by fighting criminal organised groups by strengthening

> '...international co-operation in accordance with the UN Convention against Transnational Organised Crime and its protocols on smuggling of migrants and trafficking in persons and on illicit manufacturing and trafficking of firearms. – Implementation of the UN Convention against Trans-national Organised Crime and its Protocols. – Exchange expertise and experiences, also through appropriate training on best practices in combating organised crime, including security and legal aspects'.[135]

129 Ibid. See also 'EU/Egypt Action Plan' on http://eeas.europa.eu/enp/pdf/pdf/action_plans/egypt_enp_ap_final_en.pdf, accessed on 25/2/2016.

130 Ibid

131 Above note 129, p. 28

132 Above note 129, p. 28

133 Ibid

134 Above note 129, p. 29.

135 Above note 129 p. 30.

The problem of this agreement is that does not add anything new to the fight against smuggling and trafficking because the fight against these two crimes should be enacted by cooperation in information exchange and through international legal instruments. In other terms, exchange of information without cooperation in investigations, arrest and detection of criminals, will not make the difference. Hence, exchange of information should be followed by cooperation in investigations, establishment of liaison officers in Egypt and in EU Member States, allocation of jurisdiction and common rules on extradition. These activities require the establishment of common rules on the respect of human rights as in the EU, a person cannot be extradite to a country where the death penalty has not been abolished. The first step to take to enact judicial cooperation against smuggling and THB, should be to agree common rules on the protection of human rights.

The same can be argued about the recent deal agreed between the EU and Turkey.[136] The EU-Turkey agreement has been concluded after different meetings between the EU and Turkey which eventually was implemented in March 2016.[137] The agreement states that from 20th March 2016, all new irregular migrants crossing from Turkey into Greece, will be returned to Turkey. The statement made on 18/3/2016 emphasised that the return of irregular migrants will be done in compliance with the principle of non-refoulement and in respect of the prohibition of collective expulsion. In the statement, it is declared that the Agreement is made in order 'to offer migrants an alternative to putting their lives at risk'.[138] Consequently, all migrants who have not applied for asylum or whose application has been rejected by the Greek authorities because unfounded under the Asylum Procedure Directive,[139] will be returned to Turkey. In order to achieve this objective, new irregular migrants reaching Greece, will be returned to Turkey as this 'is an essential component in breaking the pattern of refugees and migrants paying smugglers and risking their lives'.[140] On the other side, in April 2016, the Council implemented a mechanism for resettlement from Turkey to the EU which states that Syrian people who have been displaced because of

136 See http://www.consilium.europa.eu/en/press/press-releases/2016/03/18-eu-turkey-statement/ accessed on 27/4/2016.

137 See http://europa.eu/rapid/press-release_IP-16-1444_en.htm, accessed on 27/4/2016.

138 ibid note 178.

139 See Directive 2013/32/EU of 26 June 2013 (recast). On OJ EU L 180/60, 29/6/2013.

140 Ibid.

the conflict in Syria and who are in need of international protection, can be resettled to the EU if they have been registered by the Turkish authorities for the status of temporary protection, before 29th November 2015.[141] Newborns of parents registered prior that date and people suffering from a disability or in need of physical and medical protection, can also be eligible for resettlement in the EU.[142] People for resettlement will be selected on the basis of their situation. The mechanism states that people who will be resettled are women and girls, people who survived torture and/or violence, refugees with medical needs and or disabilities, minors at risk, members of the same nuclear family. People who are a threat to public policy, public security and public health and candidates who have refused to be resettled to a particular Member State, will not be eligible for resettlement. Preference will be given to migrants who have never tried to enter or have entered the EU territory, irregularly.[143] The mechanism is very strict and many people victims of human trafficking may remain without any protection. If from one side, the mechanism states that people who have suffered and other forms of violence, as women and girls, will be eligible for resettlement. From the other side, the mechanism leaves out people who are not Syrians and all categories of migrants who have tried or who have entered the EU irregularly. Victims of trafficking for the purpose of sexual exploitation, for example, if neglected or returned to their countries of origin just because they are not Syrian refugees, will face the same situation of poverty they left.[144] In addition, they will be stigmatised, excluded and with no prospect of a marriage which is very important in Sub-Saharan countries.[145] Research has shown that victims will be trapped in a vicious circle and as consequence, they will be victimised again.[146] However, the EU-Turkey deal does not support the identification of victims as if they do not make asylum claims, will be returned to their countries of origin.[147]

141 See Doc 8366/16, 27/4/2016 available on http://www.consilium.europa.eu/register/en/content/out/?&typ=ENTRY&i=ADV&DOC_ID=ST-8366-2016-INIT and accessed by http://www.statewatch.org/news/2016/apr/eu-council-eu-turkey-standard-operating-procedures-resettlement-8366-16.pdf on 5/5/2016.

142 Ibid.

143 Ibid.

144 See Triandafyllidou, A., and Maroukis... T. *Migrant Smuggling. Irregular Migration from Asia and Africa to Europe,* Palgrave Macmillian, 2012., p. 186.

145 See Triandafyllidou, A., and Maroukis, T.,...*op. cit.* note 144, p. 186 at 187.

146 Ibid note 144.

147 See section 2, p. 13, chapter 2.

Evidence shows that often victims of human trafficking do not make claims for fear of retaliation. Neglecting victims who do not make claims, may increase the number of smuggled migrants who become victims of human trafficking. There is evidence showing that criminal networks have exploited the migration crisis to target vulnerable migrants and over 60% of unaccompanied children are missing with the serious risk to become victims of human trafficking.[148] Europol has indicated that many criminal networks smuggle refugees with the aim to exploit them in the sex trade or for the purpose of forced labour.[149]

Many migrants left in the hotspots could be recruited by traffickers for the purpose of sexual exploitation or forced labour and transferred in other Member States. In the UK, for example, there is a high rate of human trafficking for the purpose of labour exploitation which statistics show, prevails over trafficking for sexual exploitation.[150] Research has revealed that forced labour is linked to trafficking and that many undocumented migrants entered to the UK via smuggling or trafficking routes, have become victims of trafficking for the purpose of sexual exploitation and forced labour.[151] Hence, it is important to understand how smuggled migrants become victims of trafficking and transferred to the UK for the purpose of forced labour and sexual exploitation. In order to achieve this objective, investigations should be initiated in hotspots. This is because the Commission stressed that the first step to protect victims and prevent trafficking is to identify actual or potential victims in the hotspots. [152] Actual or potential victims should be 'made aware of their rights and that the necessary cooperation takes place with the police and judicial authorities in order to ensure that traffickers are identified and prosecuted.' [153] This is not being put in place in hotspots and migrants have reported that victims of torture and other forms of violence hosted in Greece, for example, do not receive any information either

148 See COM (2016) 85 final, 10/2/2016, p. 16.

149 Ibid

150 See section 5, p. 36, of chapter 2.

151 See Forced Labour in the United Kingdom. On https://www.jrf.org.uk/report/forced-labour-united-kingdom, accessed on 8/6/2016. See also Clark, N. (2013) Detecting and tackling forced labour in Europe, p. 62 on https://www.jrf.org.uk/sites/default/files/jrf/migrated/files/forced-labour-europe-full.pdf, accessed on 8/6/2016. See Dwyer, P. Lewis, H., Scullion, L. and Waite, L. (2011) Forced labour and UK immigration policy: Status matters? p. 16. On https://www.jrf.org.uk/file/41487/download?token=DsgZ8vrL, accessed on 8/6/2016.

152 Ibid note 148.

153 Ibid note 148.

about their situation or on their legal options or about their rights.[154] It seems that the fact that initially, migrants have given the consent to be recruited by smugglers, justifies domestic authority to neglect them and not to investigate possible links between smuggling and trafficking.[155]

Hotspots should be improved, in order to protect vulnerable smuggled migrants.[156] Early identification systems should be launched to give assistance to smuggled migrants who have been trafficked or who can be trafficked. These vulnerable individuals should initially be given temporary protection to ensure that victims of trafficking are identified in between smuggled migrants. Subsequently, the Trafficking Directive and the protection indicated in this Directive should be applied to victims identified.

Furthermore, the EU should concentrate on long term policies to fight against smuggling and trafficking by cooperation with investigative and prosecuting authorities of Member States and third States outside the EU.

5. CONCLUSIONS

Chapter 3 focused on short-term measures adopted by the EU to fight against smuggling of migrants and the connected crime of human trafficking. The chapter, as the previous one, continued to emphasise how important is to identify victims of trafficking in between smuggled persons. For this purpose, it proposed to reform the Smuggling of Migrants Directive to ensure that international humanitarian organisations such as IOM, become engaged in the identification of victims of human trafficking. This chapter still focused on victims because the author of the book is convinced that the priority in the fight against smuggling and trafficking shall be protection of victims. One reason for this approach is because EU law and international law requires that victims are protected. Another reason is because previous research undertaken by the author of this book, has demonstrated that approaching and protecting victims can make the difference in the fighting against these two crimes as victims can be induced to

154 See 'Vulnerable lives on hold. Refugees are hardly surviving the mass camps in the Athens region'. 2016. On https://www.proasyl.de/wp-content/uploads/2015/12/2016-05-24-Vulnerable-lives-on-Hold-final.pdf, page 29, accessed on 7/6/2016.

155 See section 4.1, p. 22, chapter 2.

156 See section 7, p. 42 chapter 2.

report their traffickers and investigative authorities can understand more clearly links existing between smuggling and trafficking.

Chapter 3 highlighted that smuggling and trafficking are two separate crimes but they are interlinked between each other. This is the reason why the fight against smuggling should also include the fight against trafficking. Smuggling of migrants is being fought against by EU legal measures which may prove to be ineffective. This is because they do not address smuggling of migrants in all its complexity. This book is showing that smuggling of migrants is not only a crime committed by sea and from North African countries such as Libya and Turkey. Smuggling of migrants can take place from many different African countries as investigations conducted by public prosecutors in Palermo have shown.[157] The Sophia Operation cannot address smuggling of migrants perpetrated in many different African countries as it has been established to search, seize and eventually dispose of vessels which are engaged in smuggling of migrants by sea. It has also been highlighted that Sophia Operation is a military operation and thus, it does not have jurisdiction over investigations on smuggling. This chapter has argued that smuggling of migrants should be fought by long term policies and laws. For this purpose, JHA agencies such as Europol and Eurojust should play an important role in the fight against smuggling of migrants within the EU and outside the EU, in cooperation with African countries. However, the EU is continuing to concentrate on short-term policies such as the EU/Turkey deal which has been analysed in this chapter. The problem with this deal is that it only focuses on Syrian refugees and it neglects other categories of migrants who can be victims of human trafficking. The deal states that all people who cannot fall into the category of Syrian refugees, will be returned from Europe, particularly Greece, to Turkey and Turkish authorities will eventually return them to their countries of origin or residence. The deal does not focus on specific measures to fight against human trafficking by focusing on victims or people believed to be victims of this crime. There are no provisions requiring Turkey to identify victims of trafficking in between smuggled migrants.[158] Smuggling and Trafficking are neglected because no attention is given to potential victims of this crime.

The next chapter will focus on JHA agencies and on their role to fight against smuggling and trafficking. Chapter 4 will also focus on the external scope of these agencies because smuggling and trafficking can be seriously fighting by

157 See section 3, p. 20 chapter 2.

158 See section 4 p. 73 of this chapter.

giving more tasks to these agencies in cooperation with investigative and prosecuting authorities of origin, transit and destination countries. Unfortunately, the EPPO does not have a role in the fight against smuggling and trafficking as its scope is very limited. The next chapter will highlight that JHAs agencies should be strengthened in the fight against smuggling and trafficking and it will show how law should be amended in order to achieve this objective.

Chapter 4: Europol, Eurojust and the European Public Prosecutor roles' in the fight against smuggling of migrants and human trafficking

1. Introduction

This chapter focuses on the fight against smuggling of migrants and human trafficking. These two crimes should be fought against by applying the extra-territorial jurisdiction as requested by the UNCTOC Smuggling Protocol and the EU Framework Decision on Smuggling of Migrants.

The UNCTOC establishes different law provisions to fight against transnational organised crime, including smuggling and trafficking. In the previous chapter, provisions on the protection of victims of trafficking and on smuggled people have been examined. Therefore, this section will specifically focus on provisions to fight against smuggling and trafficking. The UNCTOC states that their provisions are addressed to structured organised criminal groups committing serious transnational crime such as trafficking and smuggling.[1] The UNCTOC promotes cooperation in investigations and prosecutions of the crimes within the respect of the principle of sovereignty.[2] Jurisdiction shall be established when the crime is committed in the territory of one State Party;[3] the crime is perpetrated 'on board a vessel that is flying the flag of that State Party or an aircraft that is registered under the laws of that State Party at the time that the offence is committed'.[4] Jurisdiction of the State Party also applies when the crime has been committed by or against a national of one of the State Parties or a stateless who has his or her habitual residence on the territory of the State Party.[5] The UNCTOC promote cooperation against these crimes between State

1 See Articles 2 and 3 of the UNCTOC.

2 See Article 4 UNCTOC.

3 See Article 15 (1) (a) UNCTOC.

4 See Article 15 (1) (b) UNCTOC.

5 See Article 2 (a) and (b) of the UNCTOC.

Parties by stating that extradition rules shall be fully applied and if States where the crime has been committed require a treaty on extradition to apply it, they may consider the UNCTOC as the legal basis for extradition concerning crimes covered by the UNCTOC.[6] Finally, the UNCTOC states that State Parties shall gather evidence by mutual legal assistance and it establishes provisions on law enforcement cooperation and the protection of victims.[7]

Paragraph 3 states that these crimes are punishable by custodial sentence and, when crimes are committed 'as an activity of a criminal organisation' and or 'while endangering the lives of the persons who are the subject of the offence', the penalties should consist of custodial sentences of no less than eight years or six years 'provided that it is among the most severe sentences available for crimes of comparable gravity'.[8] Sanctions for legal persons shall consist of 'exclusion from entitlement to public benefits or aid; temporary or permanent disqualification from the practice of commercial activities; 'placing under judicial supervision; a judicial winding-up order'.[9] Member States have to establish jurisdiction between each other by applying three criteria. One of these criteria should take into consideration where the crime has been committed in whole or in part. The other criterion has to evaluate whether the crime has been committed 'by one of its nationals or for the benefit of a legal person established in the territory of that Member State'.[10] This provision has been complied with by recent investigations conducted by Italian public prosecutors in Palermo, which have successfully detected a criminal network which smuggled migrants from Libya, Eritrea, Ethiopia, Sudan, Israel to Sicily.[11] Subsequently, the same organisation smuggled migrants to Northern Italy and eventually to Sweden, Germany, Norway, the Netherlands, France, Austria, Australia and Canada.[12] Evidence on the crime of smuggling has been gathered through wiretapping.[13]

6 See Article 16 of the UNCTOC.

7 See Articles 20 *et seq.* of the UNCTOC.

8 See Article 1 (3) and (4) of Framework Decision 2002/946/JHA. OJ L328/1, 5/12/2002.

9 See Article 3 (1).

10 See Article 4 (1).

11 See Decreto di Fermo disposto dal P.M.-art 384 c.p.p.. Procura della Repubblica press oil Tribunale di Palermo, Direzione Distrettuale Antimafia, 30/5/2014, p. 16. Document received by Public Prosecutor Dr Gery Ferrara by e mail on 23/3/2016.

12 See Decreto di Fermo...*op. cit.* note 11, p. 2.

13 See Decreto di Fermo...*op. cit.* note 11, p. 20.

The Italian Supreme Court of Cassation has admitted wiretapping as they have been made either from Italian telephones or to Italian telephones. This activity is not in breach of national sovereignty of third countries as the wiretapping has been wholly undertaken on the Italian territory[14] and it complies with the requirements of the Framework decision on Smuggling of Migrants.

Member States when conducting investigations within the EU, can rely on the EAW which was established in 2002 and amended in 2009.[15] The EAW is a judicial decision issued by a Member State to another Member State requesting to arrest and prosecute an individual ', for the purposes of conducting a criminal prosecution or executing a custodial sentence or detention order'.[16] The EAW is based on the principle of mutual judicial recognition and Member States have to execute it in compliance with this principle.[17] Mutual recognition is based on mutual trust among Member States' criminal justice systems, which is essential to give effectiveness to the EAW which 'is the first measure to be adopted in the field and the only mutual recognition measure which has been implemented fully and in detail...'.[18] Mutual recognition is "the 'cornestone' of judicial cooperation".[19] Smuggling of migrants is a crime within the scope of the EAW and Member States can rely on the EAW in order to cooperate with each other

---

14 See Decreto di Fermo...*op. cit.* note 11 pages 20 at 21. See also Cass. Sez. IV, sent n. 32924, 29/7/2004, Belforte rv. 229103; Cass. Sez. V, sent. N. 4401, 21/10/1998, Assisi.

15 See Council Framework Decision 2002/584/JHA on the European Arrest Warrant and the surrender procedures between Member States. On OJ L 190/1, 18/7/2002. The Framework Decision has been amended by Council Framework Decision 2009/299/JHA of 26 February 2009 amending Framework Decisions 2002/584/JHA, 2005/214/JHA, 2006/783/JHA, 2008/909/JHA and 2008/947/JHA, thereby enhancing the procedural rights of persons and fostering the application of the principle of mutual recognition to decisions rendered in the absence of the person concerned at the trial, OJ L 81/24, 27/3/2009.

16 See Article 1(1) of Framework Decision 2002/584/JHA.

17 See Article 1(2) of Framework Decision 2002/584/JHA.

18 See Mitsilegas, V., 'The Limits of Mutual Trust in Europe's Area of Freedom, Security and Justice: From Automatic Inter-State Cooperation to the Slow Emergence of the Individual'. On *Yearbook of European Law*, Vol. 31/1, 2012, page 323. For an in depth analysis of correlations between mutual trust and mutual recognition see E. Herlin-Karnel, 'From mutual trust to the full effectiveness of EU law: 10 years of the European arrest warrant'. On *European Law Review* 2013, 38 /1, pp. 79-91. On the shift of the EAW legislation from intergovernamentalism to supranationalism see Ventrella, M., 'European integration or democracy disintegration in measures concerning police and judicial cooperation?' *New Journal of European Criminal Law* Vol 4. Issue 3, 2013 pp. 290-309.

19 See Recital 6 of the Council Framework Decision 2002/584/JHA of 13 June 2002.

to arrest and detect smugglers.[20] However, smuggling of migrants is a transnational crime involving not only the EU but also third countries.

It has been reported that before reaching the Italian coast, for example, migrants from Africa cross the Saharan desert.[21] Many of them die in the desert and the survivors often report that they have to cross the borders of different countries at the night time and, in the meantime, they spend much time without food, water and a shelter. Many migrants take weeks, months and even years to reach the Italian coast as their money run over and they cannot pay the price of their trips to the smugglers to reach Italy or other EU Mediterranean countries. Many smuggled migrants have testified in Lampedusa that in Libya they are abused, tortured and raped.[22] However, they need the support of criminal organizations to embark from Libya to Italy and thus, they are forced to accept their conditions and the violation of their human rights otherwise, they would not be able to travel to Italy and other EU Member States. Indeed, criminal organizations have the appropriate experience and they can rely on their affiliates to choose the routes which are not under borders' checks. In this way, they are able to transfer migrants from North Africa to Europe. Migrants at sea often try to reach Europe without the support of these criminal organizations but they fail most of the time and end up to be smuggled by these criminal groups which control the smuggling of migrants by sea.[23]

Cooperation with countries of origin and transit in the fight against smuggling and trafficking is very important and this chapter analyses EU agencies in the criminal area and their support in investigations related to smuggling of migrants.

20 See Article 2(2) of Framework Decision 2002/584/JHA.

21 See "Smuggled Futures: The Dangerous path of the Migrant from Africa to Europe". On http://www.globalinitiative.net/download/global-initiative/Global%20Initiative%20-%20Migration%20from%20Africa%20to%20Europe%20-%20May%202014.pdf accessed on 18/9/2014.

22 See also De Bruycker, P., Di Bartolomeo, A., Fargues, P., 'Migrants smuggled by sea to the EU: facts, laws and policy options'. Migration Policy Centre (MPC) Report 2013/09 on http://www.migrationpolicycentre.eu/docs/MPC-RR-2013-009.pdf accessed on 18/9/2014.

23 Ibid

2. THE STOCKHOLM PROGRAMME

In 2009, the European Council in the Stockholm Programme, clearly stated that EU police and judicial cooperation between Europol, Eurojust and investigative and prosecution authorities of African countries shall be improved in order to fight against trafficking in human beings and smuggling of migrants.[24] The European Council highlighted that the external dimension of the area of freedom, security and justice shall be reinforced. In the Stockholm Programme, the Council stated that it is essential to negotiate new rules on mutual assistance and extradition agreements with third countries. EU institutions, through these important negotiations, 'should ensure...coherence between the Union and the international legal order'.[25] A particular attention is focused on Europol and Eurojust which, according to the European Council, 'should expand their work with third countries especially by forging closer links with the regions and countries neighbouring the Union'.[26] Europol should strengthen its work with the Common Security and Defence Policy (CSDP) police missions and support the promotion of European law enforcement cooperation with third countries.[27] The European Council emphasized that Europol's activities should be scrutinized by the EP and national parliaments on the basis of Articles 85 and 88 TFEU.[28] Article 85 states that cooperation and coordination between investigative and prosecuting authorities of EU Member States shall be reinforced, in order to fight effectively against serious crimes involving two or more Member States. For this purpose, the EP and the Council shall adopt regulations on the basis of the ordinary legislative procedure, on the Eurojust's structure, tasks and scope of action. These measures can consist of granting Eurojust the task to initiate investigations and of proposing the initiation of prosecution of competent authorities within Member States; strengthening coordination of investigations and prosecutions; improving judicial cooperation by overcoming conflicts of jurisdiction and by reinforcing cooperation with the European Judicial Network (EJN). Article 85 reads that efforts to improve judicial cooperation between

24 See Council of European Union The Stockholm Programme-An open and secure Europe serving and protecting the citizens. Doc. 17024/09, 2/12/2009.

25 Ibid

26 Ibid

27 Ibid

28 Ibid

Member States shall be made in order to fight crimes against the EU's financial interests. However, the same provision can be applied to trafficking in human beings and the related crime of smuggling of migrants at sea. This is because human trafficking is considered a priority crime by the European Council. [29] Smuggling of migrants can also be included in the scope of Article 85 because it is strictly linked to human trafficking.[30] Article 88 is about Europol and, as the European Council emphasised in the Stockholm Programme, the EP and national parliaments have to scrutinize Europol's activities. The same Article also states that the Council and the European Parliament have to adopt regulations on Europol's actions and tasks through the ordinary legislative procedure. Regulations can provide Europol tasks' to include 'the collection, storage, processing, analysis and exchange of information...forwarded by the authorities of the Member States or third countries or bodies'.[31] Regulations can also include in between Europol's tasks, 'the coordination, organization and implementation of investigative and operational action'[32] undertaken with Member States or thorough joint investigative teams, 'where appropriate in liaison with Eurojust'.[33] The Treaty requires more democratic accountability for Europol and Eurojust. The European Council confirms that democratic accountability is essential to reinforce police and judicial cooperation within the EU and with third countries.

The European Council stated that as organized crime is becoming more globalised, it is important that law enforcement authorities are given the tools by which 'to work effectively across borders and jurisdiction'. [34] The EU can make the difference in the fight against the serious crimes and 'widespread use of the Union agencies and investigative tools and, where necessary, the development of common investigative and prevention techniques and increased cooperation with third countries. [35] The European Council went on to highlight that smuggling of migrants and trafficking in human beings are two crimes which require cooperation 'which goes beyond the area of freedom, security and justice and...

29 Ibid

30 See section 3 *et seq.* chapter 2 of this book for the connections between human trafficking and smuggling of migrants at sea.

31 See Article 85 (2) (a) TFEU.

32 See Article 85(2) (b) TFEU.

33 ibid

34 See Council of European Union The Stockholm Programme ...*op. cit.* note 24.

35 Ibid

includes external relations'.[36] All Union migration policies require extensive cooperation with all stakeholders involved with the phenomenon. Therefore, the European Council recalled cooperation between the EU and third countries where the most important focus 'should remain on cooperation with the most relevant countries in Africa and Eastern and South-Eastern Europe.[37] The external dimension is a priority in the fight against trafficking in human beings and for this purpose, Union agencies such as Europol and Eurojust should be reinforced to fully implement the external actions and cooperation between the EU and third countries.[38] The external dimension of the Area of Freedom, Security and Justice (AFSJ) will be mainly based on principles stating that

1) The EU has a single external policy;

2) The EU and its Member States must cooperate with third countries and their neighbours;

3) The European Parliament will be involved with the EU external actions;

4) The EU's approach on external actions will be proactive.[39]

The Stockholm Programme emphasized that the CSDP and external actions in the AFSJ have common objectives and the European Council supports cooperation between the AFSJ and the CSDP in order to fight against transnational crime.[40] For this purpose, the European Council invited the European Commission to explore if cooperation agreements with specific third countries can be concluded to fight against THB and smuggling of migrants.[41] The Stockholm Programme was very ambitious and it highlighted that trafficking and smuggling are global crimes which require global cooperation with third countries where these two crimes are perpetrated. Trans-national cooperation

36 Ibid

37 Ibid

38 Ibid

39 Ibid

40 Ibid

41 Ibid

is especially important for the crime of smuggling which is more likely to be characterized by a cross-border dimension.

3. JURISDICTION TO CONCLUDE INTERNATIONAL AGREEMENTS IN THE CRIMINAL AREA

The first step to follow to enhance JHAs agencies in the criminal area, is to enhance the external scope of these agencies. The EU has competence in this area. Within the single market, before the entry into force of the Lisbon Treaty, the CJEU ruled that the EC had competence to adopt criminal penalties and thus, the EC had competence to define criminal penalties.[42] After the entry into force of the Lisbon Treaty, the EU competence in the criminal area has been further enhanced. According to Article 83(1)TFEU, the European Parliament and the Council may adopt minimum rules to define and sanction crimes with a cross-border dimension such as human trafficking, drug trafficking and terrorism. These rules can be adopted under the ordinary legislative procedure. Article 83 (2) TFEU states that Directives may also be adopted by the ordinary or special legislative procedure, if it is proved essential 'to ensure the effective implementation of a Union policy in an area which has been subject to harmonization measures…'. Article 83(2) can be adopted not only to define criminal offences but also to impose penalties in relation to these criminal offences.[43] Therefore, Framework Decision 2002/946/JHA on the strengthening of the penal framework to prevent smuggling of migrants, falls within the EU competence entirely. Two conditions must exist in order to apply Article 83(2). One of these conditions is that the criminal measure has to be essential to implement EU policy. The second condition is that the area taken into consideration must have been subject to harmonization.[44] When these conditions are met, the EU will have competence within criminal matters and the EP will have jurisdiction in adopting legislation in this area by the co-legislative procedure.

The Lisbon Treaty has also enhanced EU competence in the external relations related to the criminal area. The legal basis to conclude external agreements

42 See Case C-176/03 *Commission v. Council* [2005] ECR I-7879. See also C-440/05 *Commission v. Council* [2007] ECR I-9097. See also Peers, S., *EU Justice and Home Affairs Law*, OUP 2012, p. 536.

43 See Peers,… *op. cit.* note 42, p. 774.

44 See Article 83(2) TFEU and Peers, S.,…*op. cit.* note 42 p. 774 et 775.

can be found in Article 79(3) TFEU which states that the Union can conclude readmission agreements with third countries in order to return third-country nationals to their countries of origin. Article 216(1) TFEU states that the Union can conclude an agreement with one or more third country or international organisations not only when it is established by the Treaties but also when it is necessary in order to achieve the objectives of the Treaties or it is provided by legally binding EU acts or the agreement is likely to affect EU common rules or change their scope. Powers principle included in Article 216 are implied powers and they apply to the criminal area.[45] There are areas where the EU has exclusive competence as per Article 3(1) TFEU which lists the areas of EU exclusive competence. In these areas EU Member States can be excluded. Article 3(2) establishes that Member States do not share competence with the EU also in areas where external agreements can affect common rules or change their scope. This is the case of areas which have been internally harmonized and the criminal area is included in this scope.[46] The competence in the criminal area is shared when, according to Articles 82(2), 83(1) and (2) TFEU, the EU can only establish minimum rules in the internal area.

Article 218 TFEU states that the Commission 'where the agreement envisaged relates exclusively or principally to the common foreign and security policy, shall submit recommendations to the Council'[47] which will open the negotiation. The Council will nominate the Union's negotiator or the head the negotiation's team. Subsequently, the Council will sign and adopt the agreement.[48]

The Council can only adopt the agreement if the Parliament gives its consent unless the agreement concerns exclusively the CFSP. The Council cannot approve the agreement without obtaining the consent of the Parliament in areas, among others, concerning the association agreements; agreements related to the accession of the ECHR; agreements having important budget implications; agreements concerning areas where legislation is adopted by the ordinary legislative procedure or by the special legislative procedure.[49] In all other cases, the Council has to consult the Parliament within a time-limit established by

45 See Peers, S., *EU Justice and Home Affairs Law. Volume II: EU Criminal Law, Policing and Civil law* 2016, OUP, p. 51.

46 See Peers, S., 2016,...*op. cit.* note 45, p. 52.

47 See Article 218 (3) TFEU.

48 See Article 218 (5) and (6) TFEU.

49 See Article 218 (6) (a) TFEU.

the Council. If the Parliament does not deliver its opinion within the time-limit, the Council will be able to act.[50] The Council will act by a qualified majority vote unless the agreement covers an area which requires the unanimous vote.[51] The Parliament shall be informed at all stages of a procedure adopting by the Council which suspends an agreement on proposal of the Commission or of the High Representative of the Union for Foreign Affairs and Security Policy.[52] Finally, Article 218 (11) states that Member States, the E, the Council and the Commission can obtain 'the opinion if the Court of Justice as to whether an agreement envisaged is compatible with the Treaties'. If the CJEU does not give favourable opinion, the agreement will not enter into force unless it is amended or the Treaties are revised. These provisions of the TFEU are able to make the EU criminal area more democratic as accountable before the Parliament and subject to judicial control as Peers has emphasized.[53] However, one of the opinion that the EP role should be enhanced, in order to make the EU criminal area more democratic and more accountable. The reason for this is because JHA agencies should be able to support cooperation between police of EU Member States and police forces of third countries where the crimes of smuggling and trafficking are perpetrated. The scope of activities require that JHA agencies receive the approval of the Parliament and that their activities are accountable before the Parliament.

The next sections examine how difficult could be the extradition procedure without agreements ad hoc with third countries where smuggling and trafficking are initiated. These agreements require a high level of trust and should only be done by making EU criminal agencies accountable before the EP and national Parliaments. Some progresses have been made in reforming Europol but other agencies have not been reformed in this direction and thus, most of the fight against smuggling and trafficking is only of EU Member States' responsibility.

50 See Article 218 (6) (b) TFEU.

51 See Article 218 (8) TFEU.

52 See Article 218 (9) and (10) TFEU.

53 See Peers, S., 2016,…*op. cit.* note 45, p. 55 *et* 56.

4. THE EUROPEAN ARREST WARRANT AND THE EXTRADITION: CHALLENGES IN THE FIGHT AGAINST SMUGGLING AND TRAFFICKING

The EAW was adopted in 2002 by a framework decision.[54] The aim of the Framework Decision was to introduce 'a new simplified system of surrender of sentenced or suspected persons for the purposes of execution or prosecution of criminal sentences...to remove the complexity and potential for delay inherent in the present extradition procedure'.[55] Member States were requested to adopt the EAW Framework Decision into their legal systems no later than 31st December 2003.[56] The EAW is a judicial decision by which one Member State (the issuing Member State) requests to another Member State to arrest and surrender a requested person, with the purpose 'of conducting a criminal prosecution or executing a custodial sentence or detention order'.[57] The execution of the EAW is based on the principle of mutual recognition. [58] Mutual recognition is based on mutual trust among Member States' criminal justice systems and is "the 'cornestone' of judicial cooperation".[59] Mutual recognition is so important that the CJEU has ruled that Member States cannot rely on higher standards in the protection of human rights in particular the standards concerning trials in absentia and thus, to adopt strict provisions on the application of the EAW to respect the standards on trials in absentia.[60] The reason for this is because the EU legislation intended to harmonize rules on trials in absentia in 2009.[61] These rules are compatible with Article 53 of the Charter of Fundamental Rights which

54 See Council Framework Decision 2002/584/JHA of 13 June 2002 on the European arrest warrant and the surrender procedures between Member States. OJ L. 190/1, 18/7/2002 (EAW Framework Decision).

55 See Paragraph 5 of the EAW Framework Decision.

56 See Article 34(1) of the EAW Framework Decision.

57 See Article 1(1) of the EAW Framework Decision.

58 See Article 1(2) of the EAW Framework Decision.

59 See Recital 6 of the EAW Framework Decision.

60 See C-399/11 *Melloni* ECLI:EU:C:2013:107. See also Peers, S., 2016,...*op. cit.* note 45, p. 92.

61 See Council Framework Decision 2009/299/JHA of 26 February 2009 amending Framework Decisions 2002/584/JHA, 2005/214/JHA, 2006/783/JHA, 2008/909/JHA and 2008/947/JHA, thereby enhancing the procedural rights of persons and fostering the application of the principle of mutual recognition to decisions rendered in the absence of the person concerned at the trial, OJ L 81/24, 27/3/2009.

stats that the Charter does not restrict or adversely affect human rights and fundamental freedoms as recognised by Constitutions of Member States.[62] Mutual recognition is based on mutual trust and solidarity between Member States and for this reason, double criminality is not required.[63] The EAW Framework Dicision abolished the verification of double criminality for some crimes including human trafficking and people smuggling.[64] Specifically, the EAW Framework Decision established that a list of offences indicated in Article 2(2) which include trafficking and smuggling,

> 'if they are punishable in the issuing Member State by a custodial sentence or a detention order for a maximum period of at least three years,...shall, under the terms of this Framework Decision and without verification of the double criminality of the act, give rise to surrender pursuant to a European arrest warrant'.

The CJEU was asked whether the abolition of the double criminality is against the principle of legality, the principle of equality and non-discrimination. The Court ruled that the abolition of double criminality is not in breach of the principle of legality because the EAW Framework Decision does not intend to harmonize the criminal offences listed in Article 2(2) and the penalties to be applied.[65] It is a responsibility of the issuing Member State 'the actual definition of those offences and the penalties are those which follow from the law of 'the issuing Member State'.[66] The principle of equality and non-discrimination is not breached when comparable situations are not treated differently and when different situations are not treated in the same way unless a similar treatment is 'objectively justified'.[67] Crimes listed in Article 2(2) EAW Framework Decision are 'the categories of offences...among those the seriousness of which in terms of adversely affecting public order and public safety justifies dispensing with

62 Ibid note 60.

63 See Case C-303/05 *Advocaten voor de Wereld VZW v. Leden van de Ministerraad* [2007] ECR I-3633, para 57.

64 See Article 2(2) of the EAW Framework Decision.

65 See Case C-303/05...*op. cit.* note 63, para 51.

66 See Case C-303/05, para 52.

67 See Case C-303/05, para 56. See Case C-44/94 *Fishermen's Organisations and Others* [1995] ECR I3115, para 46, and Joined Cases C87/03 and C100/03 *Spain v Council* [2006] ECR I2915, para 48 see Case C-248/04 *Koninkijke Cooperate Cosun* [2006] ECR I-10211, para 72.

the verification of double criminality'.[68] The Court added that the abolition of double criminality can be applied 'on the basis of the principle of mutual recognition and in the light of the high degree of trust and solidarity between the Member States,...'.[69] It discerns that a distinction between crimes listed in Article 2(2) and other crimes is 'objectively justified'.[70] The EAW has been issued by Member States and as Peers emphasized, 'the EAW is frequently used in practice'.[71] Data show that in 2013 10.000 EAW had been issued and 5,900 people had been arrested and around 2.700 had been released.[72] Public Prosecutor in charge of criminal investigations against smuggling of migrants in Palermo, has also confirmed that the EAW has contributed to make investigations against smuggling successful within EU Member States.[73] In case of investigations outside the EU territory, public prosecutors have highlighted that they have relied on extradition procedure. Specifically, they have highlighted that in these cases, investigations have been based on wiretapping of telephone conversations made by criminals based on the Italian territory with criminals based outside the EU and if it was necessary to arrest individuals, they relied on the extradition.[74] However, extradition procedures are much slower than the EAW and they make investigations very slow. In Palermo, investigations have been successful because they were based on victims' testimonies and on wiretapping which confirmed what witnesses reported.[75] Public prosecutors have encountered more difficulties when they needed to gather information on criminals in their countries of origin or residence in order to carry on with investigations. The results of investigations highlighted that it was very difficult to gather personal data of criminals in countries such as Eritrea, Ethiopia, Libya and Sudan, patly because of the unstable situation of these countries and partly because the data gathered by public offices in these countries are

68 Ibid note 63.

69 Ibid.

70 See Case C-303/05 para 58.

71 Peers, S., OUP 2016,...*op. cit.* note 45, p. 98.

72 See Council Doc 11528/05, 2 September 2015.

73 E mail interview undertaken with Dr Ferrara on 8/4/2016.

74 See Decreto di Fermo disposto dal P.M.-art 384 c.p.p.. Procura della Repubblica press oil Tribunale di Palermo, Direzione Distrettuale Antimafia, 30/5/2014, p. 16 et 22. Document received by Public Prosecutor Dr Gery Ferrara by e mail on 23/3/2016.

75 See Decreto di Fermo...*op. cit.* note 11, p. 23 et seq.

either unreliable or inexistent.[76] On top of this situation, often local authorities do not cooperate.[77] Therefore, it has been noted by reading the findings of investigations that when they have been successful, it was only because of wiretapping and witnesses. In other cases, public prosecutors had to rely on extradition procedure which is complex and slow. Public prosecutors through extradition, have arrested and transferred one of the criminals responsible for the death of 366 migrants drowned in the Mediterranean Sea in October 2015. However, there were doubts about his identity.[78] In other cases, it was not possible to arrest other criminal responsible for smuggling of migrants because their data were missing and they remained at large.[79] These situations show how important is to involve activewly JHA agencies such as Europol and Eurojust and setting up a EPPO to support investigations on smuggling and trafficking perpetrated outside the EU, by criminal organisations with connections in EU Member States and thus, able to transfer migrants from Africa to Europe and America, unlawfully. Certainly, the EAW cannot be adopted outside the EU as it requires a high degree of mutual trust which is not even deeply established between law enforcement authorities of EU Member States. This is because, as Peers emphasised, substantial criminal law has not been harmonised within EU Member States.[80] Member States can also rely on the 1957 Council of Europe Convention on Extradition ratified by all Member States.[81] The situation is different for the four Protocols on extradition as they have not been ratified by all Member States.[82] The EU has also

76 See Decreto di Fermo...*op. cit.* note 11, p. 25.

77 Ibid note 75.

78 See 'Europe migrant crisis: doubt cast on identity of 'smuggler' extradited to Italy. On http://www.bbc.co.uk/news/world-europe-36488655, accessed on 14/10/2016.

79 Ibid note 75.

80 See S. Peers 2016,...*op. cit.* note 45, p. 131.

81 For the full list of States which have ratified the Convention see https://www.coe.int/en/web/conventions/full-list/-/conventions/treaty/024/signatures?p_auth=nVbvak4Y, accessed on 18/05/2018.

82 For the status of ratification of the First Protocol see https://www.coe.int/en/web/conventions/full-list/-/conventions/treaty/086/signatures?p_auth=nVbvak4Y; for the list of States which have ratified the Second Protocol see https://www.coe.int/en/web/conventions/full-list/-/conventions/treaty/098/signatures?p_auth=nVbvak4Y; for the ratification of the Third Protocol see https://www.coe.int/en/web/conventions/full-list/-/conventions/treaty/209/signatures?p_auth=nVbvak4Y; for the status of ratification of the Fourth Protocol see https://www.coe.int/en/web/conventions/full-list/-/conventions/treaty/212/signatures?p_auth=nVbvak4Y. All the four Protocols have been accessed on 14/10/2016.

adopted two Conventions on Extradition respectively in 1995 and in 1996 but they have not enterd into force as yet.[83] In any case, Member States have different legal instruments to cooperate with each other in the fight against crime, including the EAW Framework Decision. The EU has also concluded an extradition and mutual assistance agreement with the US and a Treaty with Japan on mutual legal assistance in criminal matters.[84] Finally, Member States can conclude bilateral agreements on extradition and mutual legal assistance with third countries. However, these Treaties impose restrictions to preserve national sovereignty. The issue of national soverignty may create obstacles in investigations and this is the reason why public prosecutors in Palermo, have tried to carry out investigations on smuggling of migrants by focusing mainly on investigations involving the Italian territory and invoking the Italian jurisdiction everytime the crime of smuggling was committed even only partly on the Italian territory as established by Article 6 of the Italian Criminal Code[85] and by Article 4 (1) (a) of Framework Decision 2002/946/JHA which states that a Member State can invoke jurisdiciton everytime the crime of smuggling has been committed 'in whole or in part within its territory'. However, when there are other criminals in the same organisation or in a connected criminal organisation which have perpetrated the crime outside the EU, JHA agencies should enhance their support in exchanging data on criminals perpetrating smuggling and trafficking even by cooperating in investigation, if this is necessary in order to gather information on criminals, arrest and prosecute them.

Other instruments Member States can rely on are bilateral agreements signed either by Member States or by EU with third countries. The CJEU ruled on these agreements in different occasions. In *Petruhhin* the Court ruled that

83 See respectively Council Act of 10 March 1995, adopted on the basis of Article K.3 of the Treaty on European Union, drawing up the Convention on simplified extradition procedure between the Member States of the European Union. On OJ C 78, 30/3/1995 and Council Act of 27 September 1996, adopted on the basis of Article K.3 of the Treaty on European Union, drawing up the Convention relating to extradition between the Member States of the European Union. On OJ C 313, 23/6/1996.

84 See respectively Council Decision 2009/820/CFSP of 23 October 2009 on the conclusion on behalf of the European Union of the Agreement on extradition between the European Union and the United States of America and the Agreement on mutual legal assistance between the European Union and the United States of America. On OJ L 291/40, 7/11/2009 and Council Decision 2009/933/CFSP of 30 November 2009 on the extension, on behalf of the European Union, of the territorial scope of the Agreement on extradition between the European Union and the United States of America. On OJ 325/4, 11/12/2009. See Council Decision 2010/88/CFSP/JHA of 30 November 2009 on the signing, on behalf of the European Union, of the Agreement between the European Union and Japan on mutual legal assistance in criminal matters. On OJ L39/19, 12/02/2010.

85 See Decreto di Fermo...*op. cit.* note 11, p. 21.

when a EU citzen has moved from one Member State to another Member State and the latter receives an extradition's request by a third country, the principle of non-dicrimination on grounds of nationality as established by Article 18 TFEU and Article 21 TFEU.[86] Mr Petruhhin was an Estonian national who moved to Latvia and thus,exercised his right to free movement within the EU.[87] Restrictions to free movement can only be justified when they are based on objective considerations and they are proportionate to the legitimate aims of national legislation. [88] Latvia had concluded a bilateral agreement with Russia in 1993 on Judicial Relations in Civil, Family and Criminal Matters and on the basis of this agreement, the Office of the Prosecutor-General of the Russian Federation. [89] This was not an agreement signed by the EU with Russia. Consequently, Estonia was not part of that agreement. On the basis of these facts, the CJEU ruled that according to EU rules on extradition between Mmeber States and a third country, it is necessary to protect EU nationals from measures capable of limiting their rights to free mevement and, at the same time, to fight against 'impunity in repsect of criminal offences, to apply all the cooperation and mutual assistence mechanisms provided for in the criminal field under EU law'. [90] In order to avoid discrimination on the basis of Article 18 and Article 21 TFEU, the hosting Member State shall inform the Member State of the EU person's nationality about the extradition's request and 'should the Member State so request, surrender that citizen to it,' [91] on the basis of the EAW Framework Decision.[92] In another more recent CJEU's case, this ruling was confirmed.[93] The difference between this case and *Petruhhin* is that in the latter extradition was based on a bilateral agreement, in this most recent case, the extradition was based on an international agreement signed between the EU and the US. The case was about an Italian citizen who stopped to Germany during his flight

86 See Case C-182/15 *Petruhhin* ECLI:EU:C:2016:630, paragraphs 30 et 41.

87 See Case C-182/15...*op. cit.* note 86, para. 31.

88 See Case C-182/15...*op. cit.* note 86, para. 34.

89 See Case C-182/15...*op. cit.* note 86, para. 7 et 12.

90 See Case C-182/15...*op. cit.* note 86, para. 47.

91 See Case C-182/15...*op. cit.* note 86, para. 51.

92 Ibid.

93 See Case C-191/16 *Pisciotti v. Bundesrepublik Deutschland* ECLI:EU:C:2018:222.

from Nigeria to Italy.[94] He was requested for extradition by the United States on the basis of an international agreement signed between them and the EU. [95] Mr Pisciotti expressed his opposition by stating that by allowing his extradition, Germany would be discriminatory on the basis of Article 18 TFEU. [96] The CJEU confirmed that Mr Pisciotti had exercised his rights to free movement within the EU even if he was just in transit in Germany. [97] The Court also confirmed that in order to avoid a breach of Article 18 TFEU, Germany should ask Italy whether they agree or they prefer the citizen is sureended on the baiss of the EAW Framework Decision. [98]

What is important to emphasise for the purpose of this book, is firstly that the CJEU allows extradition to third countries of EU citizens living in EU Member States not of their nationality either if there is a bilateral agreement between the Member State and the third country or if there is a bilateral agreement between the EU and the third country. Secondly, the CJEU made it clear that extradition shall be executed in accordance with Articles 4 and 19 of the Charter of Fundamental Rights. Article 4 prohibits torture and inhuman and degrading treatment, whilst Article 19 prohibits collective expulsion and returning people to countries where they may be at risk of torture, inhuman and degrading treatment and death penalty. The CJEU emphasised that before accepting a request for extradition, Member States should check whether the requesting State is party of the ECHR. [99] In any case,

> 'The existence of declarations and accession to international treaties guaranteeing respect for fundamental rights in principle are not in themselves sufficient to ensure adequate protection against the risk of ill-treatment where reliable sources have reported practices resorted to or tolerated by the authorities which are manifestly contrary to the principles of the European Convention for the Protection of Human Rights and Fundamental Freedoms'[100]

94 See Case C-191/16...*op. cit.* note 93, para. 27.

95 See Case C-191/16...*op. cit.* note 93, para. 34.

96 See Case C-191/16...*op. cit.* note 93, para. 17 at 30.

97 See Case C-191/16...*op. cit.* note 93, para. 3, 16 et 17.

98 See Case C-191/16...*op. cit.* note 93, para. 56.

99 See Case C-182/15...*op. cit.* note 86, para. 55.

100 See Case C-182/15...*op. cit.* note 86, para. 57.

Member States, before allowing extradition, shall rely on specific information that can be obtained by either the judgements of the ECtHR or by the courts of the requesting third State or on decisions and documents issues by the Council of Europe or by the UN.[101] Therefore, all bilateral agreements on extradition and on other measures related to the criminal area, can only be concluded when human rights are respected at the highest standard in the third country. This principle should also apply for the fight against human trafficking and people smuggling in cooperation with third countries. Agreements on cooperation should be monitored by the European Parliament as they will need a high consent to be legitimised. These bilateral agreements require that EU citizens are aware that human rights have to be protected at the highest level in criminal cooperation with third countries. In other terms, these agreements should be accountable before the European Parliament. A first step in this direction has been made by e reform concerning Europol. Europol and recent reformes are examined in the next section.

5. EUROPOL AND ITS ACCOUNTABILITY

Europol was established in 1995 by the Europol Convention 1995 and entered into force on 1st October 1998.[102] The main purpose of the Europol Convention was to improve the police cooperation between Member States in fighting against terrorism, drug crime and other forms of serious international crime.[103] Article 18 of the Convention established that Europol was allowed to cooperate with third countries and international organizations in the exchange of data. Data communicated by Member States, could only be exchanged with third countries or international organizations, previous the Member States' consent. The EU also established a Council Decision authorizing the Director of Europol to enter

101 See Case C-182/15...*op. cit.* note 86, para. 59.

102 See Council Act of 26/7/1995 drawing up the Convention based on Article K3 of the Treaty on the European Union, on the establishment of a European Police Office (Europol Convention), [1995] OJ C316/1, 27/11/1995 and Communication concerning the taking up of activities of Europol. [1999] OJ C 185/1, 1/7/1999.

103 See Rijken, C., 'Legal and Technical Aspects of Co-operation between Europol, Third States, and Interpol. In *The European Union and the International Legal Order: Discord or Harmony?* Asser Press, 2001, p. 577.

into negotiation agreements with third countries.[104] However, this Decision did not add anything new to the cooperation with third countries. Indeed, paragraph 5 simply stated that the Director of Europol could conclude agreements with third-countries concerning the exchange of personal, technical and operational data which are essential in order to fight against criminal organizations. Following the adoption of this Council Decision, Europol established a plan of action on cooperation with third countries that should have been based on a contract related to a strategic and technical level and on a contract concerning an operational level.[105] The contract on strategic and technical level should have consisted of exchanging data concerning information on the development and extent of criminal acts. Nevertheless, the plan of action prohibited exchange of information that could lead to the identification of the person. The contract on an operational level was also concerned with data protection and the implementation of adequate law in third countries. [106] As can be noted, Europol's material scope cannot go beyond the data exchange and protection of data. However, an effective fight against smuggling and trafficking, requires more efforts in investigative actions and thus, in cooperation with third countries in this field. Exchange of information should aim to facilitate extradition of criminals whilst preserving national sovereignty of nations where crimes have been perpetrated. Unfortunately, the Europol Convention and the following Council Decision did not address this aspect of cooperation and most importantly, the Europol Convention did not have democratic accountability, as it was not adopted by the EP's consent through the former co-decision procedure now called ordinary legislative procedure. The EP could only be consulted on the adoption of Europol's legislative measures.[107]

The Europol Convention was replaced in 2009 by a Council Decision.[108] Council Decision 2009/371/JHA states that Europol is the European Police

104 See Council Decision of 27 March 2000 authorising the Director of Europol to enter into negotiations on agreements with Third States and non-EU-related bodies, OJ 2000, C 106.

105 See Rijken, C., ...*op. cit.* note 103, p. 589.

106 See Rijken, C.,...*op. cit.* note 103, p. 590.

107 See Article 39 TEU. See also Peers, S., 'Governance and the Third Pillar: The Accountability of Europol'. In Deidre, M., Curtin and Ramsen A. Wessels, *Good Governance and the European Union*, Intersentia, 2005, p. 257 at 259.

108 See Council Decision 2009/371/JHA of 6 April 2009 establishing the European Police Office (Europol). OJ L121/37, 15/5/2009.

Office which has legal personality and which seats to the Hague.[109] Article 3 of the Council Decision establishes that the main tasks of Europol are 'to support and strengthen' cooperation between Member States in preventing and fighting against organized crime, terrorism and other forms of serious criminal activities. The list of crimes which are of Europol's competence is indicated by an Annex at the end of the Council Decision and smuggling of migrants is one of the crimes of their competence. According to Article 5, Europol has coordinating tasks as it can ask Member States to initiate investigations, although Europol cannot take this initiative. It can also support the training of national police and give technical support on methods related to the prevention of crime and coordinate actions against the euro counterfeiting.[110]

The Europol's scope on the external relations, is established by Article 23 which states that Europol can maintain cooperative relations with third States. The same Article states that Europol can conclude agreements with third-states on 'the exchange of operational, strategic or technical information, including personal data...' and that these agreements shall be approved by the Council. The problem with this Council Decision is that the EP did not play an important role in the decision-making procedure concerning the Europol's external scope and, thus, Europol does not have democratic accountability. The lack of democratic accountability is the reason why Europol does not have the extensive powers of national police such as the power of arresting, questioning and detaining suspected criminals.[111] In addition, it is unclear what powers Europol can exercise and also the position regarding judicial control.[112] There are no legal sources which clarify these powers and judicial controls over Europol. As Peers emphasized, the reports they publish annually are very informative, but they are written by Europol and only reflect their position.[113] Independent reports should be published on Europol to evaluate objectively what reforms should be proposed and put forward. This result can only be achieved by recognizing up to the EP, the power to scrutinize The Europol's work. By increasing the Europol's accountability, this agency could become more transparent and it would be more feasible to widen its scope for the purpose to strengthen police

109 See Articles 1 and 2 of Council Decision 2009/371/JHA.

110 See Article 5 (4) and (5) of Council Decision 2009/371/JHA.

111 See S. Peers, *EU Justice and Home Affairs Law, op. cit...* note 42 p. 932.

112 *ibid* note 94.

113 See Peers, S., *EU Justice and Home Affairs Law, op. cit..* note 42 p. 933.

cooperation between EU Member States and third countries. Further steps have been taken in this direction. Europol is a very important agency that could support investigations on smuggling and trafficking. A new Regulation adopted in 2016 has amended and expanded previous provisions.[114] The new Regulation has been adopted to ensure that Europol supports and strengthens the efforts made by Member States and their cooperation in preventing and fighting against serious crime affecting the territories of two or more Member States. The new Regulation introduces new provisions on the cooperation with third partners. It is not only addressed to terrorism but also to smuggling and trafficking.[115] An important amendment introduced by the Regulation is the fact that Europol will be accountable before the EP and national parliaments.[116] Europol can participate in joint investigation teams (JITs) and it can request to law enforcement authorities of Member States to initiate, conduct or coordinate criminal investigations when they fall within crimes of Europol's scope.[117] Europol will be managed by the Executive Director who will be independent and accountable before the Management Board. The Council may ask the Executive Director to report about their activities and the Executive Director will be the legal representative of Europol.[118] In relation to Europol's activities with partners, the regulation states that Europol can cooperate with international organisations, authorities of third countries and private parties. [119] Europol can exchange personal data to authorities of third countries and international organisations if these partners can assure an adequate level of protection, the respect of privacy and fundamental rights and freedom of individuals. [120] The new Regulation also allows Europol to share personal data received from private parties when they have been received by a national unit as established by Article 7 or by a contact point of the third nation or international organisation with which Europol

114 See Regulation (EU) 2016/794 of the European Parliament and of the Council of 11 May 2016 on the European Union Agency for Law Enforcement Cooperation (Europol) and replacing and repealing Council Decisions 2009/371/JHA, 2009/934/JHA, 2009/935/JHA, 2009/936/JHA and 2009/968/JHA. OJ L 135/53, 24/5/2016, para. 5.

115 See para. 6 and Annex I and Article 3 of the Regulation.

116 See para. 58 of the Regulation.

117 See Articles 5 and 6 of the Regulation.

118 See Article 23(1) of the Regulation.

119 See Article 16 of the Regulation.

120 See Article 25 (1) of the Regulation.

has concluded a cooperation agreement or when adequate level of protection is guaranteed.[121] The same criteria apply for information received by private persons.[122] Subsequently, the Regulation focuses on the protection of personal data and limits to the exchange of personal data related to persons under 18. What can be highlighted is that Europol is more transparent and accountable to the EP and national parliaments. These new provisions can make Europol more effective in the fight against smuggling of migrants and human trafficking as it is more democratic. Finally, Europol has established a European Smuggling Centre (EMSC) aiming to tackle against criminal organisations who smuggle people.[123] The EMSC coordinates and supports investigations on smuggling of migrants in cooperation with Eurojust and Frontex.

6. EUROJUST AND ITS ROLE IN THE ACTUAL JHA'S LEGAL FRAMEWORK

Eurojust was established in 2002 by Council Decision 2002/187/JHA.[124] The Council Decision 2002/187/JHA has been amended in 2003 by Council Decision 2003/659/JHA which introduced new provisions on the Eurojust's budget. Another amendment to the Council Decision of 2002 was introduced in 2009 by Council Decision 2009/426/JHA. The aim of the 2009 Decision was to make more effective its operational tasks and for this purpose, it introduced new provisions based on the working experience gained by Eurojust during the years of operation.[125] This section analyses the Council Decision of 2002 as amended by the Council Decision of 2009. The amendment of 2003 is not analysed as it concerned the Eurojust's budget and not the structure of this agency. Eurojust

121 See Article 26 (1) of the Regulation.

122 See Article 27 (1) of the Regulation.

123 See https://www.europol.europa.eu/about-europol/european-migrant-smuggling-centre-emsc, accessed on 26/4/2018.

124 See Council Decision of 28 February 2002 setting up Eurojust with a view to reinforcing the fight against serious crime. On OJ L 63/1, 6/3/2002.

125 See paragraph 2 of Council Decision 2009/426/JHA.

is a EU body which has legal personality[126] and it has its seat in the Hague.[127] Eurojust is composed by one national member for each Member State seconded to the Hague.[128] The national members will be either public prosecutors or police officers of equivalent effect or judges in the Member State where they come from.[129]

Eurojust has been established to improve judicial cooperation between Member States to fight better against trans-national criminal organisations.[130] For this purpose, in investigations and prosecutions involving two or more Member States, Eurojust shall '...stimulate and improve the coordination...of investigations and prosecutions in the Member States', '...improve cooperation between the competent authorities of the Member States...by facilitating the execution of international mutual legal assistance and the implementation of extradition requests' and give all the necessary support 'in order to render their investigations and prosecutions more effective'.[131] The Eurojust's jurisdiction covers all crimes for which Europol has competence.[132] This new Council Decision reinforced the powers of national members by stating that they will be entitled to a place of work at the Eurojust's office and they are entitled to assistance and support.[133] National members may be supported by assistants and deputies and they are subject to the national law of their Member State regarding their status.[134] Eurojust has the right to post one of its liaison magistrates to a third country to strengthen judicial cooperation.[135] In order to reinforce further judicial cooperation and settle conflicts of jurisdiction, Council Decision 2009//426/JHA emphasized that instruments based on the principle of mutual recognition should be adopted and the expression 'international mutual legal

126 See Article 1 (2) of Council Decision 2002/187/JHA.

127 See Paragraph 3 of Decision taken by Common Agreement between the Representatives of the Member States, meeting at Head of State or Government Level, of 13 December 2003, on the location of the seats of certain offices and agencies of the European Union. OJ L29/15, 3/2/2004.

128 See Article 2(1) of Council Decision 2002/187/JHA.

129 See Article 2 (1) of Council Decision 2002/187/JHA.

130 See paragraphs 1 and 3 of Council Decision 2002/187/JHA.

131 See Article 3 (1) (a), (b), (c) of Council Decision 2002/187/JHA.

132 See Article 4 of Council Decision 2002/187/JHA.

133 See Article 1 of Council Decision 2009/426/JHA.

134 See Article 2 (3), (4) and (5) of Council Decision 2009/426/JHA.

135 See Article 2 (7) of Council Decision 2009/426/JHA.

assistance and the implementation of extraditions requests" should be replaced by the expression 'request for, and decision on, judicial cooperation, including regarding instruments giving effect to the principle of mutual recognition'.[136] Eurojust can also act as a college and in this capacity, it can resolve conflicts of jurisdiction or resolving other disputes concerning mutual judicial recognition.[137] Eurojust, as a college, can ask Member States to initiate investigation or prosecution, thorough its individual members or accept that one Member State is in a better position than the other to initiate investigations or prosecute.[138] Individual members can coordinate investigations, establish JITs, exchange all the important information which can support investigation, carry out special investigative action and all relevant action which can facilitate investigation and prosecution. Competent authorities of Member States, can decide not to comply with a Eurojust's request on grounds of national security.[139] In any case, it is commendable the fact that Eurojust has an important role in coordinating investigations between investigative and prosecuting authorities of Member States. The Council Decision also introduced provisions ad hoc on mutual judicial recognition and on judicial cooperation between Eurojust and the European Judicial Network (EJN).[140]

The Council Decision stated that Eurojust shall maintain cooperation with other European bodies which are Europol, OLAF and Frontex.[141] There are specific provisions on Eurojust and the European Judicial Network which state that Eurojust and the EJN should exchange information to ensure efficient cooperation. For this purpose, national members shall inform the EJN of cases they think this agency is in a better position to deal with.[142] The secretariat of the EJN is a member of the Eurojust's staff as the secretariat of the Joint Investigation teams. Both secretariats should work as Eurojust's separate units. The same

136 See Article 2(2) of Council Decision 2009/426/JHA.

137 See Article 7 (2) of Council Decision 2009/426/JHA.

138 See Article 6 6 (1) (a) as amended by Article 6 of Council Decision 2009/426/JHA.

139 See Article 8 Council Decision 2002/187/JHA.

140 See Article 25a of Council decision 2009/426/JHA.

141 See Article 26 of Council Decision 2009/426/JHA.

142 See Article 25a of Council Decision 2009/426/JHA.

rules should be applied for any other new networks because it is stated that the secretariat shall be provided by Eurojust.[143]

Eurojust can also provide cooperation with third countries on the basis of Article 27 (3) of the Council Decision.[144] This Article states that Eurojust can conclude cooperation agreements with third countries previous the approval of the Council. Cooperation established by the Council Decision concerns the exchange of personal data. Investigative cooperation is not in the scope of the Council Decision. The same principles apply within international cooperation between Eurojust and third countries. Their cooperation will be mainly based on exchange of information, including personal data.[145] Eurojust might have an important role in the fight against smuggling and trafficking by gathering data on criminals or suspected criminals which judicial authorities in EU Member States may want to interrogate. The same principles apply for third countries which may want to request the extradition of one criminal suspected to having perpetrated smuggling or trafficking. For these purposes, Eurojust may facilitate extradition in cooperation with Europol. In the EU, Eurojust can push Member States to initiate investigation and to resolve possible conflicts of jurisdiction between each other. Conversely, in the external relations, Eurojust does not have any investigative or prosecution powers. However, Eurojust can cooperate with Europol to strengthen the EU external dimension in the area of freedom, security and justice as requested by the Stockholm Programme.[146]

---

143 See Article 25a (2) of Council Decision 2009/426/JHA.

144 See Article 3(2) of Council Decision 2002/187/JHA.

145 See Article 26a (2) of Council Decision 2009/426/JHA.

146 See The Stockholm Programme...*op. cit.* note 24.

7. COOPERATION IN CRIMINAL MATTERS BETWEEN EUROPOL, FRONTEX AND EUROJUST: CHALLENGES AND PROPOSALS

7.1 Frontex, Eurosur and their inadequacy in fighting against the crime of smuggling of migrants at sea

Frontex was established in 2004 by Regulation 2007/2004.[147] The aim of the Regulation was to set up an agency which could support Member States in the surveillance of their external borders, although the competence and responsibility for external borders checks' remained within Member States' competence.[148] The Regulation established cooperation between Frontex, Europol, international organisations and third countries.[149] Regulation 2007/2004 was amended in 2007 by Regulation 863/2007 which created Rapid Border Intervention Teams (RABITs).[150] The Regulation enforced cooperation between Member States on the external borders checks'. In any case, the Regulation did not add anything on cooperation between Frontex and JHA agencies or Frontex and third countries, specifically in the fight against smuggling of migrants by sea. Conversely, a new Regulation which established the European Agency for the Management of Operational Cooperation at the External Borders of the Member States of the European Union (Eurosur), emphasized the importance of cooperation with third parties and neighbouring third countries.[151] Eurosur was set up with the aim to exchange information with Member States and cooperate to strengthen external borders in order to prevent illegal entries. Eurosur shall also cooperate with Member States to fight against cross border crime connected with illegal

147 See Council Regulation (EC) No 2007/2004 of 26 October 2004 establishing a European Agency for the Management of Operational Cooperation at the External Borders of the Member States of the European Union. L 349/1, 25/11/2004.

148 See Articles 1 and 2 of Regulation 2007/2004.

149 See Articles 13 and 14 of Regulation 2007/2004.

150 See Regulation (EC) No 863/2007 of the European Parliament and of the Council of 11 July 2007 establishing a mechanism for the creation of Rapid Border Intervention Teams and amending Council Regulation (EC) 2007/2004 as regards that mechanism and regulating the tasks and powers of guest officers. L 199/30, 31/7/2007.

151 See Articles 18 and 20 of Regulation (EU) No 1052/2013 of the European Council and of the Council of 22 October 2013 establishing the European Border Surveillance System (Eurosur). L 295/11, 6/11/2013.

entries and to cooperate to save the lives of migrants.[152] The agency can cooperate with EU partners such as Europol and with third countries in the exchange of information. However, the problem with Eurosur and cooperation with Europol and third countries is that it is only limited to exchange information on surveillance, with the purpose to detect irregular migrants and no provisions focus on police and judicial cooperation with third countries in order to detect smuggling of migrants and trafficking when the latter crime has a cross-border dimension. There is lack of clarity on the type of cooperation nations shall be able to rely on. Article 20 states that Eurosur can conclude bilateral and multilateral agreements but there is no mention of the nature of these agreements and on the institutions of third countries which should be part of the agreements. The result is that even if the agreements are concluded, they will simply be based on exchange of information with the aim to detect irregular entries but may not support an effective fight against smuggling of migrants by sea where it would be better to establish police and judicial cooperation between EU and African countries. In addition, bilateral or multilateral agreements risk to create fragmentation in the field of smuggling of migrants at sea as they may differ with each other and this fact may increase gaps between Member States and it will advantage smugglers who will find fertile ground for their criminal activities. The EU should find a way to prevent migrants from dying in the Mediterranean.

Regulation 656/2014 has been adopted and published on the EU Official Journal on June, 27th, 2014. [153] The new Regulation clearly prohibits collective expulsion as Article 4 (3) states that the personal circumstances of people rescued in the sea, must be assessed. The place of disembarkation has to be a safe place (Member State or third country) and migrants have to be able 'to express any reasons for believing that disembarkation in the proposed place would be in violation of the principle of *non-refoulement*. The Regulation is very vague on the concept of "safe place" as it does not give a definition but it states that "the general situation of that third country" should be taken into consideration when assessing whether migrants can be disembarked in that particular place.[154]

152 See Article 1 of regulation 1052/2013.

153 See Regulation (EU) no 656/2014 of the European Parliament and the Council of 15 May 2014 establishing rules for the surveillance of the external sea borders in the context of operational cooperation coordinated by the European Agency for the Management of Operational Cooperation at the External Borders of the Member States of the European Union, L 189/93, 27/6/2014. The UK and Ireland are not bound by this Regulation (paragraphs 25 and 26).

154 See Article 4(2) Regulation 656/2014.

Article 4 (1) states that Member States shall respect the principle of non-refoulement by ensuring that no persons are disembarked to places where they could be subject to death penalty, torture or other inhuman and degrading treatment or where they could be discriminated because of their race, nationality, religion, sexual orientation or because they belong to a particular social group. These places are considered unsafe places for migrants at sea.[155] The emphasis on unsecure places is very important as it contributes to protect more efficiently migrants at sea. However, the category of people in need of subsidiary protection is not wider in the scope compared to the recast Directive. People in need of subsidiary protection are considered people who cannot be protected under the Refugee Convention but that could suffer a "serious risk" as indicated by Article 4 (1) if returned to their countries of origin.[156] The Regulation emphasizes that EU immigration and asylum policies should be based on the principle of solidarity in respect of Article 80 TFEU.[157] Principle of solidarity means that all Member States shall share responsibility in order to implement the EU policies, including policies on asylum and immigration. This is an asset in the Regulation as it can contribute to strengthen cooperation between EU Member States when facing smuggling of migrants. The Regulation also states that Frontex should fulfill its tasks in compliance with international Conventions such as UNTOC Smuggling Protocol, the United Nations Convention relating to the Status of Refugees, the European Convention for the Protection of Human Rights and Fundamental Freedoms, the International Covenant on Civil and Political Rights, the United Nations Convention against Torture and Other Cruel, Inhuman or Degrading Treatment or Punishment, the United Nations Convention on the Rights of the Child.[158] These Conventions focus on the importance of protecting irregular migrants who face war, torture or inhuman and degrading treatment. It specifies that Frontex, during the borders surveillance, has to take action in compliance with the Charter of Fundamental Rights, particularly recital 8 of the Charter on the respect of the ECHR, Social Charters adopted by the Union and case-law of

155 For a detailed analysis of this Regulation see Peers, S., "New rules on maritime surveillance: will they stop the deaths and push-backs in the Mediterranean?". On http://eulawanalysis.blogspot.be/2014/06/new-eu-rules-on-maritime-surveillance.html accessed on 11/7/2014.

156 Compare Article 4 (1) of Regulation 656/2014 with Article 2 Directive 2011/95/EU.

157 See paragraph 2 of Regulation 656/2014.

158 See paragraph 8 of Regulation 656/2014.

the CJEU and of the ECtHR.[159] The Regulation introduces new interception and rescuing rules in order to protect more effectively migrants at sea and give them the opportunity to disembark while waiting on a decision on their particular case. The Regulation addresses smuggling of migrants by establishing specific rules when one Member State suspects that one vessel is engaged in the smuggling of migrants by sea.[160] For this purpose, the Regulation introduces new rules on the interception of migrants in the territorial sea, on the high seas and in the contiguous zone. Article 6 states that the host Member State (Member States from which the sea operation takes place or is launched)[161] and the participating Member State (Member State which participate to the sea operation by providing technical equipment, border guards and other relevant staff but which is not a host Member State)[162] are responsible for checking the vessel and seize it when there is evidence that the vessel is trying to cross the borders irregularly or is committing smuggling of migrants. The host Member State and the participating Member State can be supported by participating units which will operate under their responsibility. Article 7 states that in case of interception on the high seas, the participating units will carry out the same checks and controls that can be carried out in the territorial sea, previous the authorization of the flag State, in respect of the Smuggling Protocol and other national and international law. Article 8 states that if the interception takes place in the contiguous zone, the host Member State and the neighbouring participating Member State, will still be responsible for the checks indicated by Article 6 but only 'for measures that are necessary to prevent the infringement of relevant laws and regulations within the Member State's territory or territorial sea'.[163] The measures established by Article 6 cannot be taken in the contiguous zone of a Member State which is not participating in the sea operation without its authorization.[164] Article 10 states that if the interception takes place in the territorial sea or in the contiguous zone, disembarkation will take place in the coastal Member State. In case of interception on the high seas, disembarkation will take place in the coun-

159 See paragraph 9 of Regulation 656/2014 and recital 8 of the Charter of Fundamental Rights of the European Union. OJ C83, 30/3/2010, p. 389.

160 See Articles 6 and 7 of Regulation 656/2014.

161 Article 2(2) of Regulation 656/2014.

162 Article 2(2) of Regulation 656/2014.

163 Article 8 (1) of Regulation 656/2014.

164 Article 8 (2) of Regulation 656/2014.

try from which the vessel is assumed to have departed or, if this is not possible because the place is unsafe, disembarkation will take place in the host Member State. These rules clearly establish that vessels sealing in the contiguous zone of one Member State or on the high sea and not in its territorial waters, shall be checked because actions shall be taken if there is the evidence that the vessel is involved in smuggling of migrants by sea or is trying to cross its borders. These provisions ensure that vessels are not neglected and so people in distress who may be on those vessels. Indeed, Article 9 requires that Member States

> 'observe their obligation to render assistance to any vessel or person in distress at sea and, during a sea operation...They shall do so regardless of the nationality or status of such a person or the circumstances in which that person is found'.[165]

In this way, migrants at sea are recognized the right to disembark in the host Member State and wait there for a decision on their expulsion or other claims. However, the Regulation on Frontex as the other legal instruments, have been established to coordinate rescue operations and not to prevent migrants to be smuggled. A wide approach should be preferred as smuggling of migrants has links with trafficking and it is perpetrated in many different countries and not only in countries facing the Mediterranean Sea.

7.2 The European Border and Coast Guard

Regulations No 2007/2004 and No 863/2007 have been replaced by a new Regulation establishing the European Border and Coast Guard.[166] The new Regulation states that the European Border and Coast Guard Agency (the Agency) will continue to be referred as Frontex.[167] The Agency will support Member States in providing information to ensure the border management.[168]

165 Article 9 (1) of Regulation 656/2014.

166 See Regulation (EU) 2016/1624 of the European Parliament and the Council of 14 September 2016 on the European Border and Coast Guard and amending Regulation (EU) 2016/399 of the European Parliament and of the Council and repealing Regulation (EC) No 863/2007 of the European Parliament and of the Council, Council Regulation (EC) No 2007/2004 and Council Decision 2005/267/EC. OJ L 251/1, 16/9/2016.

167 See paragraph 11 of the Regulation.

168 See paragraph 18 of the Regulation.

Information provided by the Agency will focus mainly on 'border control, return, irregular secondary movements of third-country nationals within the Union, prevention of cross-border crime including facilitation of unauthorized border crossings, trafficking in human beings…'.[169] The fight against smuggling and trafficking will be a priority for the Agency which 'should contribute to preventing and detecting serious crime with a cross-border dimension, such as migrant smuggling, trafficking in human beings'. [170] For this purpose, the Regulation states that the Agency should liaise with Europol and they should coordinate their efforts to fight against smuggling and trafficking when the crime affects two or more EU Member States.[171] The European Border and Coast Guard Agency shall also cooperate with Eurosur in the management of the external borders and with experts of Member States. [172]

Article 1 of the Regulation states that the Agency shall contribute to address 'serious crime with a cross-border dimension' in order to guarantee high level of internal security whilst respecting fundamental rights and the free movement of persons. Article 4 states that the Agency shall cooperate with Member States to manage external borders, including the participation in rescue operations, data analysis to evaluate where there is a risk for internal security. The same Article states that the Agency shall cooperate with third countries 'focusing in particular on neighbouring countries and on those third countries which have been identified through risk analysis as being countries of origin and/or transit for illegal immigration'.[173] All the operations will be undertaken in the spirit of shared cooperation where member States shall be considered fully responsible for managing their borders and the Agency shall support member States in the management of external borders.[174] According to Article 7, the Agency is accountable to the Council and the EP. Article 15 states that the Agency shall participate in joint operation and rapid border interventions at the external borders by providing technical and operational assistance and by deploying a rapid border intervention for a short time in the territory of the host Member State

169 Ibid

170 See paragraph 19 of the Regulation.

171 Ibid

172 See paragraph 20 of the Regulation.

173 See Article 4 (f) of the Regulation.

174 See Article 5 of the Regulation.

which is facing an emergency. The following Articles explain how the emergency should be tackled.[175] The Regulation then regulates the return operations where the Agency should take part, including in forced return operations.[176] Article 34 states that the Agency shall operate in the full respect of fundamental rights as established by the Charter and by international legal instruments such as the 1951 Convention Relating to the Status of refugees, the 1967 Protocol and in compliance with the principle of *non-refoulement*. The latter principle shall be respected when migrants are rescued and disembarked.[177] The Agency shall also take into account, among others, the special needs of victims of human trafficking.[178]

Article 47 states that the Agency shall process personal data concerning persons suspected to have been involved in smuggling and trafficking. Article 52 states that the Agency shall cooperate with many agencies, including Europol and Eurojust to prevent and detect smuggling and trafficking. Article 54 focuses on cooperation between the Agency and third countries but the provision mainly states that 'The establishment of cooperation with third countries shall serve to promote European border management and return standards'.[179] Article 55 (1) states that the Agency can deploy officers in third countries which 'comply with minimum human rights standards'. The deployment shall reinforce the external border management and contribute to prevent smuggling of migrants.[180]

These are the main provisions of the Regulation which describe the tasks that the Agency shall have. The new Regulation focuses specifically on external border management, although it emphasizes the importance of cooperating with other agencies and third countries of transit or of origin of migrants, in order to prevent and detect smuggling and trafficking. Smuggling and trafficking can be defeated by reinforcing cooperation between JHA agencies in investigative actions, especially Europol and Eurojust, as indicated in previous sections.[181] This chapter suggests that Europol and Eurojust should be coordinated by the EPPO.

175 See Articles 17-19 of the Regulation.

176 See Articles 28-33 of the Regulation.

177 See Article 34 (2) of the Regulation.

178 See Article 34 (3) of the Regulation.

179 See Article 54 (1) of the Regulation.

180 See Article 54(2) and (3) of the Regulation.

181 See section 5, p. 92 and p. 6 p. 95 of this chapter.

The EPPO should reinforce the support to be given by Europol and Eurojust in investigations among EU Member States investigative authorities and investigative teams of third countries such as the African countries.

7.3 Existing specific legal framework on cooperation between Europol, Eurojust and Frontex

JITs have been established by a Council Framework Decision.[182] JITs can be set up by competent authorities of two or more EU Member States with the intent to carry out criminal investigations in one or more Member States setting up the JITs.[183] JITs can be concluded with non-EU States as established by a Council Resolution which permits the establishment of JITs with non-EU countries on the basis of relevant international instruments.[184] JITs could be established with countries of origin and transit of smuggled migrants to carry out investigations on smuggling. However, JITs as such could be of concern for human rights if they are established with countries which do not have a high standard in the respect of human rights. On the basis of what the CJEU has ruled above,[185] bilateral agreements in the criminal area cannot be concluded with States which do not respect human rights at a high level.

Article 1(12) the JITs Framework Decision, authorize Eurojust and Europol to participate in investigations either separately or jointly.[186]

The Framework Decision allows officials or bodies established by the Treaty and therefore, Eurojust and Europol to participate in JITs. However, they will not be conferred the rights of members and seconded members of the JITs, unless established otherwise.[187] On the basis, of this provision, it can be stated that the support these two agencies can give to JITs, is very limited as the Framework Decision allows JITs of Member States to prevent these agencies from participating effectively to criminal investigations. This provision adds more fragmenta-

182 See Council Framework Decision 2002/465/JHA of 13 June 2002 on joint investigation teams. On OJ L 162/1, 20/6/2002.

183 See Article 1 of Framework Decision 2002/465/JHA.

184 See Council Resolution on a Model Agreement for setting up a Joint Investigation Team (JIT) OJ C 18/1, 19/1/2017.

185 See section 4 of this chapter.

186 See Article 1 (12) Council Framework Decision 2002/465/JHA.

187 ibid note 112.

tion and lack of coordination in investigations and in the context of smuggling of migrants at sea, they will not make any difference. Conversely, strengthening the powers of Eurojust and Europol can certainly make the difference because if these two agencies were given investigative powers to work jointly, their force task will be reinforced and cooperation with African countries may be addressed more seriously. It is not disputed that the EU has adopted some measures on JHA agencies such as Eurojust, Europol and it has emphasized how important their cooperation is in the fight against smuggling of migrants at sea.[188] In addition, the Council has highlighted that cooperation with third countries such as West Africa, is very important in the fighting against criminal organisations facilitating smuggling of migrants and human trafficking. However, the efforts made are not sufficient. The legal framework is very fragmented as there are many different regulations, framework decisions and agreements which seem to be a duplication of each other and do not give the agencies effective competence. An example of what it is stressed in this section, can be found in the agreement between Eurojust and Europol.[189] The agreement is just a repetition of the other legal instruments on these two agencies analysed in the previous sections of this chapter. The language is the same and the agreement does not add anything which could support an effective fight against smuggling of migrants at sea. The agreement states that Europol and Eurojust 'will develop priorities and strategies' to fight effectively the crime of their competence.[190] Article 4 of the same agreement states that 'Eurojust shall promote the coordination of and facilitate the cooperation between the competent judicial authorities'. This expression is just a repetition of the current legal framework on Eurojust. Article 4 also adds that 'Europol shall promote the widest possible cooperation among the competent law enforcement authorities through National Units'. However, Europol's tasks are very limited compared to those tasks of Eurojust as Europol can only gather information on personal data and exchange with other JHA partners or Member States'. It is believed that the agreement concluded between Eurojust and Europol will not make the difference in the fight against criminal organisations and in particular against smuggling of migrants at sea, because

188 See http://register.consilium.europa.eu/doc/srv?l=EN&f=ST%2012095%202013%20INIT, accessed on 16/4/2015.

189 See http://www.eurojust.europa.eu/doclibrary/Eurojust-framework/agreements/Agreement%20between%20Eurojust%20and%20Europol%20(2010)/Eurojust-Europol-2010-01-01-EN.pdf accessed on 16/4/2015.

190 See Article 3 of the Agreement between Eurojust and Europol.

Europol's tasks are very limited. Article 9 of the Agreement states that 'Europol shall inform Eurojust on the opening of an analysis work file' and Europol can refuse to open it. Article 10 of the Agreement states that Europol can ask Eurojust to provide assistance when it believes that there is the need to launch judicial cooperation between national authorities of Member States. Europol can require Eurojust to provide assistance 'through coordination with national authorities participating in the analysis work files supporting the execution of European Arrest warrant' and other instruments in order to achieve mutual recognition and mutual legal assistance between judicial authorities of Member States. Therefore, Europol's role is limited to requests to address to Eurojust but it cannot take its own investigative and police tasks. Eurojust's scope in investigation is also very limited because even if Article 6 of the Agreement states that Eurojust and Europol may participate to JITs, *de facto* their scope of participation is very limited because, as shown in the previous section, they cannot be considered seconded in the Member State where the investigation will be carried out and thus, their participation is very marginal. On the basis of this analysis, it can be asserted that the competence on investigation and prosecution in the fight against serious crime and in particular smuggling of migrants and trafficking, remains mainly of Member States' jurisdiction and when no solutions have been proposed for when the crime has been perpetrated outside the territory of Member States. The fight against this crime requires a global approach because it involves the EU and different States in Africa. More effective can instead be the memorandum of Understanding Regulating Cooperation between Frontex and Eurojust[191] which was stipulated in 2013 to reinforce cooperation in the fight against smuggling of migrants and human trafficking.[192] Article 2 states that Eurojust and Frontex shall establish a contact point whose tasks will be coordinated among the two agencies. The contact points shall promote effective cooperation between the two agencies. They shall exchange strategic information on cross-border crime and technical information in order to contribute to improve judicial and law enforcement cooperation in the fight against smuggling and trafficking. The parties can organize seminars conference and other trainings in

191 See http://eurojust.europa.eu/doclibrary/Eurojust-framework/agreements/Memorandum%20of%20Understanding%20between%20Eurojust%20and%20Frontex%20%282013%29/Frontex-Eurojust-2013-12-18_EN.pdf accessed on 16/04/2015.

192 See Article 1 of the Memorandum of Understanding...*op. cit.* note 191.

order to improve investigative and judicial cooperation between each other.[193] This agreement reinforces the scope of these two agencies in the exchange of information. Nevertheless, the memorandum should have clarified what information should be exchanged, with the aim to improve law enforcement and investigative cooperation between EU Member States and third countries. This measure is lacking on this point as all the previous legal instruments which have been analysed in this chapter. It would be ideal to recognize up to Eurojust more powers compared to the other two agencies. All initiatives and new legislation enhancing the powers of JHA agencies in the fight against smuggling and trafficking, shall grant coordination powers' to Eurojust which should cooperate with the other agencies within the EU and outside the EU under the direction of the EPPO. In this way, EU JHAs' agencies participation in the fight against smuggling and trafficking, could be more effective as it would guarantee more uniformity in the response to these criminal threats.

A similar project should be adopted after all EU agencies become accountable before the EP. Cooperation in criminal investigations within and outside the EU, can only be adopted if human rights are respected at a high standard in all nations where investigations should be carried out. In fact, the CJEU has ruled that a bilateral agreement can take place if the third country prohibits torture, inhuman and degrading treatment and death penalty. The EP should inform EU citizens on the importance of the respect of human rights in cooperation in criminal investigations. By making EU agencies accountable before the EP, this institution would ensure that investigations are carried out where human rights are respected at the highest standard.

8. THE EUROPEAN PUBLIC PROSECUTOR'S OFFICE

8.1 Background

In 2001, the European Commission published a Green Paper on the establishment of the European Public Prosecutor (EPP).[194] The Green Paper was followed

193 See Articles 3, 4 and 5 of the Memorandum of Understanding *op. cit.* note 191.

194 See Green paper on the criminal-law protection of the financial interests of the Community and the establishment of a European Prosecutor. COM (2001) 715 final, 11/12/2001.

by another report of the Commission published in 2003 which showed an update on the EPP.[195] These two reports showed the results of a research project supported by the Commission and that focused on the possibility of setting up the EPP to protect the financial interests of the Community. The *Corpus Juris* was established in 2000. Its aim was to set up a European Judicial Area in order to investigate, prosecute, trial and execute sentences concerning financial crimes committed against the EU budget. The EPP should have been part of a criminal law code called *Corpus Juris 2000*.[196] The *Corpus Juris 2000* set up the EPP to fight against crimes listed in Articles 1-8. Those crimes were fraud, market-rigging, money laundering, conspiracy between or more persons working together with the purpose to harm the EU financial interests'. This initiative was commendable because, for the first time, it was seriously considered the establishment of a single legal area to fight against financial crimes. Certainly, the *Corpus Juris* was very limited in its scope as it only focused on financial crimes and not on other crimes such as human trafficking and people smuggling, but the idea was commendable. Article 18 stated that in order to investigate, prosecute, trial and execute sentences against financial crimes affecting the EU, the territory of the Member States should have been considered 'a single legal area'. The EPP should have been considered the authority responsible for actions against financial crimes and it should have acted independently from national authorities and EU institutions. Their office should have included a European Director of Public Prosecution (EDPP) based in Brussels and European delegated Public Prosecutors (EDelPPS) whose offices should have been based in each capital of EU Member States. The EPP should have been indivisible in the sense that the action taken by one of its members should have been considered to be taken by all the other members. The EPP would also have been considered interdependent with the different EDelPPs. They would have been under the obligation to assist each other. Article 19 established that the EPP could open a proceeding when an investigation conducted by a national authority revealed that a financial crime against the EU budget had been committed or the EPP learned about one of these crimes committed within one of the Member States independently. Article 20 granted to the EPP powers of investigation in cooperation

195 See Follow-up report on the Green paper on the criminal-law protection of the financial interests of the Community and the establishment of a European Prosecutor. COM (2003) 128 final, 19/3/2003.

196 See http://ec.europa.eu/anti_fraud/documents/fwk-green-paper-corpus/corpus_juris_en.pdf accessed on 22/4/2015.

with EdelPPs. Articles 22 and 26 stated that after the end of investigations, the EPP would have been able to prosecute the offenders before independent and impartial courts based in each Member State and appointed by them on the basis of their domestic law. The *Corpus Juris 2000* was very advanced because Article 27 also gave the opportunity to appeal against the conviction to national courts. Article 28 stated that the CJEU had jurisdiction in preliminary questions concerning the interpretation and implementation of the *Corpus Juris*, on dispute concerning its application and on conflicts of jurisdiction between national and European prosecutors related to European territoriality and on the request of the accused concerning the choice of jurisdiction. Article 29 *et seq.* concerned the rights of the accused and the gathering and admissibility of evidence. The project aimed to fight against cross-border crimes by establishing a common criminal area in the EU and a public prosecutor which could have overcome problems related to conflict of jurisdiction and combat effectively them. The Green Paper of the Commission, inspired by the *Corpus Juris 2000*, proposed to insert Article 280a in the EC Treaty. However, the proposal stated that the EPP would have been set up only to fight against financial crime against the EU budget. In order to avoid conflicts of jurisdiction with investigative and prosecuting authorities of Member States, the proposal stated that the Community could have adopted legislation within the respect of the principles of subsidiarity.[197] Principle of subsidiarity means that the EU action cannot go beyond what is necessary to achieve the single market. If Member States can achieve the object by acting alone, the EU should not intervene.[198] Many scholars and governments such as the UK, criticized the Green Paper on two aspects. First of all, the EPP's project received much criticism because it left too much independence to its office.[199] Secondly, the project was criticized because the EPP was not accountable before the European Parliament and/or national Parliaments. [200] Therefore, the project was abandoned not only because many scholars and many Member

197 See Green Paper...*op. cit.* note 194, p.20.

198 See Article 5 TEC.

199 See Fijnaut, C., and Groenhuijsen, M.S., *A European Public Prosecutor: comments on the Green Paper.* P. 10. Available at http://ec.europa.eu/anti_fraud/documents/fwk-green-paper-contributions/gp_fijnaut_nl_en.pdf, accessed on 27/4/2015.

200 See Zwiers, M., *The European Public Prosecutor's Office* 2011, Intersentia, p. 372. See also United Kingdom Response to the Commission Green Paper, p. 1. The United Kingdom Parliament, Select Committee on European Communities, Ninth Report, *Prosecuting Fraud on the Communities' Finances-The Corpus Juris*, 18/5/1999, para 62.

States showed their opposition to it, but also because they preferred to wait for the outcome of Eurojust's activities and OLAF just established in the same period.[201] The AFSJ continued to develop by the establishment of other instruments such as the EAW examined above.[202] These new instruments adopted to support Member States in the fight against cross-border crime, are certainly less ambitious than the previous EPP. The project should have been carry on as it could have been a very good instrument to fight against the cross-border crimes of smuggling and trafficking. The EPP could have facilitated police and judicial cooperation between investigative and judicial authorities of Member States, with investigative and judicial authorities of origin and transit countries of criminal organisations perpetrating smuggling and trafficking. These objectives could be achieved by making the EPP accountable before the EP and national parliaments.[203] This is because establishing a EPP who should cooperate in investigations, requires a wide mandate and the involvement of the EP and national parliaments as issues related to encroachment of national sovereignty may become very problematic. New legislation should indicate what mandate the EPP should acquire and whether it will be established to undertake investigations within the EU or outside the EU or support and facilitate cooperation between police and judicial authorities of EU member States and third countries, especially if investigations concern smuggling and trafficking.

The Lisbon Treaty has improved the powers of the EP and it has introduced a way to ensure that national Parliaments are taken into consideration when new legislation is drafted.[204] Furthermore, as it will be highlighted in chapter 5,[205] the CJEU has pointed out, in different rulings, that the involvement of people in the decision-making procedure is very important to guarantee that all decisions are taken democratically.

201 See Zwiers, M., *The European Public Prosecutor's Office* 2011,... *op. cit.* note 200, p. 356.

202 See section 5 of this chapter.

203 See Protocol No 1 on the Role of National Parliaments in the European Union and Protocol No 2 on the Application of the Principles of Subsidiarity and Proportionality. C 326/201, 26/10/2012.

204 Ibid

205 See section 2, p. 116 of chapter 5.

8.2 The Lisbon Treaty and the establishment of the European Public Prosecutor's Office

The EPP's project had not been shelved by the Lisbon Treaty. Indeed, Article 86 TFEU established the European Public Prosecutor's Office (EPPO). Article 86 established the EPPO '...to combat crimes affecting the financial interests of the Union'. The EPPO shall be established from Eurojust, by a Regulation. The Council has to act unanimously after having obtain the EP's consent.

> 'In the absence of unanimity in the Council, a group of at least nine Member States may request that the draft regulation be referred to the European Council. In that case, the procedure in the Council shall be suspended. After discussion, and in case of a consensus, the European Council shall, within four months of this suspension, refer the draft back to the Council for adoption.
>
> Within the same timeframe, in case of disagreement, and if at least nine Member States wish to establish enhanced cooperation on the basis of the draft regulation concerned, they shall notify the European Parliament, the Council he Council and the Commission accordingly. In such a case, the authorisation to proceed with enhanced cooperation referred to in Article 20(2) of the Treaty on European Union and Article 329(1) of this Treaty shall be deemed to be granted and the provisions on enhanced cooperation shall apply.
>
> 2. The European Public Prosecutor's Office shall be responsible for investigating, prosecuting and bringing to judgment, where appropriate in liaison with Europol, the perpetrators of, and accomplices in, offences against the Union's financial interests, as determined by the regulation provided for in paragraph 1. It shall exercise the functions of prosecutor in the competent courts of the Member States in relation to such offences.
>
> 3. The regulations referred to in paragraph 1 shall determine the general rules applicable to the European Public Prosecutor's Office, the conditions governing the performance of its functions, the rules of procedure applicable to its activities, as well as those governing the admissibility of evidence, and the rules applicable to the judicial review of procedural measures taken by it in the performance of its functions.

> 4. The European Council may, at the same time or subsequently, adopt a decision amending paragraph 1 in order to extend the powers of the European Public Prosecutor's Office to include serious crime having a cross-border dimension and amending accordingly paragraph 2 as regards the perpetrators of, and accomplices in, serious crimes affecting more than one Member State. The European Council shall act unanimously after obtaining the consent of the European Parliament and after consulting the Commission.'[206]

It can be noted that the EPPO's scope has been widened compared to the project drafted in the *Corpus Juris 2000*. The EPPO can be established not only to fight against financial crimes but also to fight against other serious crimes. Definitely, smuggling of migrant and human trafficking are included in the EPPO's scope. Article 86 states that the EPPO has to liaise with Europol.

It must be added that the EPPO will be established by a regulation and that the EP will play a role as the Council will not be able to approve a regulation on the EPPO's establishment without the EP's consent. Therefore, in order to approve the Regulation, it is necessary that Council acts unanimously on the EP's consent. There will be applied the special ordinary procedure which means that the Council and the EP will not act upon the Commission's proposal and thus its role will be very marginal.[207]

Nevertheless, unanimity in order to set up the EPPO is not necessary as if nine Member States will be in agreement, enhanced cooperation ex Article 20 TEU, will be established and the Regulation on the EPPO will be agreed by the co-decision procedure on the basis of Article 289 TFEU. However, enhanced cooperation will not be launched to fight against other cross-border crimes but only to fight against financial crimes. In order to fight against other serious crimes, it is necessary that the Council acts unanimously, after having obtained the consent of the EP and after having consulted the Commission. Zwiers thinks that the provision may be subject to a different interpretation which would permit to widen the mandate by the participating European Council members which would act unanimously. [208] It is thought that the EPPO may be a very effective office to support investigations against smuggling and trafficking, and to contribute to prosecute perpetrators either in the EU or outside the EU.

---

206 See Article 86 TFEU.

207 See Zwiers, M., *The European Public Prosecutor's Office* 2011,... *op. cit.* note 200, p. 387.

208 Ibid

Therefore, the EPPO should be given adequate powers to achieve this objective. Zwiers highlights that the EPPO could have the same mandate of Eurojust as this agency has jurisdiction over serious cross-border crime otherwise it would be necessary to make a differentiation in between cases where the EPPO can prosecute and cases where it cannot prosecute.[209] An alternative, as Zwiers suggests, could be to permit EPPO and Eurojust to coexist and share their tasks on the basis of their competence.[210] A solution could be to establish the EPPO to coordinate Europol and Eurojust efforts in exchanging data between EU member States and third countries. A particular emphasis should be given on crimes of trafficking and smuggling. However, drafters of the Lisbon Treaty seemed more concentrated to establishing the EPPO to fight against EU fraud and financial crimes connected to fraud, rather than to fight against other serious crimes such as smuggling and trafficking. [211] This limited material scope had already been criticized when the Green Paper was published in 2001 and it can be further criticized now as the AFSJ has as its objectives to fight against any serious cross-border crime and not only against fraud.[212] However, at the moment proposals on the establishment of the EPPO are only concentrating on fraud against EU budget and corruption within the EU.[213]

There is no intention to widen the scope of EPPO, although there is the intention to grant it external competence. According to Article 82(2), the EPPO will have the competence to investigate, prosecute and bring to judgement perpetrators and accomplices of crimes affecting the EU financial interests and, on the basis of Article 86(4), also other serious crimes. The dilemma is how this competence will be exercised. For the purpose of smuggling and trafficking, it is definitely going to impact the role of Europol. In addition, should the EPPO be able to issue instructions to national police? There might be two alternatives to follow. As shown above,[214] Europol does not have coercive powers ex Article 88 TFEU, it cannot become a European Police and will never have these powers. On the basis of these facts, there is who proposes to give the

209 See Zwiers, M., *The European Public Prosecutor's Office* 2011,... *op. cit.* note 200, p. 389.

210 See Zwiers, M., *The European Public Prosecutor's Office* 2011,... *op. cit.* note 200, pp. 389 et 390.

211 See Zwiers, M., *The European Public Prosecutor's Office* 2011,... *op. cit.* note 200, p. 390 et 391.

212 See M. Zwiers *The European Public Prosecutor's Office* 2011,... *op. cit.* note 200, p. 391.

213 See COM (2013) 534 final 17/7/2013, p. 4.

214 See section 5.

EPPO investigative powers.[215] However, a proposal as such, would be contrary to Article 88 which never intended to accord coercive powers to Europol as they shall remain of national police competence.[216] Therefore, it would be better to concentrate on a less ambitious project by not giving the EPPO investigative and prosecuting powers. The EPPO should aim to accelerate investigations with national authorities of third countries on smuggling and trafficking by ensuring that data on criminals are exchanged between the different domestic authorities investigating smuggling and trafficking within the EU and outside the EU. The EPPO should be the point of contact for domestic authorities. When they contact the EPPO, this office should be able to provide information gathered by Europol and Eurojust. The role of the EPPO should be to ensure that information are exchanged uniformly, in order to proceed with extradition requests'. These decisions should be taken by domestic police of States where smuggling and trafficking have been perpetrated by concluding agreements with law enforcement authorities of different nations. These agreements should be overseen and controlled by the EPPO in cooperation with enforcement authorities of third countries. EU Member States should delegate these tasks to the EPPO on the basis of mutual trust and mutual judicial cooperation. No investigative tasks should be given to the EPPO as these tasks would risk to compromise cooperation when issues related to national sovereignty are raised. The EPPO should be established to avoid that issues related to national sovereignty can compromise investigations with third countries. The EPPO should also monitor whether all requests of extradition are processed in the respect of human rights as protected by the ECHR and the Charter of Fundamental Rights. No suspected criminals should be extradited to third countries where the standard in the respect of human rights is low and the EPPO should ensure that extradition will not be processed on those cases. Most importantly, the EPPO should be accountable before the EP to ensure that human rights are respected at the highest standard in investigations on smuggling and trafficking.

215 See Zwiers, M., *The European Public Prosecutor's Office* 2011,... *op. cit.* note 200, pp. 389 *et* 390.

216 *ibid* note 198.

Chapter 4 has focused on possible long term procedures to fight against smuggling and trafficking. For this purpose, Europol, Eurojust, Frontex and changes adopted on this agencies and a possible establishment of the EPPO have been analysed. It has been noted that the EU is concentrated in securing and controlling external border managements rather than in fighting against smuggling and trafficking by enhancing the scope of Europol and Eurojust And by establishing the EPPO to fight against these two crimes. Police and judicial cooperation is essential to fight against smuggling of migrants and trafficking. However, the scope of JHAs agencies such as Europol and Eurojust has not been widened and there is no intention to widen their scope in the future. Therefore, this chapter has suggested to work on the basis of the EU legal framework which has established Europol and Eurojust and it has suggested to give them an important role in the investigative cooperation between police forces of Member States and police forces of third countries of transit or of residence of migrants. Europol and Eurojust should facilitate extradition between different police forces. The chapter highlighted that the EPPO should also have a role, although there is not scope for its establishment to fight against smuggling and trafficking in the near future. This chapter has emphasized this problem which will make the fight against smuggling and trafficking in cooperation with third countries, very difficult.

This chapter has also shown that agreements with non-EU countries on criminal investigations, can jeopardise human rights when they are not respected at the level of the ECHR. Therefore, it is very important to enhance the EP's role by making EU agencies accountable before the EP. The EP's task should be to monitor whether the setting up of JITs comply with the human rights as protected by the ECHR and the EU Charter of Fundamental Rights. The CJEU has emphasized in established case-law that it is a fundamental democratic principle that EU citizens have to participate in the measures adopted at EU level through their representatives who sit in the Parliament.[217] External cooperation may have many implications as investigations may require authorities of third countries to access the territory of Member States and the handle of information on suspected criminals who are EU citizens. This mandate should be given by the

217 See Case C-138/79 *Roquette Freres v. Council*, EU:C:1980:249, para 33. See Case C-300/89 *Titanium Dioxide* EU:C:1991:244, para. 20. See Case C-130/10, *Parliament v. Council* EU:C:2012:472, para. 81.

EP and by making Europol and other JHA agencies, accountable before the EP. In this way, criminal investigations against these criminals based in Europe and in Africa, will be carried out effectively. Certainly, as it will be shown below,[218] the EP can only be consulted in the Common Foreign and Security Policy (CFSP) as it cannot negotiate and conclude international agreements. The CJEU has ruled that the Parliament shall scrutinize measures related to the EU policy.[219] However, if the CFSP has an impact on the AFSJ, the EP has to consent to the negotiation concluded by the Council as established by Article 218 (6) TFEU and which is examined below.[220]

The next and conclusive chapter will focus on the EP's role and on cooperation between the EU and African countries to eradicate the root causes of irregular migration and to sustain African countries to develop economies which could prevent irregular migration and that many migrants become victims of smuggling and trafficking.

218 See section 2, p 116 chapter 5.

219 See Case C-658/11, *Parliament v. Council,* EU:C:2014:2025, para. 85.

220 See section 2, p. 116 of chapter 5.

Chapter 5: Extra-territorial cooperation against smuggling and trafficking

1. Introduction

The absolute priority to fight against smuggling and trafficking should be to identify root causes for migration and address them by measures preventing people from leaving irregularly their countries of origin.

The EP, the European Council and the Council in their Joint Report, emphasised that smuggling of migrants involving criminal organisations, can be effectively defeated by addressing the root causes of irregular migration.[1] For this reason, support should be given to 'municipalities located along the migration route (in particular, in 'migration hubs' and coastal cities)'. An effective and durable result could only be achieved by giving socio-economic support to origin and transit countries. The EU should enhance extra-territorial cooperation and responsibility in order to provide durable solution to smuggling of migrants and human trafficking. This chapter focusses on extra-territorial cooperation between the EU and African countries in order to fight against smuggling of migrants and human trafficking. This chapter emphasises that smuggling and trafficking can be fought against by enhancing criminal investigations between the EU and African countries and especially by identifying root causes of irregular migration. However, this latter objective can be achieved by prosecuting criminals involved with smuggling because this crime can be perpetrated by governments.[2] If governments are corrupted, it will be very difficult to reduce the root causes of migration as it will not be convenient for their criminal business. Corrupted governments prefer to opt for restrictive immigration controls rather than on economic development. Recent research conducted in Niger has shown that since the 2000s and thus since irregular migration became a concern

1 See JOIN (2017) 4 final 25/1/2017, p. 9.

2 See Zhang, S.X., Sanchez, G. E., Achilli, L., 'Crimes of Solidarity in Mobility: Alternative Views on Migrant Smuggling'. ANNALS, AAPSS, 676, March 2018, Vol. 676, issues 1 p. 10.

in the relationships between Sub-Saharan Africa, Northern Africa and European governments, tough immigration controls have been adopted.[3] During the immigration controls on people coming from Agadez to southern Libya, migrants are taxed many times by the Nigerien police and military.[4] Since migration policies have changed, 'West African elites no longer envisaged migration as a factor of development, but as a bargaining chip in their relations with the EU'.[5] The Economic Community of West African States (ECOWAS), in January 2008 adopted migration policies more focused on controlling external borders rather than on free movement of people within the African region.[6] This orientation was 'influenced by European assumptions BOUT West African migration, which are more ideological than based on facts'.[7]

Chapter 5 analyses different agreements concluded in between the EU and Africa which are the EUCAP Sahel Niger, the EU Horn of Africa Migration Route Initiative (from now on Khartoum Process) and the Valletta Summit on migration in order to identify root causes of irregular migration and tackle them and in order to fight against smuggling and trafficking, bearing in mind that although smuggling and trafficking are two separate crimes, they can overlap and in this latter case, EU measures in cooperation with African countries, should prioritize the protection of victims rather than their return to their countries of origin and residence.

The European Commission in the Action Plan against migrants smuggling stressed that smuggling and trafficking should be fought against by cooperation at EU level and with origin and transit countries, strategic partners, civil society and international organisations.[8] The aim of cooperation should be to dismantle criminal activities, seize their assets and prosecute smugglers. The approach should be multi-lateral in order to fight against these two crimes and to prevent them by addressing the root-causes of irregular migration. The Commission stated that Member States' efforts should be strengthened and EU agencies should give support to Member States in the fight against criminal net-

3 See Brachet, J., 'Manifacturing Smugglers: From Irregular to Clandestine Mobility in the Sahara'. ANNALS, AAPSS, 676, March 2018, p. 17.

4 See Brachet, J.,...*op. cit.* note 3, p. 21.

5 See Brachet, J.,...*op. cit.* note 3, p. 24.

6 Ibid

7 Ibid

8 See COM (2015) 285 final, 27/5/2015, p. 2.

works.[9] In order to achieve this objective, the Commission proposed to establish a 'single point of contact on migrant smuggling' to improve cooperation with each other and with EU agencies.[10] The Commission will set up a 'Contact Group of EU Agencies on migrant smuggling' to strengthen operational cooperation and share of information between the different EU agencies.[11] Member States should cooperate through JITs and mutual legal assistance. Eurojust can contribute by financing the investigation teams and by supporting mutual legal assistance in criminal matters. Europol, CEPOL and the European Training Judicial Network will organise training for law enforcement authorities, judicial authorities, border guards and consulate authorities on cross-border cooperation against smuggling of migrants.[12]

The Commission highlighted that information on the modus operandi of criminal networks is very important as at the moment exchange of information is sporadic and thus, it needs to be improved by reinforcing the capacity of EU agencies to gather, collect and analyse information on people smuggling. As announced by the European Agenda on Migration, Europol focal point on smuggling of migrants and its Joint Operational Team (JOT) MARE, should become the information hub for smuggling of migrants by sea.[13] The Commission highlights that cooperation with Interpol, Regional Bureaus and key African countries should be strengthened and the Africa Frontex Intelligence Community (AFIC) should be developed to share and analyse information with third countries. In hotspots, Europol, Eurojust and Frontex should deploy joint mobile teams to provide support and information to frontline Member States.[14]

Root causes of migration should be addressed by cooperation between the EU and third countries on border management, mobility, youth and employment.[15] The European Union External Action (EEAS) and the Commission will either launch or reinforce the bilateral and regional cooperation frameworks which include the Rabat, Khartoum, Budapest and Prague Processes, the

9 See COM (2015)...*op. cit.* note 8, pp. 2 at 3.

10 See COM (2015)...*op. cit.* note 8, p. 3.

11 See COM (2015)...*op. cit.* note 8, p. 4.

12 Ibid

13 See COM (2015)...*op. cit.* note 8, p. 5.

14 Ibid

15 See COM (2015)...*op. cit.* note 8, p. 9.

African, Caribbean and Pacific Group of States (ACP) and its dialogue with the EU (ACP-EU Dialogue), the EU-Africa Migration AND Mobility Dialogues and the Malta Summit focussed on migration.[16] The Commission and the EEAS will also develop national and regional strategies to fight against smuggling and to adopt anti-corruption policies 'that address smuggling of migrants as well as the setting up of integrated border management systems'.[17]

At the end of the Communication the Commission indicated the specific actions that should be taken to fight against smuggling. They include, among others, the promotion of bilateral cooperation with transit and origin irregular migrants' third countries; financing projects which can support third countries to establish strategies on smuggling of migrants, police and judicial responses against this crime and which can support the development of an integrated border management. [18]

The EEAS should be adopted under the Common Security and Defence Policy (CSDP) which should adopt measures to identify, capture and dispose of vessels used by smugglers. [19] Under CFSP, the EU has launched the EUNAVFOR Med which has been analysed earlier on in the book.[20] External cooperation with third countries, will remain intergovernmental and this means that the EP will have a marginal role in the conclusion of these agreements. Conversely, the EP should play a more important role in the CFSP because CFSP, cooperation of EU in developing economies of origin and transit countries and cooperation in criminal matters with these countries require initiatives of human rights' concerns. Cooperation between police of different nations with differ legal systems and different perceptions of human rights' protection, require that the EU receives a democratic mandate and that its action is accountable before democratic institutions. Hence, the EP should play a very important role in scrutinising the EU external initiatives. This chapter will focus on the role of the EP in the external cooperation and in particular in CFSP. It will also analyse external agreements with transit and origin third countries to address smuggling of migrants in the long term by reinforcing investigative actions against criminal networks and by addressing the root causes of irregular migration which must be

16 Ibid

17 Ibid

18 See COM (2015)...*op. cit.* note 8, p. 10.

19 Ibid note 8.

20 See sections 3.1 p. 66 and 3.2, p. 68 of chapter 3.

a priority. This is because initiatives aimed to dismantle smuggling of migrants have contributed to professionalize criminal networks as the more checks are established, the more journeys become unsafe and risky.[21] Therefore, criminal networks have to become more professional and sophisticated, in order to make journeys more secure. It must be added that the business of people smuggling has a positive impact on local economies where, for instance, shop owners have made a profit by selling life jackets.[22] EU external policies such as the EU-Turkey Agreement and the establishment of EUNAVFOR Med, 'did not address either the root causes of or the local economic factors in migration'. [23] As explained in chapter 3, these measures only focus on short term solutions against smuggling of migrants. Conversely, EU policies should focus on long term policies which could benefit the local populations and the economies of countries of origin and transit otherwise, the African populations will not be willing to dismantle criminal networks as they are a source of profit for them. EU policies and thus, external cooperation with African countries and other legal systems in Africa such as the African Union (AU), should focus on eradicating the root causes of migration and on enhancing local economies rather than on the fight against smuggling of migrants. The EU should make its citizens aware that criminal initiatives without the involvement of local populations, will not contribute to defeat smuggling of migrants and the related crime of human trafficking. Awareness can be created by involving the civil society and the EP because in this institution there are the representatives of EU citizens and they can create awareness by informing EU citizens on what it really involves smuggling and trafficking. Simple acts of repression will not reduce smuggling and trafficking unless local economies grow and root causes of migration are addressed seriously. The EP should create awareness and establish points of contact with the civil society in African countries. They should cooperate together in shaping EU external policies tackling irregular migration by creating opportunities in transit and origin countries. The EP represents EU citizens and aims to protect the general interests of EU citizens. Other institutions such as the Council are democratic but they are representative of the Member States' governments and thus, they act in the particular interests of their governments rather than in the

21 See Triandafyllidou, A., 'Migrant Smuggling: Novel Insights and Implications for Migration Control Policies'...*op. cit.* note 2, p. 216.

22 Ibid

23 Ibid

interest of all EU citizens. However, at the moment the role of the EP is very marginal in the EU external action.

2. THE ROLE OF THE EUROPEAN PARLIAMENT IN EXTERNAL AGREEMENTS

In different judgements the CJEU has emphasised that the Parliament has not the legislative competence in the CFSP if measures adopted in this area do not have an influence or affect internal EU policies. This is because Article 218 (6), as highlighted in the previous section, has established that the EP has a mere consultative role in the CFSP. In different cases the CJEU has clarified when a measure shall be adopted by the Council in cooperation with the Parliament through the co-decision procedure now called ordinary legislative procedure. Initially and before the Lisbon Treaty was adopted, the CJEU clarified that the European Community (EC) did not have the competence to conclude international agreements when they relate to activities of public authorities in the area of public security. Before the entry into force of the Lisbon Treaty, the EU was divided into three pillars. The first pillar included the EC and it was supranational as the EP, Council and Commission participated together to the adoption of legislation. The other two pillars which included the CFSP (second pillar) and EU police and judicial cooperation, were inter-governamental as the Council enacted legislation alone. The EP and the Commission had a merely consultative role. The Lisbon Treaty abolished the pillar structure and made the criminal area more democratic by establishing that most measures in the area shall be adopted by the Council and the EP through the ordinary legislative procedure. However, the CFSP has remained inter-governmental. Instead, the EP should legislate with the Council in the area concerning immigration and economic development of migrants' countries of nationality and residence.

In 2006, under the pillar structure, the CJEU was called to clarify whether the United States customs authorities could be authorized to access the Passenger Name Records (PNR data) of flights operating to or from the United States (US).[24] The Commission adopted two Decisions. One Decision was the conclusion of an agreement between the EC and the US on the processing and transit of PNR

24 See Joined Cases C-317/04 and C-318/04 *Parliament v. Council* ECR 2005 I-4721.

data by Air carriers to the US.[25] The other Decision concerned the protection of personal data contained in the PNR data of air passengers (the Decision on adequacy).[26] The EP asked the annulment of both Decisions as they had been adopted outside the scope of Community law.[27] The first Decision was based on Article 95 (1) EC which stated that the Council by the co-decision procedure, adopts 'the measures for the approximation of the provisions laid down by law, regulation or administrative action in Member States which have as their objective the establishment and functioning of the internal market'. Specifically, the EP argued that the Decision was in breach of Article 3(2) of Directive 95/46/EC on the protection of individuals with regard to the processing of personal data and on the free movement of such data.[28] Article 3(2) of the Directive states that it shall not apply to the processing of personal data concerning public security, defense, State security and the activities of a Stat in the criminal area. The EP argued that the Commission by adopting the Decision allowing the release of personal data to the United States was going beyond the scope of the Community. [29] The CJEU ruled that the Commission's decision went beyond the scope of the Community because the transfer of personal data 'falls within a framework established by the public authorities that relates to public security'. [30] The CJEU confirmed what it already stated in *Lindqvist*.[31] Specifically, the CJEU stated that the activities mentioned in Article 3(2) Directive 95/46/EC are activities of the State and not activities of individuals.[32] Consequently, the transfer of

25 See Council Decision 2004/496 of 17 May 2004 on the conclusion of an Agreement between the European Community and the United States of America on the processing and transfer of PNR data by Air Carriers to the United States Department of Homeland Security, Bureu of Customs and Border Protection. OJ 2004, L.183/83, 25/5/2004 and corrigendum at OJ 2005 L 255/168, 30/9/2005.

26 See Commission Decision 2004/535/EC of 14 May 2004 on the adequate protection of personal data contained in the Passenger Name Record of air passengers transferred to the United States Bureau of Customs and Border Protection. OJ 2004 L 235/11.

27 See Joined Cases C-317/04 and C-318/04...*op. cit.* note 24, paras 43, 50 *et* 51.

28 See OJ 1995 L 281/31 as amended by Regulation (EC) No 1882/2003 of the European Parliament and of the Council of 29 September 2003 adapting to Council Decision 1999/468/EC the provisions relating to committees which assist the Commission in the exercise of its implementing powers laid down in instruments subject to the procedure referred to in Article 251 of the EC Treaty. OJ L 284/1, 31/10/2003.

29 See Joined Cases C-317/04 and C-318/04...*op. cit.* note 24, paras 51 et 52.

30 See Joined Cases C-317/04 and C-318/04...*op. cit.* note 24, para 58.

31 See Case C-101/01 *Lindqvist* [2003] ECR I-12971, para 43.

32 Ibid

personal data, even if it is carried out by private companies for commercial aims, it is an activity exercised by public authorities and which concerns public security.[33] It follows that the Commission Decision is outside the scope of Community competence as reported by the EP and on the basis of these facts, the CJEU ruled that the Directive was infringed.[34] The CJEU in Case C-317/04, joined to the one examined, confirmed that the Commission Decision was adopted on the incorrect legal basis as adopted on the basis of Article 95 EC.

In 2007, the EP sought the annulment of a Commission Decision on a project concerning the securitization of Philippines borders to be financed by part of the EC general budget and adopted to implement Council Regulation (ECC) No 443/92 of 25 February on financial and technical assistance to, and economic cooperation with, the developing countries in Asia and Latin America as amended by Council Regulation (EC) No 807/2003 of 14 April 2003.[35] The EP argued that the Commission adopted the Decision with the aim to fight against terrorism and international crime and this aim 'goes beyond the framework set out by Regulation No 443/92 which serves as its legal basis and, more particularly, Article 7 and 8 relating to economic cooperation'.[36] An amendment to the Regulation should be added, in order to include the fight against international crime and terrorism in its scope. [37]

The CJEU in settled case-law has established that the EC can act only within powers conferred by the Treaty.[38] The Council in this case brought before the Court by the EP, conferred to the Commission 'the power to administer the financial and technical assistance as well as the economic cooperation'[39] with Asian and Latin American countries. The contested Commission's decision goes beyond the scope of the Regulation and for this reason the Commission exceeded the powers conferred by the Council through Article 15 of the Regulation and it discerns that the Decision must be annulled.[40]

33 Ibid note 30.

34 See Joined Cases C-317/04 and C-318/04...*op. cit.* note 24, para 59 at 60.

35 See L 122/36, 16/5/2003. See Case C-403/05 *Parliament v. Commission,* [2007] ECR I-9045, para. 1.

36 See Case C-403/05...*op. cit.* note 35, para 39.

37 See Case C-403/05...*op. cit.* note 35, para 40.

38 See Case C-93/00 *Parliament v. Council* [2001] ECR I-10119, para 39. See Case C-110/03 *Belgium v. Commission* [2005] ECR I-2801, para 57. See also Case C-403/05...*op. cit.* note 35, para 49.

39 Case C-403/05...*op. cit.* note 35, para 52.

40 Case C-403/05...*op. cit.* note 35, paras 68 at 70.

More recently, the CJEU clarified further the EP's competence in the external relations. The EP asked for the annulment of Council Regulation (EU) No 1286/2009 of 22 December 2009 amending regulation (EC) No 881/2002 imposing certain specific restrictive measures directed against certain persons and entities associated to Usama Bin Laden, the Al-Qaeda and Taliban criminal organisations (contested regulation).[41] The contested regulation was based on Article 215 (2) TFEU.[42] The Parliament sought the annulment of the Regulation as it is not based on the correct legal basis which should be Article 75 TFEU rather than Article 215 TFEU.[43] Article 75 TFEU states that administrative measures related to capital movements and payments used to finance terrorism and related activities, shall be adopted by regulations enacted by the Council and the EP through the ordinary legislative procedure. Article 215 TFEU states that interruptions or reductions partially or wholly of financial relations with one or more third country, shall be adopted by the Council 'acting by qualified majority on a joint proposal from the High Representative of the Union for Foreign Affairs and Security Policy and the Commission'.[44] The EP has only a mere consultative role as, according to Article 215(1), the Council 'shall inform the European Parliament thereof'. The EP argued that the correct legal basis should be Article 75 TFEU as it concerns prevention of terrorism and other connected activities.[45] In regards to this point, the CJEU has ruled that two legal bases can be used for one legal measure if the legal measure which in this case is a regulation, has more components or aims. [46] However, the CJEU has established that if one component is merely incidental, the adopted legal measure shall be based only on the basis which is predominant and if the components are incompatible with each other, even if one is not predominant on the other, the principle of dual legal basis cannot be applied. [47] The CJEU has adopted this approach, before the entry into force of the Lisbon Treaty, when there was an incompatibility between the coop-

41 See Case C-130/10 *Parliament v. Council* Judgement of 19 July 2012 ECLI:EU:C:2012:472, para 1.

42 See Case C-130/10...*op. cit.* note 41, para 5.

43 See Case C-130/10...*op. cit.* note 41, para 10.

44 See Article 215 (1) TFEU.

45 See Case C-130/10...*op. cit.* note 41, para 12.

46 See Case C-130/10...*op. cit.* note 41, paras 43 *at* 44. See also Case C-155/07 *Parliament v. Council* [2008] ECR I-8103, para 36.

47 See Case C-130/10...*op. cit.* note 41, para 42. See also Case C-300/89 *Commission v. Council* [1991] ECR I-2867 *(Titanium dioxide)* paras 17 at 21. See also Case C-155/07...*op. cit.* note 46, para 37.

eration procedure and the procedure concerning the Council acting alone and unanimously after merely having consulted the EP.[48] In *Titanium dioxide,* the CJEU clarified that the aim of the cooperation procedure was to involve the EP in the legislative process by permitting it to request amendments to the common position made by the Council.[49] The CJEU stated that the same approach can be adopted when there are incompatibilities between a procedure consisting of the Council acting alone after having consulted the EP and the co-decision procedure where the EP and the Council adopted legislation together and it was established by Article 251 of the EC Treaty.[50] The CJEU ruled that this approach is still valid after the entry into force of the Lisbon treaty and thus, it is applicable to the ordinary legislative procedure replacing the co-legislative procedure.[51] In the present case, there is an incompatibility between Article 215 (2) TFEU and Article 75 TFEU. The CJEU explains that the incompatibility is caused by the fact that Article 75 TFEU requires the application of the ordinary legislative procedure, whilst Article 215(2) TFEU only requires that the Council consults the EP.[52] The CJEU emphasized that another difference between Article 75 and Article 215 is that the latter requires that a previous restrictive decision is adopted in the CFSP and the adoption of a decision in the CFSP requires the unanimity of votes in the Council who will act alone.[53] Hence, the two provisions cannot be cumulated and one should prevail on the other.[54] In *Kadi and Al Barakaat International Foundation v. Council and Commission,* the Court stressed that a link had been made 'between the actions of the Community involving economic measures...and the objectives of the EU Treaty, as it stood before the Treaty of Lisbon...in the sphere of external relations, including the CFSP'.[55] However, the CJEU stated that in the present case the link has not been established because Article 75 TFEU and Article 215 TFEU pursue two different objectives. In order

48 See *Titanium dioxide...op. cit.* note 47, para 18 at 20.

49 See *Titanium dioxide...op. cit.* note 47, para 19 at 20.

50 See Case C-130/10...*op. cit.* note 41, para 46. See Case C-178/03 *Commission v. Parliament and Council* [2006] ECR I-107, paras 58 *at* 59. See Case C-155/07...*op. cit.* note 46, para 76 at 79.

51 See Case C-130/10...*op. cit.* note 41, para 46.

52 See Case C-130/10...*op. cit.* note 41, para 47.

53 Ibid

54 See Case C-130/10...*op. cit.* note 41, para 49.

55 See Case C-130/10...op. cit. note 41, para 59. See also Joined Cases C-402/05 P and C-415/05 P *Kadi and Al Barakaat International Foundation v. Council and Commission* [2008] ECR I-6351, para 197.

to explain this point, the CJEU cited the opinion of Advocate General in this case who stated that these two Articles are related to different policies which do not have the same scope.[56] The scope of Article 215 is to preserve peace and international security by fighting against terrorism as this criminal activity can be a threat to these values.[57] Article 75 TFEU has, instead, as its object the creation of an area of freedom security and justice. [58] The CJEU stressed that Regulation No 881/2002 as amended by the contested regulation 'intended to preserve international peace and security'. [59] Hence, it is based on the correct legal basis which is Article 215 TFEU and for this reason the EP can only be consulted by the Council as the ordinary legislative procedure does not apply to the CFSP. [60] The CJEU recognized that the EP's participation in the legislative procedure at EU level, is a fundamental democratic principle which ensures that people participate in the exercise of power through their representatives. [61] However, the choice of the framers of the Lisbon Treaty was to confer a more limited power to the EP in the legislative process related to the CFSP.[62]

The CJEU added that it cannot even be accepted the argument made by the EP that it would be contrary to EU law to adopt measures on fundamental rights without the EP's participation. [63] The Court emphasized that the duty to respect fundamental rights on the basis of Article 51 (1) of the Charter of Fundamental Rights, is an obligation imposed on all EU institutions and bodies.[64] This means that measures contained in the contested regulation including safeguards for the respect of fundamental rights, can be adopted on the basis of Article 215 (2) TFEU. [65] This interpretation has been confirmed by the Court when it asserted

56 See Case C-130/10...*op. cit.* note 41, para 66.

57 See Case C-130/10...*op. cit.* note 41, para 63.

58 See Case C-130/10...*op. cit.* note 41, para 58.

59 See Case C-130/10...*op. cit.* note 41, para 67.

60 See Case C-130/10...*op. cit.* note 41, para 79.

61 See Case C-130/10...*op. cit.* note 41, para 81. See also Case 138/79 *Roquette Freres v. Council* [1980] ECR 3333 para 33 and *Titanium dioxide...op. cit.* note 47, para 20.

62 See Case C-130/10...*op. cit.* note 41, para 82.

63 See Case C-130/10...*op. cit.* note 41, para 83.

64 Ibid

65 See Case C-130/10...*op. cit.* note 41, para 84.

that even measures which give effects to Security Council resolutions must be adopted in the respect of fundamental rights.[66]

The CJEU has further clarified the EP's role in the conclusion of international agreements.[67] The issue concerned the EU-Mauritius Agreement which established the general principles and modality to be followed in order to transfer suspected pirates from the EUNAVFOR to the Republic of Mauritius. The EP contested that the Joint Agreement was concluded by the Council acting alone, whilst the EP should have participated in the legislative process by the ordinary legislative procedure, because the agreement related not only to the CFSP but also 'to judicial cooperation in criminal matters, police cooperation and development cooperation'.[68] The EP also argued that the Council did not inform it immediately of the Joint Agreement concluded with the republic of Mauritius and by neglecting this obligation, the Council acted in breach of Article 218 (10) TFEU.[69] The CJEU, although rejected the allegation made by the EP on the plea that the international agreement should have been concluded by the ordinary legislative procedure, it ruled that the Council had acted in breach of Article 218 (10) by not informing the EP of all the stages of the procedure and therefore, ruled that the Council Decision should have been annulled.[70] The CJEU clarified when an international agreement can be adopted without the ordinary legislative procedure and thus, and what role does the EP have even when it cannot co-legislate in the adoption of a decision on an international agreement. The CJEU ruled that 'where the decision concluding the agreement in question is legitimate founded exclusively on a substantive legal basis falling within the CFSP'[71] the Council has exclusive competence. The interpretation of Article 218 proposed by the Council will have as its effect to introduce 'a degree of uncertainty and inconsistency into that choice'.[72] In any case, the Council cannot fail to inform the EP immediately and fully because it has to be in the position 'to exercise the right of scrutiny...in relation to the CFSP or, where appropriate, to make known its views as

66 See Joined Cases C-402/05 P and C-415/05...*op. cit.* note 55, paras 285, 299 et 326.

67 See Case C-658/11 *European Parliament v. Council*, Judgment of 24/6/2014, ECLI:EU:C:2014:2025.

68 See Case C-658/11... *op. cit.* note 67, para 25.

69 See Case C-658/11... *op. cit.* note 67, paras 65 and 68.

70 See Case C-658/11...*op. cit.* note 67, paras 85, 86 and 87.

71 See Case C-658/11...*op. cit.* note 67, para 59.

72 See Case C-658/11...*op. cit.* note 67, para 60.

regards,...the correct legal basis for the act concerned'.[73] As Peers pointed out, if the EP had won its argument on the competence to co-legislate with the Council in the CFSP, it would have gained the power to enact legislation in most aspects of the CFSP treaties because of their links with other aspects of EU external policies.[74] The EP was trying to assert 'a more general legal base point'[75] in the CFSP. However, it did not achieve this result and the CJEU missed the opportunity to clarify the external scope of EU police and judicial cooperation. It is thought that international agreements with African countries to strengthen investigative cooperation against smuggling of migrants by sea should not fall exclusively or mainly in the CFSP's scope because they concern the AFSJ and the Parliament should enact legislation with the Council in this area. The Advocate General in the same case, has clarified when the AFSJ has an external dimension and thus, the Parliament can legislate in EU external policies. The Advocate General stated that a measure in this area shall have as aim 'to further freedom, security and justice inside the Union'.[76] This is because Article 67 TFEU states that the Union shall establish an AFSJ without internal border controls where the different legal systems, cultures and traditions of Member States are fully respected. Article 3 (2) TEU reflects and reiterates what is established in Article 67. The Advocate General clarified that it is on the basis of the objectives established in these 2 Articles that the external dimension of the AFSJ could be identified.[77] The Advocate General explained that

> 'The internal and external policies in the field of the AFSJ are inextricably linked. In order to define the substance of the external aspect in the field of the AFSJ, utmost account should be taken of the internal policy function of the AFSJ'.[78]

---

73 See Case C-658/11 *op. cit.* note 67, para 86.

74 See Peers, S., 'The CJEU ensures basic democratic and judicial accountability of the EU's foreign policy'. On http://eulawanalysis.blogspot.co.uk/2014/06/the-cjeu-ensures-basic-democratic-and.html accessed on 14/10/2014.

75 Ibid note 73.

76 See Opinion of Advocate General Bot delivered on 30/1/2014 in Case C-658/11...*op.cit.* note 67, para 109.

77 See Opinion of Advocate General Bot delivered on 30/1/2014 in Case C-658/11 *supra* note 67, para 111.

78 Ibid note 70.

On the basis of this assertion, it can be argued that the EP could have competence in the CFSP with the aim to strengthen EU criminal cooperation with countries outside the EU, when this cooperation could benefit the EU internal security. This is reiterated by the Advocate General who states that '...the connection with the AFSJ is justified where there is a direct link between the aim of the internal security of the Union and the judicial and/or police cooperation which is developed outside the Union'.[79] Conversely, when the objectives of the Union are the achievements of '...peace, stability and democratic development in a region outside the Union'[80] the action will fall within the CFSP's scope and the EP will not be able to co-legislate in this area with the Council. The CJEU did not clarify this point but on the basis of what the Advocate General has stated, it could be concluded that strengthening the JHA agencies external competence to cooperate in criminal investigations against smuggling of migrants with African countries, should fall within the scope of the AFSJ as it would positively impact in this area. Indeed, criminal cooperation as such would contribute to reduce irregular migrants by sea and the death of many migrants in the sea who die because they rely on criminal organizations which organize their trips from the desert to the EU. Nevertheless, it is desirable that in future judgments, the CJEU clarifies the scope of AFSJ in the EU external relations as it has clarified the EP position and its right to be informed on CFSP adopted by the Council. By ruling in this way, the CJEU has contribute to ensure democracy and accountability within the CFSP as the EP has the right to be informed immediately in order to scrutinise whether the Council is respecting the fundamental EU democratic principles when adopting international agreements. The EP's right to be informed could also contribute to influence a public debate on whether the Europol should be strengthened to reduce smuggling of migrants. This public debate and a wider Europol's scope in fighting against smuggling of migrants are very important because it is thought that the Europol's role, for example, is essential to fight against smuggling of migrants by supporting investigations between police of Member States and police of third countries and it could contribute to a better management of migration flows.

However, in a more recent case, the CJEU has confirmed that in the CFSP, the Parliament has a mere consultative role. The case concerned Council

79 See Opinion of Advocate General Bot delivered on 30/1/2014 in Case C-658/11 *supra* note 67, para 112.

80 Ibid note 77.

Decision 2014/198/CFSP of 10 March 2014 on the signature and conclusion of the Agreement between the European Union and United Republic of Tanzania on the conditions of transfer of suspected pirates and associated seized property from the European Union-led naval force to the United Republic of Tanzania.[81] The EP sought the annulment of the Decision (contested decision) as it argued that it was adopted on the basis of Article 37 TEU only even if the agreement did not only concerned the CFSP but also judicial and police cooperation in criminal matters.[82] Hence, the contested decision should have been based not only on Article 37 TEU but also on Articles 82 and 87 TFEU and thus, the procedure should have been adopted under the procedure established by point (a) (v) of the second subparagraph of Article 218(6) TFEU.[83] Article 37 TEU states that the Union can conclude international agreements. Article 82 TFEU states that measures concerning judicial cooperation in criminal matters shall be adopted by the ordinary legislative procedure (EP and Council acting together). Article 87 TFEU establishes that measures related to the collection, storage, processing and analysis of information, support for the training of staff and cooperation on exchange of staff, on equipment and on research concerning crime-detection and measures on common investigative techniques relating to detection of serious forms of organized crimes, shall be adopted by the ordinary legislative procedure.[84] Measures related to operational cooperation shall be adopted by the special legislative procedure by the Council acting unanimously after having consulted the EP.[85] Article 218 (6) (v) TFEU states that the Council shall conclude an agreement covered either by the ordinary legislative procedure or by the special legislative procedure not related to the CFSP after having obtained the EP's consent. The EP claimed that the EU-Tanzania Agreement does not only concern the CFSP and the EU mission to preserve peace, but also criminal measures as the purpose of the agreement 'is also to transfer persons suspected of criminal activities,...to the judicial and police authorities of a third State in order to enable them to exercise their powers to investigate and prosecute, with

81 See OJ L 108/1, 11/4/2014. See Case C-263/14 *European Parliament and Commission v. Council* ECLI:EU:C:2016:435.

82 See Case C-263/14...*op. cit.* note 81 paras 25 at 27.

83 See Case C-263/14...*op. cit.* note 81 para 26.

84 See Article 87 (2) TFEU.

85 See Article 87 (3) TFEU.

regard to those suspects'.[86] From the other side, the Council argued that the EU-Tanzania Agreement was correctly based solely on Articles 37 TEU and on Article 218 (5) TFEU as the agreement was only related to the CFSP which did not need the EP's consent.[87] The CJEU stated that apparently, the EU-Tanzania Agreement may fall within the area of cross-border judicial and police cooperation in criminal matters, if they are considered individually.[88] However, this is not sufficient to determine the correct legal basis as the provisions of the EU-Tanzania Agreement on the respect of the rule of law, human rights and human dignity is requested in all areas of EU, including the area concerning the CFSP.[89] In addition, the CJEU pointed out that the contested decision is based on Article 12 of Joint Action 2008/851 which falls within the scope of the CFSP.[90] Article 12 states that people suspected to have committed piracy should be transferred with seized assets to the flag Member States or a third Member State participating in the operation or to any third State wishing to exercise jurisdiction over the suspected individual and his or her assets.[91] The EU-Tanzania Agreement has as objective to strengthen international cooperation to prevent acts of piracy by adopting legal framework which permits to transfer suspected individuals to a country participating in the operation and ensure that the individual does not remain unpunished, in accordance with the mandate indicated by the Security Council Resolution.[92] Preventing that individuals who commit piracy do not remain unpunished by transferring persons arrested or detained and their assets, is an operation adopted 'to preserve international peace and security'.[93] Therefore, the EP's request was rejected by the CJEU as the contested decision was adopted on the correct legal basis. The EP also contested that the Council acted in breach of Article 218(10) TFEU as it was not informed of all

86 See Case C-263/14...*op. cit.* note 81 para 28.

87 See Case C-263/14...*op. cit.* note 81 para 33.

88 See Case C-263/14...*op. cit.* note 81 para 47.

89 Ibid

90 See Council Joint Action 2008/851/CFSP of 10 November 2008 on a European Union military operation to contribute to the deterrence, prevention and repression of acts of piracy and armed robbery off the Somali coast. On OJ L 301/33, 12/11/2008.

91 See Case C-263/14...*op. cit.* note 81 para 48.

92 See Case C-263/14...*op. cit.* note 81 para 49.

93 See Case C-263/14...*op. cit.* note 81 para 54.

stages of the procedure as established by this provision.[94] The CJEU stated that established case-law (analysed in this section) has stated that the EP has to be informed of all stages of procedures concerning the negotiation and conclusion of international agreements even if they relate exclusively to the CFSP.[95] The CJEU emphasized that informing the EP ensures that the EU external action is coherent and consistent.[96] The CJEU noted that the EP had not been fully informed of all stages of the procedure, including the negotiation stage.[97] Therefore, the CJEU found 'detrimental to the ability of the Parliament to perform its duties in the area of the CFSP' the lack of information that should have been provided by the Council.[98] For this reason, it stated that the Council infringed 'an essential procedural requirement.[99]

On the basis of the analysis of these cases, it can be concluded that the EP does not have competence in the CFSP unless it is related to other areas such as the AFSJ. However, it is very difficult to demonstrate that a legal measure adopted by the Council covers partly the CFSP and partly other areas of EU policy. The EP has been recognized the right to be informed of all the procedure to conclude an international agreement even if the agreement falls only within the CFSP area. The CJEU has explained that this right has been established by Article 218(10) TFEU

> 'in order to ensure that the Parliament is in a position to exercise democratic scrutiny of the European Union's external action and, more particularly, to verify that its powers are respected specifically as a result of the choice of legal basis for a decision on the conclusion of an agreement'.[100]

The EP can guarantee accountability and that EU legal measures are adopted by involving people either through the ordinary legislative procedure or by the EP's consent in all measures related to the CFSP. A step forward would be to

---

94 See Case C-263/14...*op. cit.* note 81 para 57.

95 See Case C-263/14...*op. cit.* note 81 para 68. See Case C-658/11...*op. cit.* note 67, paras 83 *et* 84.

96 See Case C-263/14...*op. cit.* note 81 para 72.

97 See Case C-263/14...*op. cit.* note 81 para 77 *et* 84.

98 See Case C-263/14...*op. cit.* note 81 para 84.

99 Ibid. See also See also Case C-658/11...*op. cit.* note 67, para 86.

100 See Case C-263/14...*op. cit.* note 81 para 80. See Case C-658/11...*op. cit.* note 67, para 79.

adopt measures related to the criminal area and cooperation with third countries against smuggling and trafficking, by the ordinary legislative procedure. The first step to take in this direction should be to adopt specific law on Europol, Eurojust and the EPPO. This is because these agencies can facilitate investigations and the transfer of criminals perpetrating smuggling and trafficking from one State to another within the EU and outside the EU. EU Member States are relying on the EAW, whilst cooperation between EU Member States and third countries is based on the extradition.

However, at the moment the EP's role has only been reinforced on the Europol's accountability and the EP has a marginal role compared to the Council in the conclusion of international agreements for the economic development of countries of origin of irregular migrants. These international agreement could contribute to identify the root causes of irregular migration and defeat smuggling of migrants and human trafficking.

3. THE RABAT PROCESS, THE BUDAPEST PROCESS, THE PRAGUE PROCESS

The Rabat Process was established in July 2006 in Morocco by Europe and African Ministers responsible to manage immigration.[101] The objectives of the Rabat Process include management of migration, the fight against poverty, the promotion of sustainable development and the respect of migrants and refugees dignity. The Budapest Process has the same aims of the Rabat Process but it is focusses on cooperation in the management of migration with Asian countries.[102] The Budapest Process was established in 2003 to enhance cooperation in the migration management between Europe and Eastern European countries and subsequently it focussed on management of migration from Asian countries. In 2013, the Budapest Process witnessed the adoption of the Istanbul Ministerial Declaration on a Silk Routes Partnership for Migration.[103] The Declaration had the aim to reinforce cooperation between Asia and Europe in managing migra-

101 See 'Rabat Process'. International Centre for Migration Policy Development (ICMPD) on https://www.icmpd.org/our-work/migration-dialogues/rabat-process/ accessed on 15/11/2016.

102 See 'Budapest Process'. ICMPD on https://www.icmpd.org/our-work/migration-dialogues/budapest-process/ accessed on 15/11/2016.

103 See https://www.icmpd.org/our-work/migration-dialogues/budapest-process/ministerial-conferences/ accessed on 15/11/2016.

tion and in protecting refugees in respect of the 1951 UN Refugee Convention and its 1967 Protocol.[104] In between the aims of the Declaration, there is the fight against smuggling and trafficking.[105] A particular emphasis is given to the prevention of human trafficking by identifying the root causes and by providing support and protection to victims of trafficking.[106]

The Prague Process was launched in April 2009 in Prague with the aim to prevent and fight against irregular migration, to facilitate voluntary return, to promote readmission and reintegration.[107] The fight against irregular migration includes the fight against criminal networks perpetrating smuggling and trafficking and awareness raising campaigns in countries of origin to prevent people from becoming victims of these two crimes. Readmission agreements include the sharing of best practices concerning the return and reintegration of victims of human beings and unaccompanied minors. The Process also aimed to facilitate legal immigration and to reinforce capacities of the asylum and international protection systems in cooperation with UNHCR.[108]

The most relevant agreement concluded by the EU for the purpose of this book is the ACP-EU Dialogue.[109] The ACP-EU Dialogue focussed specifically on smuggling of migrants and human trafficking. An important meeting was held on 9th and 10th July 2014 in Brussels between EU experts and ACP countries.[110] During these meetings, the EU and ACP countries stressed how important is to cooperate between each other to fight against criminal networks which smuggling and traffic people from origin countries to their destinations in Europe. For this reason, cooperation should be strengthened between origin, transit and destination countries. In the meetings, the parties agreed that they will cooperate with each other in compliance with the UNCTOC Protocols against

104 See Istanbul Ministerial Declaration on a Silk Routes Partnership for Migration. Available on https://www.icmpd.org/fileadmin/ICMPD-Website/Budapest_Process/November_2013_Update/Istanbul_Ministerial_Declaration_Silk_Routes_Partnership_EN.pdf, accessed on 15/11/2016.

105 See Paragraph 1(d) and (e) of the Declaration.

106 See Paragraph 1 (e) of the Declaration.

107 See '2nd Ministerial Conference of the Prague Process Action Plan 2012-2016' on https://www.pragueprocess.eu/en/documents/category/3-programme-key-documents, accessed on 15/11/2016.

108 Ibid

109 See the Council of European Union ACP-EU Dialogue on Migration and Development, 11/5/2015, ACP-UE 2111/15. On http://data.consilium.europa.eu/doc/document/ST-2111-2015-INIT/en/pdf, accessed on 15/11/2016.

110 Ibid

smuggling and trafficking. National legislation on trafficking and smuggling should be implemented with the aim to identify victims and detecting criminal networks. This is because, most victims remain unidentified and criminal networks remained unpunished. Bilateral memoranda of understanding between North-South and South-South countries shall be promoted as international cooperation between origin, transit and destination countries.

The EU and Africa signed the Declaration of the Ministerial Conference of the Khartoum Process in 2014. The Khartoum Process aims to fighting against smuggling of migrants and human trafficking which is perpetrated from African countries to Europe.[111] The Ministerial Conference was joined by the EU High Representative/Vice-President of the European Commission, the European and African Union (AU) Commissioners in charge of migration and development and the following nations: Austria, Belgium, Bulgaria, Croatia, Cyprus, Czech Republic, Denmark, Djibouti, Egypt, Eritrea, Estonia, Ethiopia, Finland, France, Germany, Greece, Hungary, Ireland, Italy, Kenya, Latvia, Lithuania, Luxembourg, Malta, Netherlands, Poland, Portugal, Romania, Slovakia, Slovenia, Somalia, South Sudan, Spain, Sudan, Sweden, Tunisia and United Kingdom. Norway and Switzerland were present to the Conference. The EU its Member States and AU agreed to establish the EU-Horn of Africa Migration Route Initiative called the Khartoum Process which will focus on the development of bilateral and regional cooperation between origin, transit and destination countries to fight against irregular migration and criminal networks. For this purpose, cooperation will consist of 'concrete measures on a voluntary basis such as initiatives in the area of information-sharing, focused training and capacity building, technical assistance and the exchange of best practices'.[112] Cooperation shall also promote 'prevention measures such as information campaigns to improve awareness of risks of irregular migration, with special regards to trafficking in human beings and smuggling of migrants'. [113] Different nations in the EU and in the AU shall cooperate with each other in order to identify and prosecute members of criminal organisations. Cooperation shall include strengthening of law enforcement authorities, including judicial systems responses, 'enhancing, and where appro-

111 See Declaration of the Ministerial Conference of the Khartoum Process (EU-Horn of Africa Migration Route Initiative) Rome, 28th November 2014. On http://italia2014.eu/media/3785/declaration-of-the-ministerial-conference-of-the-khartoum-process.pdf, accessed on 16/11/2016.

112 Ibid

113 Ibid

priate, setting up systems of proper financial investigations and measures to prevent laundering of proceeds of crime as well as tackling corruption more effectively'.[114] States shall ensure the establishment of criminal law frameworks and they shall be committed to implement the UNCTOC Protocols against smuggling and trafficking.[115] They shall promote victim-centred approach, sustainable development in countries of origin and transit with the aim to identify the root causes of irregular migration. Regional framework for return of migrants including their voluntary return shall be agreed by the EU and transit and origin countries in Africa.

The Declaration clarifies that all the initiatives to tackle against smuggling and trafficking, shall be taken on a voluntary basis 'without prejudice to the sovereignty of the participating States.[116]

The examined instruments have highlighted the importance of developing extraterritorial cooperation between the EU and other regions in the world, in order to fight against smuggling and trafficking not only by enhancing cooperation in between law enforcement and judicial authorities but also by identifying the root causes of irregular migration. The initiatives have emphasised that an important step to fight effectively against smuggling and trafficking is to implement the Smuggling and Trafficking Protocols. In addition, it has been stressed that the protection of victims is a priority as most of them remain unidentified and thus, vulnerable to criminal networks. These initiatives should be adopted in the long term to ensure that smuggling and trafficking are completely defeated.

4. THE EUROPEAN UNION EXTERNAL ACTION

The EEAS has focused on short term measures and by them it has established the EUNAVFOR Med and the European Border and Coast Guard.[117] These measures are short term as they do not focus on the identification of root causes for irregular migration. In addition, they are mainly rescue operations as neither EUNAVFOR Med nor the European Border and Coast Guard have investigative powers against smuggling and trafficking.

114 Ibid

115 Ibid

116 Ibid

117 See sections 3.1, p. 66 and 3.2, p. 68, chapter 3. See section 7.2, p. 100, chapter 4.

Root causes for irregular migration can only be identified by focussing on long term policies and agreements with countries of transit and origin. On this direction is the Sahel Strategy put forward by the EU in the regions of Burkina Faso, Chad, Mali, Mauritania end Niger[118] which are part of the Sahel region. This region which is the Sahara is extended across the African country and includes part of Mauritania and Senegal on the West coast and Mali, Algeria, Burkina Faso, Niger, Nigeria, Chad, Sudan, South Sudan and Eritrea.[119] These countries experience extreme poverty, irregular migration and smuggling and trafficking. This is because Sahelian countries have not provided economic and social development and polices adopted mainly by the international community, have destroyed pastoralism. Hence, people in the Sahelian states mainly depending on pastoralism, have experienced famine and have 'became increasingly dependent on cross-border smuggling'.[120] In 2011, the EU adopted a comprehensive approach called the EU Strategy for Security and Development (the Sahel Strategy) which should tackle these difficult situations in the Sahel region.[121] In 2015, the EU Sahel Strategy was implemented through the Sahel Regional Action Plan (RAP). [122] The RAP has identified different priorities which shall focus on creating opportunities for youth, migration mobility, border management and the fight against illicit trafficking and transnational organised criminal networks.[123] The EU is promoting developing policies which can support the fight against extreme poverty by a holistic strategy which could address security concerns and development in the area which consequently, will strengthen EU security.[124] The Sahel Strategy aims to improve political stability, security, good governance, economic and education opportunity and social cohesion in five years. Improving these areas will create economic opportunity and the region will not be targeted anymore by criminal networks and extremist groups such

118 See https://eeas.europa.eu/diplomatic-network/sahel-region/4094/sahel-region_en, accessed on 16/11/2016.

119 See P. Tinti and S. Reitano *Migrant Refugee Smuggler Savior.* OUP 2017, p. 149.

120 See P. Tinti and S. Reitano...*op. cit.* note 119, p.151.

121 Ibid note 119.

122 Ibid

123 Ibid

124 See 'European Union External Action Service Strategy for Security and Development in the Sahel', available on https://eeas.europa.eu/sites/eeas/files/strategy_for_security_and_development_in_the_sahel_en_0.pdf, p.2, accessed on 16/11/2016.

as Al-Qaida in the Maghreb (AQIM).[125] The Action Plan 2015-2020, confirms the priorities indicated by the Strategy and emphasises that more actions should be taken to fight against smuggling and trafficking.[126] In 2016 the EU has allocated funds in the Sahel Region to tackle root causes of irregular migration.[127] At regional level, the EU is supporting the establishment of West African police information system/WAPIS to combat trafficking, terrorism and criminal organisations and to ensure that national administrations improve their methods to collect, centralise, manage and share information gathered by police. At national level, the EU has allocated funds to strengthen national economies. In Burkina Faso, funds aim to improve socio-economic conditions of women and youth in rural areas and, in Northern Burkina Faso, funds will focus on improving the living conditions of the most vulnerable people, especially in the area of health and food security. Improving the economy in Cameroon, Central Africa, Mali, Nigeria, Senegal, Niger and Mauritania is also the aim of funds allocated in these nations by the EU. In Mauritania, the EU is also launching a project to protect children from human trafficking and exploitation. These objectives will be achieved by managing migration flows through actions on the protection of children by criminal networks which intend to exploit them or recruit in extremist criminal groups. In Senegal, the reduction of irregular migration will be supported through programmes aimed to improve living conditions of people by combating poverty. In Niger, the EU intends to launch a pilot project on setting up joint investigations teams to fight against irregular migration, smuggling and trafficking. The project has been identified in the Valletta Action Plan and intends to improve the ability of Nigerien Police to fight against irregular migration, trafficking, smuggling and document fraud whilst protecting victims from criminal organisations and enhancing the effectiveness of borders' management.

125 See 'European Union External Action Service Strategy for Security and Development in the Sahel'... *op. cit.* note 124, p. 4.

126 See Council Conclusions on the Sahel Regional Action Plan 2015-2020. Doc 7823/15, 20/4/2015, p. 10.

127 See European Commission- Fact Sheet 'Description of the new measures adopted to tackle the root causes of irregular migration and displaced persons in the Sahel region and Lake Chad Basin, 18/4/2016. On http://europa.eu/rapid/press-release_MEMO-16-1426_en.htm, accessed on 16/11/2016.

The Valletta Action Plan was launched in 2015 and aimed to focus on sixteen priorities.[128] The Action Plan will focus on the benefit of migration and on the fight against irregular migration, smuggling and trafficking by identifying the root causes for irregular migration. For the purpose of development and eradication of poverty, the EU will cooperate with African countries and with the AU to strengthen migration strategies at national and regional level by taking into consideration individual countries characteristics. In order to eradicate poverty, the EU and Africa will conduct an analysis on the root-causes of irregular migration and forced displacement. The EU will also focus on boosting socio-economic development by increasing economic opportunities and by creating jobs for women and youth. The EU will address instability and crises by preventing new conflicts and new forms of radicalization in Sahel, Lake Chad, Horn of Africa and North Africa. The EU will support the establishment of the rule of law and good governance.

Legal migration and mobility will be supported and promoted through bilateral cooperation agreement as the Mobility Partnerships and the Common Agendas on Migration and Mobility. Migration and Mobility will also be supported by continental, regional, sub-regional frameworks such as the Joint Labour Migration Programmes adopted by the AU in 2015 and other initiatives adopted by Economic Community of West African States (ECOWAS) and the Intergovernmental Authority and Development (IGAD).[129] The fight against smuggling and trafficking will be supported by implementing the UNCTOC Protocols against these two crimes and by implementing the 2014 Protocol to the Forced Labour Convention. The Valletta Summit highlights the importance of cooperating against irregular migration, smuggling and trafficking by improving information exchange between the EU and African countries. The EU supports police and judicial cooperation and the establishment of Joint Investigation Teams between countries affected by smuggling and trafficking. The EU also promotes police cooperation to investigate smuggling and trafficking with the support of Interpol and other EU agencies, especially Europol. Police and judicial cooperation through mutual legal assistance against smuggling and trafficking is also promoted by the Valletta Action Plan.

128 See Valletta Summit on Migration, 11-12 November 2015. On http://www.consilium.europa.eu/en/meetings/international-summit/2015/11/action_plan_en_pdf/, accessed on 18/11/2016.

129 Ibid. For the work of ECOWAS and IGAD, see http://www.ecowas.int/ and https://igad.int/, accessed on 18/11/2016.

The EU is committed to fight against smuggling and trafficking by global actions which include the identification of root causes of irregular migration, socio-economic development in origin and transit countries and police and judicial cooperation between countries where smuggling and trafficking are perpetrated by criminal organisations. In the Valletta Summit, the EU and African countries also agreed an agenda on return policies and admission agreements. For this purpose, the EU and African countries aim to strengthen cooperation between each other in order to return nationals of third countries to their places of origin by ensuring that Article 13 of the Cotonou Agreement is fully complied.[130] The Cotonou Agreement states that ACP/EU countries agree that they

> 'shall accept the return of and readmission of the readmission and return of their nationals any of its nationals who are illegally present on These agreements shall also cover, if deemed the territory of an ACP State, at that State's necessary by any of the Parties, arrangements request and without further formalities'.[131]

In the Valletta Action Plan it is emphasised that Readmission agreements shall take into consideration the best interest of unaccompanied children and shall promote reintegration of migrants in their countries of origin. The EU and countries of origin will cooperate to identify migrants, return them and provide reintegration programmes. Civil society should cooperate with transit and origin countries in supporting voluntary return and reintegration of migrants. Reintegration measures should be taken in cooperation with IOM.

The implementation of these measures, including police and judicial cooperation and mutual legal assistance, require that the EU and African countries agree common rules on the protection of human rights as exchange of information on criminals require that when they are transferred from one EU Member State to an African standard, his or her human rights are fully respected. The same can be asserted on readmission agreements and voluntary returns. Programmes to ensure the reintegration of migrants by giving them socio-economic opportunities, require that African countries and EU Member States are fully committed

130 See Partnership Agreement between the members of the African, Caribbean and Pacific Group of States of the one part, and the European Community and its Member States, of the other part, signed in Cotonou on 23 June 2000. On OJ L 317/3, 15/12/2000.

131 See Article 13 (c) (i) of the Cotonou Agreement.

to the achievement of these objectives. These ambitious programmes can be effective if common agreements on the protection of human rights, democracy, governance, the respect of rule of law and socio-economic stability are achieved democratically. In order, to achieve these objectives, the European Parliament should be involved in decisions related to EU external relations. It has already been shown that the EP has a very marginal role in the EU external action.[132] Consequently, initiatives taken by the EU to fight against smuggling and trafficking in cooperation with third countries, will not be accountable before the Parliament as it will only have a consultative role. Decisions on cooperation between the EU and investigative authorities of third countries, will be taken without the EP's active involvement. The EP will not even be involved in decisions which can affect the respect of human rights during investigations. The area related to external cooperation with third countries will remain intergovernmental. It must be added that smuggling of migrants will not be defeated if the EU does not address the needs of people who are benefiting from smuggling of migrants.[133] It has also been reported that anti-smuggling measures jeopardise the safety of migrants because smugglers will use more dangerous routes and demand higher prices for the journey to ensure that migrants reach the EU.[134] In other terms, EU policies only aimed at fighting against smugglers and traffickers cannot be effective if they do not address poverty in transit and origin countries. There are different programmes and agreements concluded to identify the root causes of migration and they include cooperation with the AU and the ECOWAS. Is this cooperation feasible at the moment? In order to address this concern, the next sections focus on the AU's structure.

132 See section 2, p. 116 of this chapter.

133 See P. Tinti and S. Reitano...*op. cit.* note 119, p.180.

134 See P. Tinti and S. Reitano...*op. cit.* note 119, p.181.

5.1 Structure and organs of the African Union

The AU is formed by all African countries apart from Morocco.[135] The AU organs comprise different institutions which form the Executive, the Parliament and the Judiciary of the AU. Their functions are explained in the Constitutive Act of the African Union. Article 1 of the Constitutive Act states that the AU is composed by the Assembly of Heads of States, the Commission which is the Secretariat of the AU, the Court of Justice of the AU and the Executive Council of Ministers of the AU. [136] Articles 5 and 17 have set up the Pan-African Parliament in order to ensure the full participation of all AU's citizens 'in the development and economic integration of the continent'.[137] Article 3 establishes the objectives of the AU which mainly are the achievement of great solidarity and unity between African countries and African people; the encouragement of international cooperation on the basis of the Charter of the United Nations and the Universal Declaration of Human Rights; the promotion and protection of human rights in compliance with the African Charter on Human and Peoples' Rights and other human rights instruments; the promotion of economic development and the cooperation with other Regional Economic Communities for the gradual attainment of the AU's objectives. By the wording of the Constitutive Act, it can be deducted that the AU will not interfere with the national sovereignty of its members. This fact can be deducted by Articles 3(b) which states that one of the AU's objectives are 'to defend the sovereignty, territorial integrity and independence of its Member States'. In addition, Article 4 (a) and (b) state that the AU shall function in compliance with 'sovereign equality and interdependence among Member States...' and the 'respect of borders existing on achievement of independence'. In comparison with the EU and on the basis of the Constitutive Act, it can be noted that the AU is not a new legal system of international law for the benefit of which its Member States have accepted to

135 See http://au.int/en/member_states/countryprofiles, accessed on 23/6/2015.

136 See Constitutive Act of the African Union adopted on 11/7/2000 available on http://au.int/en/sites/default/files/ConstitutiveAct_EN.pdf accessed on 23/6/2015.

137 See Article 17 of the Constitutive Act.

limit national sovereignty as it is in the EU according to the CJEU's case *Van Gend en Loos*. Therefore, the AU is not as advanced as the EU which has developed principles of EU primacy and direct effect. The Assembly is the supreme organ of the AU which will take decision either by consensus or by a two-third majority of Member States.[138] Procedural decisions can be taken by a simple majority.[139] Article 9 states that the Assembly can determine the AU's common policies; take into consideration and decisions on reports and recommendation received by other organs; establish new organs, monitor how the AU's policies are implemented by Member States; adopt the AU's budget and 'give directives to the Executive Council (Council) on the management of conflicts, war and other emergency situations and the restoration of peace'.[140] The Council is composed by the Ministers of Foreign Affairs or by other ministers as designated by the government.[141] Finally, the Assembly can appoint judges of the Court of Justice and the Chairman of the Commission, the Chairman's deputy and their functions and terms of office. The meetings of the Assembly shall be formed by a quorum of two-thirds of the total AU's members.[142] The fact that the Council is formed mainly by Ministers of Foreign Affairs is another signal indicating the fact that the AU is not a new legal system forming part of the legal systems of its Member States but an international organization external to internal legal systems. Decisions of the Council which are not procedural can be taken by consensus or by 'a two-third of majority of the Member States' and the quorum is two-thirds of the total membership and the same established for the Assembly.[143] The Council's functions are listed in Article 13. This provision states that the 'Council shall coordinate and take decisions on policies in areas of common interest to the Member States'.[144] In between the policies of Council's responsibility, there are 'nationality, residency and immigration matters'.[145] The Council is responsible before the Assembly for its decisions and it shall considered issues

138 See Article 6(2) and Article 7(1) of the Constitutive Act.

139 See Article 7(2).

140 See Article 9 (1) (g).

141 See Article 10 (1).

142 See Article 9 (2).

143 See Article11.

144 See Article 13 (1).

145 See Article 13 (2).

referred by the Assembly and monitor the compliance of policies formulated by it.[146] The involvement of people 'in the development and economic integration of the continent'[147] is ensured by the Pan-African Parliament whose composition, powers, functions and organisations are defined by a protocol which is the 2000 Protocol to the Treaty establishing African Economic Community relating to the Pan-African Parliament.[148] According to the Protocol, members of the Pan-African Parliament are either elected or designed by national parliaments of AU Member States or any other deliberative organs of Member States.[149] The terms of members of the Pan-African Parliament will 'run concurrently with his or her term in the National Parliament or other deliberative organ'.[150] The role of members of the Pan-African Parliament is incompatible 'with the exercise of executive or judicial functions in a Member State'.[151] When the Pan-African Parliament was established in 2000, it was expressly stated that in its first term, the Parliament would have had 'advisory and consultative powers only'.[152] After the first term, it was recognized that the Parliament would have 'be vested with legislative powers'.[153] Finally, it has been established that the Pan-African Parliament will work in cooperation with national Parliaments and with Parliaments of the Regional Economic Communities or other deliberative organs of Member States.[154]

Another institution expressly established by the Constitutive Act of the AU is the Court of Justice.[155] The Act recalls the Protocol of the Court of Justice of

146 See Article 9 (1) (g).

147 See Article 17 (1).

148 See Article 17 (2). The Protocol on the Pan-African Parliament can be found on this website http://www.au.int/en/sites/default/files/PROTOCOL_TREATY_ESTABLISHING_THE_AFRICAN_ECONOMIC_COMMUNITY_RELATING_PAN_AFRICAN_PARLIAMENT.pdf accessed on 25/6/2015.

149 See Article 5(1) of the Protocol.

150 See Article 5(3) of the Protocol.

151 See Article 7 of the Protocol.

152 See Article 11 of the Protocol.

153 ibid note 174.

154 See Article 18 of the Protocol.

155 See Article 18 of the Constitutive Act.

the African Union, adopted by the Assembly of the Union on 11 July 2003.[156] The Court consists of eleven judges who are nationals of Member States.[157] Judges are elected by the Assembly which votes 'by secret ballot and by two-thirds majority of the Member States eligible to vote'. [158] Judges can be elected for a period of six years renewable only once.[159] The Court will also have a President and a Vice-President eligible for three years and re-eligible only for another mandate.[160] In order to guarantee the Court's independence, it has been established that judges cannot participate in decisions where they have been agents, advocates or counsels for any of the parties in the trial or as a member of a national or international court or as a member of a commission of enquiry or in any other capacity. [161] There is also a provision on incompatibility which states that the role of the judge is incompatible 'with any activity that might interfere with the independence or impartiality of such a judge or the demands of the office'.[162] The provision seems too vague as it does not specifically state when there could be incompatibility, leaving the decision to the Court's discretion. [163] The disputes of Court's jurisdiction can be related to the interpretation and application of the Constitutive Act and to the interpretation, application and validity of the AU Treaties and subsidiary legal instruments. [164] In between the areas where the Court has jurisdiction, can be included 'any question of international law'. [165] Furthermore, the list is not exhaustive as the Protocol states that 'The Assembly may confer on the Court power to assume jurisdiction over any dispute other than those referred to in this Article'. [166] In any case, the Court's jurisdiction does not include the merit of a question but only points of law. The Court's decisions

156 The Protocol on the Court of Justice of the African Union can be accessed by this website: http://www.au.int/en/sites/default/files/PROTOCOL_COURT_OF_JUSTICE_OF_THE_AFRICAN_UNION.pdf accessed on 25/6/2015.

157 See Article 3(1) of the Protocol on the Court of Justice of the African Union.

158 See Article 7 (1) of the Protocol on the Court of Justice of the African Union.

159 See Article 8 (1) of the Protocol on the Court of Justice.

160 See Article 10 (1) of the Protocol on the Court of Justice.

161 See Article 13 (2) of the Protocol on the Court of Justice.

162 See Article 15 (1) of the Protocol on the Court of Justice.

163 See Article 15 (2) of the Protocol on the Court of Justice.

164 See Article 19 (1) (a) and (b) of the Protocol on the Court of Justice.

165 See Article 19 (1) (c) of the Protocol on the Court of Justice.

166 See Article 19 (2) of the Protocol on the Court of Justice.

shall be in compliance with international law and thus, decisions have to be taken in accordance with the Constitutive Act, special or general International Treaties and international customs, the general principle of law 'recognized universally or by African States.'[167] The Protocol on the Court of Justice states that decisions of the Court are binding 'for the parties and in respect of that particular case'.[168] However, the Court can refer to 'judicial decisions and the writing of the most highly qualified publicists of various nations' and to 'regulations, directives and decisions of the Union as subsidiary means for the determination of the rule of law'.[169] Decisions of the Court can be revised when new facts have been discovered and they have to be factors without which, the Court would not have made that decision.[170]

The Constitutive Act has also established an AU Commission 'which shall be the Secretariat of the Union and its functions and regulations will be determined by the Assembly.[171]

AU organs are the African Court of Human and Peoples' Rights[172] and the African Commission of Human and People's Rights (ACHPR).[173] Both these organs have been established by the African Charter on Human and People's Rights and Protocols.[174]

5.2 The protection of human rights in the African Union

The African Charter on Human and People's Rights also known as the Banjul Charter (thus, from now on the Charter will be referred as Banjul Charter), was established in 1982 and entered in to force in 1986.[175] The Banjul Charter

167 See Article 20 (1) of the Protocol on the Court of Justice.

168 See Article 37 of the Protocol on the Court of Justice.

169 See Article 20 (1) (e) of the Protocol on the Court of Justice.

170 See Article 41 (1) of the Protocol on the Court of Justice.

171 See Article 20 of the Constitutive Act.

172 See http://au.int/en/organs/cj accessed on 23/6/2015.

173 See http://www.achpr.org/ accessed on 23/6/2015. See also http://www.achpr.org/instruments/achpr/ratification/, accessed on 1/7/2015.

174 See for the Charter http://www.achpr.org/instruments/achpr/ accessed on 23/6/2015. For the Protocol, see http://www.achpr.org/files/instruments/court-establishment/achpr_instr_proto_court_eng.pdf accessed on 23/6/2015.

175 See African (Banjul) Charter on Human and Peoples' Rights http://www.achpr.org/files/instruments/achpr/banjul_charter.pdf accessed on 26/6/2015.

is an instrument of international law which aims to protect human rights and fundamental freedoms in African countries.[176] The ACHPR was set up in 1987 in Banjul in Gambia, with the task to interpret the Banjul Charter.[177] The Charter comprises 68 Articles and recognizes 'the enjoyment of the rights and freedoms' indicated in it 'without distinction...such as race, ethnic group, color, sex, language, religion, political or any other opinion, national and social origin, fortune, birth or other status'.[178] The Charter recognizes the principle of equality,[179] the right to life,[180] the right to liberty and security,[181] the right to a fair trial,[182] freedom of religion and of association,[183] freedom of movement and residence within the limits concerning the protection of national security, morality, law and order and public health.[184] The same provision recognizes the right to asylum and the prohibition of collective expulsion, although the Charter refers to 'massive expulsion of non-nationals' which means expulsion 'aimed at national, racial, ethnic or religious groups'.[185] The other provisions recognizes human rights which can be found in the ECHR such as the right to private and family life which in the Banjul Charter, is recognized in a different way. It is established that 'The family shall be the natural unit and basis of society'.[186] The Banjul Charter states that the family shall be assisted and protected. In addition, the same provision states that discriminations based on sex and age shall be prohibited. Conversely, the ECHR protects the right of individuals to have a private life and family and it states that these rights can be limited to protect the national security and other superior interests. The ECHR does not consider the family as 'the natural unit and basis of society' as the Banjul Charter does. However, the

176 See http://www.achpr.org/instruments/achpr/ accessed on 26/6/2015.

177 ibid note 199.

178 See Article 2 of the Banjul Charter.

179 See Article 3.

180 See Article 4.

181 See Article 6.

182 See Article 7.

183 See Articles 8 and 10.

184 See Article 12(1) and (2).

185 See Article 12 (5).

186 See Article 18 (1) and (2) of the Banjul Charter.

ECHR as the Banjul Charter, recognize that family life can be limited for reasons concerning national security.

In Articles 27-29 can be found principles which are common to the EU. This part of the Charter indicates the duties that individuals have in order to preserve the respect of human rights. Individuals are under the duty to promote, safeguard and reinforce 'mutual respect and tolerance'.[187] The Charter also requires that individuals' action is taken in accordance and compliance with the principle of solidarity. [188] Common rules on the respect of human rights could be agreed on the basis of this principle and the common fundamental rights protected by the Banjul Charter, the ECHR and the EU Charter of Fundamental Rights.

The AU, as the ECHR, has established a Commission called the High Commission on Human and Peoples' Rights (the AU Commission). The AU Commission has been set up by the Banjul Charter. The Commission has the task 'to promote human and peoples' rights and ensure their protection in Africa'.[189] The AU Commission is composed by eleven members who are of high morality, integrity and impartiality and they are chosen in between the citizens of Member States who have extensive legal experience. [190] In order to promote the respect human rights, the AU Commission shall organize conferences, seminars, symposia, disseminate information and 'encourage national and local institutions concerned with human and peoples' rights, and should the case arise, give its views or make recommendations to Governments'. [191] Despite the AU Commission can only make recommendation, it can influence AU governments to respect human rights. In addition, the AU Commission has other important roles such as laying down rules and procedures 'aiming at solving legal problems related to human and peoples' rights and fundamental freedoms upon which African Governments may base their legislation'.[192] The Banjul Charter gives the AU Commission the chance to cooperate with African and international organisations in order to promote and reinforce the protection of human rights in

187 See Article 28 the Banjul Charter.

188 See Article 29 (4) of the Banjul Charter.

189 See Article 30 of the Banjul Charter.

190 See Article 31 of the Banjul Charter.

191 See Article 45(1) (a) of the Banjul Charter.

192 See Article 45 (1) (b) of the Banjul Charter.

African countries.[193] This is a very important provisions which ought to be one of the legal basis to launch cooperation and common agreements between the EU and the AU in the protection of human rights. The establishment of common rules on the protection of human rights, might be the first step to sign and ratify further agreements on police and judicial cooperation against criminals who smuggle migrants by sea.

Violations of human rights can be reported to the Commission from one Member State against another Member State. [194] The two Member States will try to resolve the dispute between each other through bilateral negotiation. [195] If the negotiation does not resolve the issue, the AU Commission can be requested to deal with the matter but only after the local remedies have been exhausted, unless the local procedure will prolong unnecessarily the time to take the issue before the AU Commission. [196] Subsequently, the AU Commission will evaluate whether there have been breaches of the Charter and it will write a report where it will describe the facts and its findings. [197] The report will be sent to the Assembly of Heads of State and governments and in this report, the AU Commission can also add its recommendations. [198] In this way, Member States keep their control over the AU Commission. The African Court on Human and Peoples' Rights was established by Protocol to the Banjul Charter adopted in 1998 and entered into force in 2004.[199] The Court has the task to 'complement the protective mandate' of the Commission.[200] The Courts' jurisdiction includes disputes and case-law related to 'the interpretation and application of the Charter, this Protocol and any other relevant Human Rights instrument ratified by the States concerned'.[201] Cases can be submitted before the Court

193 See Article 45 (1) (c) of the Banjul Charter.

194 See Article 47 of the Banjul Charter.

195 See Article 48 of the Banjul Charter.

196 See Article 50 of the Banjul Charter.

197 See Article 52 of the Banjul Charter.

198 See Article 53 of the Banjul Charter.

199 See http://www.african-court.org/en/index.php/about-the-court/brief-history accessed on 1/7/2015. The Protocol can be accessed on the following website: http://www.african-court.org/en/images/documents/Court/Court%20Establishment/africancourt-humanrights.pdf both websites have been accessed on 1/7/2015.

200 See Article 2 of the Protocol to the African Charter on Human and Peoples' Rights on the Establishment of an African Court on human and Peoples' Rights.

201 See Article 3(1) of the Protocol.

by the Commission, the Member State which has lodged a complaint to the Commission or against which the complaint has been lodged.[202] A Member State whose citizen may have been victim of human rights' breaches can also lodge a case before the Court as African intergovernmental and governmental organisations, even though the latter must be entitled by the Court. [203]State parties which may have an interest in the case, may be allowed by the Court to join it.[204] The Court may ask the AU Commission's opinion before declaring a case admissible and the AU Commission has to deliver its opinion without delay. [205] The Court is composed by eleven judges who are citizens of AU Member States, although they do not have to belong to the same State. [206] Judges are elected by secret ballot by the Assembly from a list prepared by the Secretary General of the AU for a period of six years only renewable for once. [207] Their independence must be ensured by the respect of international law and by monitoring possible incompatibility between the judge and other activities which may be in conflict with his office.[208] The Court shall hear all the submission and, if necessary, it can hold an enquiry and Member States shall provide all the facilities to ensure that the Court handle the case. [209] In order to fulfil its tasks, the Court can hear oral and written evidence. [210] If the Court finds that the human rights protected by the Banjul Charter have been breached, it can 'make appropriate orders, including the payment of fair compensation or reparation'. [211] The judgement shall be made in ninety days and the Court has to give reasons for the decision which cannot be appealed but it can be reviewed. [212] If the Court does not reach the judgment by unanimous votes, the judges in disagreement, can write a dissenting opinion.

202 See Article 5 (1) (a), (b) and (c) of the Protocol.

203 See Article 5 (1) (d), (e) and (3) of the Protocol.

204 See Article 5 (2) of the Protocol.

205 See Article 6 (1) of the Protocol.

206 See Article11 of the Protocol.

207 See Article 13 (1) 14 (1) and 15(1) of the Protocol.

208 See Article 17 (1) and 18 of the Protocol.

209 See Article 26 (1) of the Protocol.

210 See Article 26 (2) of the Protocol.

211 See Article 27 (1) of the Protocol.

212 See Article 28 (1), (2), (3) and (6) of the Protocol.

[213] The Court shall submit a regular report to the Assembly, especially to notify Member States which are not complying with its judgments.[214]

The Protocol on the Court have not been ratified by all Member States and neither it is possible to know whether this is still the situation because the website is not updated.[215] The status of ratification shows that there are still Member States which do not recognize the authority of the Court as they have not ratified the Protocol.

The AU has adopted other instruments to protect human rights. These legal instruments could lead to adopt common rules on human rights and cooperation with the EU.

5.3 Other legal instruments and developing case-law on the protection of human rights in the African Union and on international cooperation

In 2008, the Assembly of the Heads of State and Government of the Union adopted the Protocol on the Statute of the African Court of Justice and Human Rights.[216] This new Protocol ought to replace a previous Protocol which established the AU Court of Justice in 2003 and the Protocol setting up the African Court on Human and Peoples' Rights adopted in 1998 and entered into force in 2004.[217] The reason for the replacement of these two Courts is because there is the intention to create a single court called the African Court of Justice and Human Rights.[218] For this purpose the reference made in the AU Constitutive Act to the Court of Justice, shall be replaced by 'African Court of Justice and Human Rights'. [219] The 2008 Protocol states that the new Court shall have competence 'in the interpretation and application of the Constitutive Act'; 'the

213 See Article 28 (7) of the Protocol.

214 See Article 31 of the Protocol.

215 See http://www.african-court.org/en/images/documents/Court/Ratification_and_Deposit_of_the_Declaration.pdf to check the status of ratification of the Protocol on the Court but it is updated to 1/2/2013.

216 See http://www.au.int/en/sites/default/files/PROTOCOL_STATUTE_AFRICAN_COURT_JUSTICE_AND_HUMAN_RIGHTS.pdf accessed on 1/7/2015.

217 See Article 1 of the 2008 Protocol on the Statute of the African Court of Justice and Human Rights.

218 See Article 2 of the 2008 Protocol.

219 See Article 3 of the 2008 Protocol.

interpretation, application or validity of other Union Treaties' and other legal instruments adopted by the AU including the African Charter, the Protocol to the African Charter on Human and Peoples' Rights, the Charter on the Rights and Welfare on the Child and the Charter on the Rights of Women in Africa; questions concerning international law; all legal instruments adopted by the AU organs; other facts which could be considered a violation of Member States or AU laws; the Court has also jurisdiction on the extent of reparation to be made for the violation of international obligations. [220] The scope of the new Court seems very wide as it includes many topics and issues related to Member States and international law. Court's decisions shall be based on the Constitutive Act, ratified International treaties, International customs accepted as law, general principles of law recognized by the AU Member States as well as the opinion of established scholars of different nations, AU directives, regulations and decisions and any other relevant law. [221] The Court's judgment shall consist of a remedy of the situation of violation of human rights, including a compensation.[222] The judgment shall be binding and judges in disagreement with the decision, can issue a dissenting opinion. [223] The Statute of the African Court of Justice and Human Rights has been ratified by very few African nations.[224] The status of the Protocol in February 2014 was that only 5 African States ratified it and these States were: Libya, Mani, Burkina Faso, Benin and Congo. Therefore, the Statute has not entered into force and African people of most AU Member States, can rely on the Banjul Charter and previous Courts described above.[225]

Another legal instrument which could lead the AU to agree common rules on human rights with the EU is the African Charter on Democracy, Elections and Governance of 2007.[226] The objectives of the 2007 Charter are to promote and comply with 'the universal values and principles of democracy and respect

220 See Article 28 of the 2008 Protocol.

221 See Article 31 (1) of the 2008 Protocol.

222 See Article 45 of the 2008 Protocol.

223 See Articles 44 and 46(1) of the 2008 Protocol.

224 See http://www.africancourtcoalition.org/index.php?option=com_content&view=article&id=87:ratification-status-protocol-on-the-statute-of-the-african-court-of-justice-and-human-rights&catid=7:african-union&Itemid=12 accessed on 9/7/2015.

225 See sections 5.1, p. 132 and 5.2, p. 135.

226 See http://www.ipu.org/idd-E/afr_charter.pdf accessed on 9/7/2015.

for human rights',[227] the rule of law, the respect of the principle of 'supremacy of, the Constitution and constitutional order in the political arrangements of the State Parties'.[228] Other objectives are the promotion of free elections in Member States, the prohibition of unconstitutional change of government in Member States as it can be a serious threat to their peace, stability, development and security, [229] the promotion and protection of judiciary independence,[230] the promotion of democracy, regional and continental integration, the fight against corruption, the promotion of gender equality and of principles of transparency, access to information, freedom of press and the enhancement of cooperation between the AU, Regional Economic Communities and the International Community on democracy, elections and governance.[231] Other provisions of the Charter state that State Parties shall be committed to implement principles of democracy, respect of human rights and the rule of law in their territories. For this purpose, State Parties may seek advice to the Commission 'for strengthening and developing their electoral institutions and processes'.[232] According to the Charter, the AU can sanction all means by which democratic governments in Member States are elected, including coup d'Etat. [233] Finally, State Parties, through the support of the Commission, shall evaluate the implementation of the Charter in cooperation with other organs of the AU, 'including the Pan-African Parliament, the peace and Security Council, the African Human Rights Commission'. [234] The African Charter on Democracy, Elections and Governance has been ratified by few Member States which are Burkina Faso, Ethiopia, Ghana, Guinea, Lesotho, Mauritania, Sierra Leone, South Africa and Zambia.[235]

The AU has also adopted the African Union Border Programme (AUBP) to ensure peace, security and prosperity within the African continent.[236] In addi-

227 See Article 2(1) of the African Charter on Democracy, Elections and Governance.

228 See Article 2(2) of the African Charter.

229 See Article 2(3) and (4) of the African Charter.

230 See Article 2(5) of the African Charter.

231 See Article 2(6), (7), (8), (9), (10), (11) and (12) of the African Charter.

232 See Article 18(1) of the African Charter.

233 See Article 23 of the African Charter.

234 See Article 45(c) of the African Charter.

235 See http://www.achpr.org/instruments/charter-democracy/ratification/ accessed on 9/7/2015.

236 See http://www.peaceau.org/en/page/27-au-border-programme-aubp accessed on 9/7/2015.

tion, the Member States have devoted themselves to the respect of human rights within their territories. It has been reported that efforts are being made to abolish the death penalty in African countries.[237] Emerging jurisprudence is based on Article 4 of the Banjul Charter which protects the right to life of individuals.[238] One of the reasons why African countries are abolishing the death penalty is because countries of refuge may refuse to extradite a person in the requesting State if the death penalty is considered one of the penalties to be applied to defendants. [239] Indeed, EU Member States, for instance, cannot extradite a defendant to a country where they apply the death penalty. Not only because EU Member States' criminal justice prohibits extradition, but also because case-law of the ECtHR prohibits to extradite an individual in a country where he may suffer torture, inhuman and degrading treatment or where he may face the death penalty.[240] Furthermore, EU Member States, in order to apply provisions on the EAW, agreed to abolish the death penalty in their domestic criminal justice systems. This is confirmed by the EAW framework decision which states that 'No person should be removed, expelled or extradited to a State where there is a serious risk that he or she would be subjected to the death penalty, torture or other inhuman or degrading treatment or punishment'.[241] Therefore, EU Member States not only have abolished the death penalty in their legal systems, but they have also been forbidden from extraditing a person to a country where the death penalty is applied. This fact means that cooperation in criminal matters between the EU and the AU, in order to detect, arrest and prosecute smugglers of migrants ought to be agreed by establishing common rules on the abolition of the death penalty. The African Union is committed to the abolishment of the death penalty and this is confirmed by the Commission's jurisprudence on Article 4 of the Banjul Charter.

> ...the jurisprudence of the Commission shows that deprivation of life would be arbitrary where life is taken away in disregard of fair trial procedures or in

---

237 See Anyangwe, C., 'Emerging African jurisprudence suggesting the desirability of the abolition of capital punishment'. In *African Journal of International and Comparative Law*, 2015, 23/1, pp. 1-28.

238 See C., Anyangwe...*op. cit.* note 237, p. 6.

239 See C., Anyangwe...*op. cit.* note 237, p. 2.

240 See, for instance, the key cases *Soering v. United Kingdom,* Application no. 14038/88 Judgment of 7/7/1989; *Chahal v. the United Kingdom,* Application no. 22414/93, judgment of 15/11/1996.

241 See paragraph 13 of Council Framework Decision 2002/584/JHA of 13 June 2002 on the European arrest warrant and the surrender procedures between Member States, OJ L 190/1, 18/7/2002.

> circumstances of extrajudicial killing. Deprivation of life would also be arbitrary where death results from, or where the methods of execution of a capital offender would amount to, torture or other cruel, inhuman and degrading treatment or punishment'.[242]

In Sudan, on a case related to the execution of rebels belonging to the Sudanese People's Liberation Army, the Commission ruled that the Sudanese government violated Article 4 of the Banjul Charter as prisoners were executed without trial as unarmed civilians who were also executed.[243] Evidence was carried out from reports written by the United Nations Special Rapporteur and the Sudanese government did not provide specific information on the executions.[244] In another case, the Commission stated that the right to life, being 'the supreme right of human beings' includes 'the right to dignity and the right to livelihood'.[245] Consequently, it is a duty of the State to protect individuals against abuses committed by public bodies such as the arbitrary killings committed by agents of State.[246] In other cases, the Commission confirmed that States could be responsible for killing perpetrated by non-State actors.[247] The protection against the death penalty has also been made by the interpretation of the Charter's provisions on the fair trial.[248] The Commission stated that the decision of the Martial Court in Sierra Leone to execute twenty-four soldiers found guilty of an attempted coup without recognizing up to them the right of appeal, was in breach of the right to life in conjunction with the right to fair trial. It was stated that

> 'The right to life is the fulcrum of all other rights. It is the fountain through which other rights flow, and any violation of this right without due process amounts to arbitrary deprivation of life. Having found above that the trial of

242 See C., Anyangwe...op. cit. note 237, p. 7.

243 See Case No. 48/90 *Amnesty International v. Sudan*, para 47.

244 See Case No. 48/90 *Amnesty International v. Sudan*, para 48.

245 See Case No. 279/03-296/05, *Sudan Human Rights Organisation & Centre on Housing and Evictions (COHRE) v. Sudan*, para 146.

246 See Case No. 279/03-296/05, para 147.

247 See Case No. 245/2002 *Zimbabwe Human Rights NGO Forum v. Zimbabwe*. See also Case No 204/97 *Association of Victims of Post-Electoral Violence & Interights v. Cameroon*, 1999.

248 See Case No. 223/98 *Forum of Coscience v. Sierra Leone*, 2000.

> the 24 soldiers constituted a breach of due process of law as guaranteed under Article 7(1)(a) of the Charter, the Commission consequently finds their execution an arbitrary deprivation of their rights to life provided for in Article 4 of the Charter'.[249]

Violations of the fair trial which eventually caused the breach of Article 4 of the Charter, were found in other cases, where the Commission stated that the lack of respect of the fair trial caused a breach of Articles 4 and 7 of the Charter.[250] These cases show that the AU is contributing to abolish the death penalty, although the Commission's case law does not state that death penalty is prohibited in all circumstances but only in some cases. It has been emphasised that the imposition of death penalty itself is not unlawful.[251] It can only be prohibited in some cases where the death penalty was in breach of the right to life. Two circumstances had been indicated. One of these circumstances is when the death penalty sentence follows a trial that does not respect the procedure on the fair trial as established by Article 7 of the Charter. The other circumstance was when a mandatory death penalty was imposed by law and not 'by a court of law in the light of all relevant circumstances'.[252] This fact may create obstacles in the fight against smuggling of migrants by sea in cooperation with the EU as in the EU, the death penalty has been abolished in all cases.

Other general considerations are that the AU is not well developed as an international legal system. Principles of primacy, direct effect and rule of law have not been established by the AU. Hence, it is very difficult to launch cooperation with the AU on investigations and prosecution concerning smuggling and trafficking. The fight against these crimes rises issues related to the protection of human rights of defendants which shall be guaranteed when the person is extradited and when the person is trialed, pled guilty and jailed. These are the reasons why at the moment police and judicial cooperation between the EU and the AU is not possible and it is better to prioritise bilateral agreements between States

249 See Case 223/98, para 19.

250 See Case no 54/91 *Malawi African Association v. Mauritania*; Case no. 61/91 *Amnesty International v. Mauritania*; Case 98/93 *Ms Sarr Diop, Union Interafricaine des Droits de l'Homme and RADDHOM v. Mauritania;* Case 164/97 to 196/97 *Collectife de Veuves et Ayants-droit v. Mauritania;* Case 210/98 *Association Mauritanienne des Droit de l'Homme v. Mauritania.* An in depth analysis of all these cases can be found in C., Anyangwe...*op. cit.* note 237, pp 10 and 11.

251 See C., Anyangwe...*op. cit.* note 237, p.13.

252 Ibid

in the EU and outside the EU where smuggling and trafficking are perpetrated. Europol and Eurojust, as indicated in chapter 4,[253] should give support in enacting extradition by exchanging information on criminals to the different police and investigative forces of states involved. In this way, they will cooperate to identify criminal groups and to ensure that they are punished for the crimes committed. The way Europol and Eurojust support criminal cooperation should be supervised by the EP to which these EU agencies should be accountable.

Economic cooperation to identify root causes of migration and address them by appropriate policies, is more feasible as there are not the challenges related to limitation of national sovereignty and issues related to the protection of human rights. Regional cooperation between the EU and African organisations can support a reduction of irregular migration by identifying root causes of migration. One of the organisations the EU should conclude agreements with is the ECOWAS.

6. ECOWAS AND OTHER INITIATIVES

The ECOWAS was established in 1975 by the Treaty of Lagos with the purpose to promote economic development in the participating countries which are Benin, Burkina Faso, Cape Verde, Cote d'Ivoire, Gambia, Ghana, Guinea, Guinea Bissau, Liberia, Mali, Nigeria, Niger, Sierra Leone, Senegal and Togo.[254] The ECOWAS also includes specialized agencies which are ECOWAS Gender and Development Centre, Youth and Sports development Centre and the Water Sources Coordination Centre. Member States will work together 'as a single regional economic block'.[255] The Treaty was revised in 1993 to strengthen economic cooperation between the different signing sovereign states. The signing states took into consideration the African Charter of Human and People's Rights and the Declaration of Political principles of the Economic Community of West African States adopted in Abuja in 1991. The ECOWAS promotes economic agreements at bilateral and multilateral levels.

253 See section 5, p. 92 and 6, p. 95, chapter 4.

254 See http://www.ecowas.int/about-ecowas/basic-information/, accessed on 23/11/2016.

255 See http://www.ecowas.int/ecowas-law/treaties/, accessed on 23/11/2016.

Chapter 10 of the revised Treaty focusses on immigration policies.[256] The Treaty recognizes the right of entry, residence and establishment to citizens of the ECOWAS. Hence, the Treaty recognizes the free movement of citizens within the Community and Member States shall ensure that the rights recognized by the revised Treaties are fully implemented within their legal systems. The ECOWAS publishes annual reports on the economic, social and political situation in African countries belonging to this organization.[257] However, at the moment no reports show that the ECOWAS is cooperating with the EI in preventing smuggling and trafficking through development policies. The EU is launching cooperation but only with single countries.

Niger and Horn of Africa: In 2011 the EU opened EU Operation Centres (EU OpCen) in the Horn of Africa.[258] The aim of the EU OpCen were to improve cooperation and strengthen civil-military actions between the Common Foreign and Security Policy (CFSP) actions in the Horn of Africa.

On 1st December 2014 the mandate was extended until the end of 2016 and the CFSP actions were expanded to the Sahel Region. The CFSP missions supported by the EU OpCen are EUTM Mali, EUCAP SAHEL Mali, and EUCAP SAHEL NIGER.

The EU OpCen provide crisis managements in these regions. At the moment, the EU OpCen are not focussed on addressing smuggling and trafficking.

The EU also put forward the Sahel Strategy in the regions of Burkina Faso, Chad, Mali, Mauritania end Niger.[259] The Sahel region experiences extreme poverty, irregular migration and smuggling and trafficking. For this reason in 2011, the EU adopted a comprehensive approach called the EU Strategy for Security and Development (the Sahel Strategy) which should tackle these difficult situations in the Sahel region. In 2015, the EU Sahel Strategy was implemented through the Sahel Regional Action Plan (RAP). The RAP has identified different priorities which shall focus on creating opportunities for youth, migration mobil-

256 See Article 59 of the revised Treaty, ECOWAS Commission Abuja Nigeria. On http://www.ecowas.int/wp-content/uploads/2015/01/Revised-treaty.pdf, accessed on 23/11/2016.

257 See http://www.ecowas.int/documentation/ecowas-commission-annuel-report/ accessed on 8/1/2018.

258 See Common Security and Defense Policy EU Operations Centre Horn of Africa & Sahel (EU OPCEN), June 2015. Available on http://eeas.europa.eu/csdp/structures-instruments-agencies/eu-operations-centre/docs/factsheet_eu_opcen_23_06_2015.pdf, accessed on 16/1/2017.

259 See https://eeas.europa.eu/diplomatic-network/sahel-region/4094/sahel-region_en.

ity, border management and the fight against illicit trafficking and transnational organised criminal networks. The EU is promoting developing policies which can support the fight against extreme poverty by a holistic strategy which could address security concerns and development in the area which consequently, will strengthen EU security.[260] The Sahel Strategy aims to improve political stability, security, good governance, economic and education opportunity and social cohesion in five years. Improving these areas will create economic opportunity and the region will not be targeted anymore by criminal networks and extremist groups such as Al-Qaida in the Maghreb (AQIM).[261] The Action Plan 2015-2020, confirms the priorities indicated by the Strategy and emphasises that more actions should be taken to fight against smuggling and trafficking.[262] In 2016 the EU has allocated funds in the Sahel Region to tackle root causes of irregular migration.[263] At regional level, the EU is supporting the establishment of West African police information system/WAPIS to combat trafficking, terrorism and criminal organisations and to ensure that national administrations improve their methods to collect, centralise, manage and share information gathered by police. At national level, the EU has allocated funds to strengthen national economies. In Burkina Faso, funds aim to improve socio-economic conditions of women and youth in rural areas and, in Northern Burkina Faso, funds will focus on improving the living conditions of the most vulnerable people, especially in the area of health and food security. Improving the economy in Cameroon, Central Africa, Mali, Nigeria, Senegal, Niger and Mauritania is also the aim of funds allocated in these nations by the EU. In Mauritania, the EU is also launching a project to protect children from human trafficking and exploitation. These objectives will be achieved by managing migration flows through actions on the protection of children by criminal networks which intend to exploit them or recruit in extremist criminal groups. In Senegal, the reduction of irregular migration will be supported through programmes aimed to improve living con-

260 See 'European Union External Action Service Strategy for Security and Development in the Sahel', available on https://eeas.europa.eu/sites/eeas/files/strategy_for_security_and_development_in_the_sahel_en_0.pdf, p.2.

261 See 'European Union External Action Service Strategy for Security and Development in the Sahel'... *op. cit.* note 260, p. 4.

262 See Council Conclusions on the Sahel Regional Action Plan 2015-2020. Doc 7823/15, 20/4/2015, p. 10.

263 See European Commission- Fact Sheet 'Description of the new measures adopted to tackle the root causes of irregular migration and displaced persons in the Sahel region and Lake Chad Basin, 18/4/2016. On http://europa.eu/rapid/press-release_MEMO-16-1426_en.htm.

ditions of people by combating poverty. In Niger, the EU intends to launch a pilot project on setting up joint investigations teams to fight against irregular migration, smuggling and trafficking. The project has been identified in the Valletta Action Plan and intends to improve the ability of Nigerien Police to fight against irregular migration, trafficking, smuggling and document fraud whilst protecting victims from criminal organisations and enhancing the effectiveness of borders' management.

The Valletta Action Plan was launched in 2015 and aimed to focus on sixteen priorities.[264] The Action Plan will focus on the benefit of migration and on the fight against irregular migration, smuggling and trafficking by identifying the root causes for irregular migration. For the purpose of development and eradication of poverty, the EU will cooperate with African countries and with the AU to strengthen migration strategies at national and regional level by taking into consideration individual countries characteristics. In order to eradicate poverty, the EU and Africa will conduct an analysis on the root-causes of irregular migration and forced displacement. The EU will also focus on boosting socio-economic development by increasing economic opportunities and by creating jobs for women and youth. The EU will address instability and crises by preventing new conflicts and new forms of radicalization in Sahel, Lake Chad, Horn of Africa and North Africa. The EU will support the establishment of the rule of law and good governance.

Legal migration and mobility will be supported and promoted through bilateral cooperation agreement as the Mobility Partnerships and the Common Agendas on Migration and Mobility. Migration and Mobility will also be supported by continental, regional, sub-regional frameworks such as the Joint Labour Migration Programmes adopted by the AU in 2015 and other initiatives adopted by ECOWAS and IGAD.[265] The fight against smuggling and trafficking will be supported by implementing the UNCTOC Protocols against these two crimes and by implementing the 2014 Protocol to the Forced Labour Convention. The Valletta Summit highlights the importance of cooperating against irregular migration, smuggling and trafficking by improving information exchange between the EU and African countries. The EU supports police

264 See Valletta Summit on Migration, 11-12 November 2015. On http://www.consilium.europa.eu/en/meetings/international-summit/2015/11/action_plan_en_pdf/, accessed on 18/11/2016.

265 Ibid. For the work of ECOWAS and IGAD, see respectively http://www.ecowas.int/ and https://igad.int/.

and judicial cooperation and the establishment of Joint Investigation Teams between countries affected by smuggling and trafficking. The EU also promotes police cooperation to investigate smuggling and trafficking with the support of Interpol and other EU agencies, especially Europol. Police and judicial cooperation through mutual legal assistance against smuggling and trafficking is also promoted by the Valletta Action Plan.

The EU is committed to fight against smuggling and trafficking by global actions which include the identification of root causes of irregular migration, socio-economic development in origin and transit countries and police and judicial cooperation between countries where smuggling and trafficking are perpetrated by criminal organisations. In the Valletta Summit, the EU and African countries also agreed an agenda on return policies and admission agreements. For this purpose, the EU and African countries aim to strengthen cooperation between each other in order to return nationals of third countries to their places of origin by ensuring that Article 13 of the Cotonou Agreement is fully complied.[266] The Cotonou Agreement states that ACP/EU countries agree that they

> 'shall accept the return of and readmission of the readmission and return of their nationals any of its nationals who are illegally present on These agreements shall also cover, if deemed the territory of an ACP State, at that State's necessary by any of the Parties, arrangements request and without further formalities'.[267]

Sudan: The EU has launched cooperation with Sudan to address the root causes of migration and for this purpose has announced a 100 million euros development package.[268] Sudan also benefits from additional funding under the EU Emergency trust Fund for Africa.[269] The major beneficiaries of these funds will be refugees, displaced people, returnees and local communities hosting them.[270]

266 See Partnership Agreement between the members of the African, Caribbean and Pacific Group of States of the one part, and the European Community and its Member States, of the other part, signed in Cotonou on 23 June 2000. On OJ L 317/3, 15/12/2000.

267 See Article 13 (c) (i) of the Cotonou Agreement.

268 See http://europa.eu/rapid/press-release_IP-16-1206_en.htm.

269 See http://ec.europa.eu/europeaid/regions/africa/eu-emergency-trust-fund-africa_en.

270 See http://ec.europa.eu/europeaid/countries/sudan_en.

7. CONCLUSIONS

The chapter examined the external scope of the EU in concluding agreements with EU countries of transit and origin of smuggled migrants. The chapter focused on these agreements because the EU has made a priority the identification of root causes of migration because in this way, the crime of people smuggling and human trafficking can be effectively defeated. The chapter explained the challenges that the EU can face in concluding international agreements with third countries with the aim to develop their economies to prevent irregular migration and with the aim to cooperate with police forces in order to fight against smuggling and trafficking. The main challenge is that human rights have different standards in third countries and for this reason it is important to give the EP the power to scrutinize the EU external action in order to ensure that international agreements maintain high standard in the respect of human rights. The high respect of human rights should be maintained by the EU and the EU should also monitor that third countries reform their law in order to ensure high respect of human rights. By doing this, international agreements will be more feasible.

At the moment the EU is reaching some agreements which have been analysed in this chapter. However, as it can be noted by previous chapters, the EU is more focused on short term actions such as the establishment of Sophia Operation. More efforts should be made in the identification of root causes of migration. In this way, smuggling of migrants could be defeated in the long term. However, long term initiatives require much time because the EU should be committed in improving the economic conditions of third countries and the EU should also cooperate with the AU and ECOWAS. The AU does not have the same scope and competence of the EU. Therefore, shorter solutions addressing smuggling and trafficking seem more feasible for the EU. However, short term initiatives could not resolve these issues for a prolonged time and if the EU does not make the necessary efforts to concentrate on long term initiatives, smuggling and trafficking will not be defeated because criminal organisations will always have people to smuggle. Indeed, people will look for them as they will not have alternatives to their poor conditions but emigrate and if regular routes will be closed by the EU and its Member States, people will emigrate irregularly.

Chapter 6: Conclusions

This book considered smuggling of migrants by sea and human trafficking as two crimes which although are different between each other, can overlap. For this reason the book proposed to fight against trafficking in human beings by targeting criminal organisations which commit the crime of smuggling. The book has shown that often migrants look for smugglers to leave their countries of origin in Africa to travel to Europe. However, during their journeys, smuggled people can become victims of human trafficking as the consent initially given did not include exploitation and therefore, smuggled migrants are forced to work as slave or to become prostitutes during their trips and when eventually reach the countries of destination.

The book proposed to fight against these two crimes by applying the law on legal migration, the prohibition of collective expulsion and the application of the European Convention on Human Rights. These legal instruments can permit not to return vulnerable migrants to their countries of origin where they risk to be targeted again by smugglers and traffickers.

The book gave particular attention to the identification of victims and potential victims of human trafficking and it argued that victims should be identified in between smuggled migrants by law enforcement authorities of countries of arrival. The book explained that identification at the moment is not being undertaken by competent authorities and this is the reason why trafficking in human beings is increasing. Many victims are returned to their countries of origin because of their unlawful migration status and it is not ascertained whether they are victims of human trafficking. Their unlawful immigration status poses an obstacle to their identification as victims. From one side, the case-law of the ECtHR states that law enforcement authorities have the legal obligation to identify and protect victims of human trafficking. Hence, law enforcement authorities shall not return irregular migrants without investigating whether they are victims of human trafficking. Returning irregular migrants without investigating whether they may be entitled to stay in the country of arrival would amount to collective expulsion which is prohibited by Article 4 Protocol 4 of the ECHR. From the other side, the CJEU ruled that that EU Member States, according to the EU Return Directive, have only the legal obligation to ascertain that the migrants does not have the right to stay on their territory. Once, it is proved that the migrant is not entitled to enter the territory of the Member State, competent authorities can return him or her to his or her country of origin or residence. There is a gap in the EU Return Directive as it does not refer to law on trafficking and it does not state that the competent authorities should ascertain whether the migrant is a victim of human trafficking. Certainly, this is established by the EU Trafficking Directive but all these legal instruments seem isolated because no reference is made in the EU Return Directive to EU legislation on human trafficking.

The book then gives particular attention to the fight against smuggling and trafficking by analysing short term and long term measures. It emphasises that short term measures cannot defeat the two crimes in the long term because long term solutions require that the root causes of migration are identified and adequately addressed. Therefore, the book states that the fight against smuggling and trafficking should be done by EU Member States with the support of EU agencies such as Europol and Eurojust. Investigations should be primarily of Member States' responsibility. Subsequently, external cooperation with third countries should be supported by EU agencies. The EU should promote economic and social development in countries where there is poverty to prevent people from leaving these countries. Indeed, improving economic conditions of countries of origin and residence of migrants, should be the priority for the EU as it can be a deterrent to irregular migration.

At the moment measures adopted by the EU appear fragmented because the EU is more concentrated on short term solutions and external agreements with countries facing the Mediterranean such as Libya. Conversely, the EU should take more initiatives in transit and origin countries to prevent that migrants leave them by trusting criminal organisation which may exploit them. Preventing people from leaving their countries of origin should be an effective way to fight against smuggling and trafficking. These initiatives should include cooperation with the AU and ECOWAS. However, cooperation should not have as aim to restrict migration further as initiatives as such, push people to look for smugglers when legal routes are closed. Cooperation should consist of supporting the AU and ECOWAS initiatives in promoting democracy, respecting human rights and tacking poverty in the African continent. Adopting common rules in the respect of human rights is important to establish cooperation against smuggling and trafficking by setting up JITs. The CJEU has ruled that bilateral agreements on extradition wit third countries can only be actioned if third countries prohibit torture, inhuman and degrading treatment and the death penalty. The same principles can be applied to all agreements on cooperation in the criminal area. Eurojust and Europol can give their support in investigations but this book argues that they should be accountable before the EP. The reason is because EU citizens should be informed on ay agreements which may have concerns related to human rights. The EP, on behalf of its citizens, should monitor human rights are respected at the highest standard. The EP should co-legislate with the Council in the CFSP to ensure that all initiatives of cooperation in the criminal area are fully respectful of human rights.

Unfortunately, the EP has only a marginal role in the CFSP, although some progress has been made as Europol is now accountable before the EP. However, no real efforts are being made to address root causes of migration to prevent irregular migration by the support of smugglers. It is desirable that the EU concentrates on long and effective term measures to fight against smuggling and trafficking.

BIBLIOGRAPHY

Achilli, L., *The smugglers: hero or felon?* Migration Policy Centre, European University Institute, June 2015. On http://cadmus.eui.eu/bitstream/handle/1814/36296/MPC_2015_10_PB.pdf?sequence=1.

http://www.achpr.org/

http://www.achpr.org/instruments/achpr/ratification/

http://www.achpr.org/instruments/achpr

http://www.achpr.org/instruments/charter-democracy/ratification

http://www.achpr.org/files/instruments/court-establishment/achpr_instr_proto_court_eng.pdf

http://www.africancourtcoalition.org/index.php?option=com_content&view=article&id=87:ratification-status-protocol-on-the-statute-of-the-african-court-of-justice-and-human-rights&catid=7:african-union&Itemid=12

http://www.african-court.org/en/images/documents/Court/Ratification_and_Deposit_of_the_Declaration.pdf to check the status of ratification of the Protocol on the Court

Anyangwe, C., 'Emerging African jurisprudence suggesting the desirability of the abolition of capital punishment'. In *African Journal of International and Comparative Law,* 2015, 23/1, pp. 1-28.

http://www.au.int/en/sites/default/files/PROTOCOL_STATUTE_AFRICAN_COURT_JUSTICE_AND_HUMAN_RIGHTS.pdf

Acosta Arcarazo, D., 'The Charter, detention and possible regularization of migrants in an irregular situation under the Return Directive: *Mahdi'.* On *Common Market Law Review* 52, 2015, pp. 1361-1378.

African (Banjul) Charter on Human and Peoples' Rights http://www.achpr.org/files/instruments/achpr/banjul_charter.pdf

African Charter on Democracy, Elections and Governance. On http://www.achpr.org/instruments/charter-democracy/

http://www.african-court.org/en/index.php/about-the-court/brief-history

http://www.african-court.org/en/images/documents/Court/Court%20Establishment/africancourt-humanrights.pdf both

Annison, R., *In the dock. Examining the UK's criminal Justice Response to Trafficking,* Anti-Trafficking Monitoring Group, June 2013.

http://www.ansa.it/sito/notizie/magazine/numeri/2014/10/10/africa-take-away_9037661f-41a5-4e68-9ebf-686a1486678c.html.

Article 20 of Directive 2011/36/EU on preventing and combating trafficking in human beings and protecting its victims {SWD (2016) 159 final}. COM (2016) 267 final, 19/5/2016.

Associazione per gli Studi Giuridici sull'Immigrazione (Asgi) http://www.asgi.it/wp-content/uploads/2015/06/proposte_ASGI-su-agenda-europea-migrazione.pdf, accessed on 21/7/2015.

http://au.int/en/member_states/countryprofiles

http://au.int/en/organs/cj

Basilien-Gainche, M.L., "The EU immigration and asylum policy in the post-Lisbon institutional context", in Rubini, L., and Robertson, D., (ed.), *The Treaty of Lisbon and the Future of European Law, London*, Edward Elgar Publishing, 2012, pp. 355-378.

Bett, A., 'Towards a 'Soft 'Law framework for the Protection of Vulnerable Irregular Migrants'. On *International Journal of Refugee Law*, (2010) 22/2, pp. 209-236.

Budapest Process'. ICMPD on https://www.icmpd.org/our-work/migration-dialogues/budapest-process/

Brachet, J., 'Manufacturing Smugglers: From Irregular to Clandestine Mobility in the Sahara'. On ANNALS, AAPSS, 676, March 2018, pp. 16-35.

Campana, P., 'Out of Africa: The organization of migrant smuggling across the Mediterranean'. On *European Journal of Criminology* 2017, pp. 1-22.

'Can Schengen be suspended because of Greece?. Should it be?'. On http://eulawanalysis.blogspot.co.uk/2015/12/can-schengen-be-suspended-because-of.html.

Case 26/62 *Van Gend & Loos v Netherlands Inland Revenue Administration* [1963] ECR 3-Court of Justice.

Case 6/64 *Costa v E.N.E.L.* [1964] ECR 1194-Court of Justice.

Case C-67/74 *Bonsignore*, ECLI:EU:C:1975:34.

Case 41/74 *Van Duyn* ECLI:EU:C:1974:133.

Case C-30/77 *Regina v. Bouchereau* ECLI:EU:C:1977:172.

Case C-138/79 *Roquette Freres v. Council*, EU:C:1980:249.

Case C-300/89 *Titanium Dioxide* EU:C:1991:244.

Case C-269/90 *Technische Universitat Munchen*, EU:C:1991:438.

Case C-44/94 *Fishermen's Organisations and Others* [1995] ECR I3115.

Case C-60/00 *Carpenter* [2002] ECR I-6279.

Case C-101/01 *Lindqvist* [2003] ECR I-12971.

Case C-109/01 *Akrich* [2003] ECR I-9607.

Cases C-482/01 and 493/01 *Orfanopoulos and Oliveri* ECLI:EU:C:2004:262

Joined Cases C87/03 and C100/03 *Spain* v *Council* [2006] ECR I2915.

Case C-105/03 *Criminal proceedings against Maria Pupino.* [2005] 2 ECR I-5285.

Case C-176/03 *Commission v. Council* ECR 2005, ECR I-7879.

Case C-178/03 *Commission v. Parliament and Council* [2006] ECR I-107.

Case C-408/03 *Commission v Belgium*, ECR 2006 I-2647.

Case C-540/03 *Parliament v. Council*, ECLI:EU:C:2006:429.

Case C-248/04 *Koninkijke Cooperate Cosun* [2006] ECR I-10211.

Joined Cases C-317/04 and C-318/04 *Parliament v. Council* ECR 2005 I-4721.

Case C-303/05 *Advocaten voor de Wereld VZW v. Leden van de Ministerraad* [2007] ECR I-3633.

Joined Cases C-402/05 P and C-415/05 P *Kadi and Al Barakaat International Foundation v. Council and Commission* [2008] ECR I-6351.

Case C-403/05 *Parliament v. Commission*, [2007] ECR I-9045.

Case C-440/05 *Commission v. Council* [2007] ECR I-9097.

Case C-50/06 *Commission v Netherlands* ECLI:EU:C:2007:325.

Case C-155/07 *Parliament v. Council* [2008] ECR I-8103.

Case C-349/07 *Sopropé* EU:C:2008:746.

Case C-578/08 *Chakroun*, ECR I-1839, 2010.

Case C-317/08 to C-320/08 *Alassini and Others*, EU:C:2010:146.

Case C-130/10, *Parliament v. Council* EU:C:2012:472.

Case C-482/10 *Cicala*, EU:C:2011:868.

Case C-508/10 *Commission v. Netherlands*, ECLI:EU:C:2012:243.

Case C-61/11 PPU, *El Dridi*, EU:C:2011:268 and case C C-329/11 *Achughbabian* EU:C:2011:807.

C-399/11 *Melloni* ECLI:EU:C:2013:107.

Case C-430/11 *Sagor* ECLI:EU:C:2012:777.

Case C-658/11, *Parliament v. Council* EU:C:2014:2025

Cases C-141/12 and C-372/12 *YS and Others*, EU:C:2014:2081.

Case C-129/13 *Kamino International Logistics* EU:C:2014:2041.

Case C-166/13 *Mukarubega*, EU:C:2014:2336.

Case C-249/13 *Boudjlida*, EU:C:2014:2431.

Case C-383/13 PPU, *G. and R.*, EU:C2013:533 and case C-418/11 *Texdata Software*, EU:C:2013:588.

Case C-579/13 *P and S*, ECLI:EU:C:2015:369.

Case C-263/14 *European Parliament and Commission v. Council* ECLI:EU:C:2016:435.

Case C-643/15, *Slovakia v. Council* ECLI:EU:C:2017:631.

Case C-647/15, *Hungary v. Council*, ECLI:EU:C:2017:618.

Case C-182/15 *Petruhhin* ECLI:EU:C:2016:630

Case C-191/16 *Pisciotti v. Bundesrepublik Deutschland* ECLI:EU:C:2018:222

Case No IT-96-23-T *Prosecutor v. Kunarac, Kovac and Vukovic*

Case No. 48/90 *Amnesty International v. Sudan*

Case No 204/97 *Associaiton of Victims of Post-Electoral Violence & Interights v. Cameroon*, 1999.

Case no 54/91 *Malawi African Association v. Mauritania;*

Case no. 61/91 *Amnesty International v. Mauritania;*

Case 98/93 *Ms Sarr Diop, Union Interafricaine des Droits de l'Homme and RADDHOM v. Mauritania;*

Case 164/97 to 196/97 *Collectife de Veuves et Ayants-droit v. Mauritania*

Case 210/98 *Association Mauritanienne des Droit de l'Homme v. Mauritania.*

Case No. 223/98 *Forum of Coscience v. Sierra Leone*, 2000.

Case No. 245/2002 *Zimbabwe Human Rights NGO Forum v. Zimbabwe.*

Case No. 279/03-296/05, *Sudan Human Rights Organisation & Centre on Housing and Evictions (COHRE) v. Sudan*

Case No. 223/98 *Forum of Coscience v. Sierra Leone*, 2000.

Case *Ahmut v. the Netherlands*, Application no. 21702/93, judgment of 28 November 1996.

Case *Chahal v. the United Kingdom*, Application no. *22414/93*, judgment of 15/11/1996.

Case *Chowdury and others. V. Greece*, Application no. 21884/15, judgement of 20 March 2017.

Case *Conka v. Belgium*, Application no. 51564/99, 5 February 2002.

Case *De Souza Ribeiro v. France*, judgement of 18 December 2012 Application no. 22689/07.

Jabari v. Turkey, Judgement of 11 July 2000, Application no. 40035/98.

Case *Gebremedhin [Gaberamadhien] v. France*, judgement of 26 April 2007, Application no. 25389/05.

Case *Gül v. Switzerland*, Application no. 23218/94, judgment of 19 February 1996.

Case *Hirsi Jamaa and Others v. Italy*, Application no. 27765/09, judgement of 23 February 2012.

Case *Khlaifia and others v. Italy*, judgement of 1/9/2015, Application no. 16483/12.

Case *Kudla v. Poland [GC]*, Application no. 30210/96, judgement of 20 October 2000.

Case *L.E. v.Greece*, Application no. 71545/12, Judgement of 21 January 2016.

Case *Moustaquim v. Belgium*, Application no. 12313/86, judgment of 18 February 1991.

Case *Pretty v. United Kingdom*, Application no. 2346/02, 29 April 2002.

Case *Rantsev v. Cyprus and Russia*, Application no. 25965/04, judgement of 7 January 2010.

Case *Sen v. the Netherlands*, Application no. 31465/96, judgement of 21 December 2001.

Case *Siliadin v. France*, Application no. 73316/01, judgement of 26 October 2010.

Case *Soering v. UK*, Application no. 14038/88, judgement of 7 July 1979.

Case *Tyrer v. United Kingdom*, Application no. 5856/72, judgement of 25 April 1978.

Case *X. v. Denmark*, Application no. 7011/75, judgement of 3 October 1975.

Cass. Sez. IV, sent n. 32924, 29/7/2004, Belforte rv. 229103.

Cass. Sez. V, sent. N. 4401, 21/10/1998, Assisi.

Cholewinski, R., 'Family Reunification and Conditions Placed on Family Members: Dismantling a Fundamental Right'. On *European Journal of Migration and Law* Vol 4, 2002, pp. 271-290.

Clark, N. (2013) Detecting and tackling forced labour in Europe on https://www.jrf.org.uk/sites/default/files/jrf/migrated/files/forced-labour-europe-full.pdf

https://www.coe.int/en/web/conventions/full-list/-/conventions/treaty/024/signatures?p_auth=nVbvak4Y

https://www.coe.int/en/web/conventions/full-list/-/conventions/treaty/086/signatures?p_auth=nVbvak4Y

https://www.coe.int/en/web/conventions/full-list/-/conventions/treaty/098/signatures?p_auth=nVbvak4Y

https://www.coe.int/en/web/conventions/full-list/-/conventions/treaty/209/signatures?p_auth=nVbvak4Y

https://www.coe.int/en/web/conventions/full-list/-/conventions/treaty/212/signatures?p_auth=nVbvak4Y

Commission Decision 2004/535/EC of 14 May 2004 on the adequate protection of personal data contained in the Passenger Name Record of air passengers transferred to the United States Bureau of Customs and Border Protection. OJ 2004 L 235/11.

Common Security and Defense Policy EU Operations Centre Horn of Africa & Sahel (EU OPCEN), June 2015. Available on http://eeas.europa.

eu/csdp/structures-instruments-agencies/eu-operations-centre/docs/factsheet_eu_opcen_23_06_2015.pdf

Communication concerning the taking up of activities of Europol. [1999] OJ C 185/1, 1/7/1999.

Communication from the Commission to the European Parliament, the Council, the European Economic and Social Committee and the Committee of the Regions On circular migration and mobility partnerships between the European Union and third countries COM(2007) 248 final, 16/5/2007.

Communication from the Commission to the European Parliament and the Council on guidance for better transposition and application of Directive 2004/38/EC on the right of citizens of the Union and their family members to move and reside freely within the territory of the Member States COM (2009) 313 final, 2/7/2009.

Communication from the Commission to the European Parliament, the Council, the European Economic and Social Committee and the Committee of the Regions. The Global Approach to Migration and Mobility {SEC (2011) 1353 final} COM (2011) 743 final, 18/11/2011.

Communication from the Commission to the European Parliament and the Council on the Task Force Mediterranean. COM (2013) 869 final, 4/12/2013.

Communication from the European Commission to the European parliament and the Council on guidance for application of Directive 2003/86/EC on the right to family reunification. COM (2014) 210 final, 3/4/2014.

Communication from the Commission to the Council and the European Parliament On the application of Directive 2004/81 on the residence permit issued to third-country nationals who are victims of trafficking in human beings or who have been the subject of an action to facilitate illegal immigration, who cooperate with the competent authorities. COM (2014) 635 final, 17/4/2014.

Communication from the Commission to the European Parliament and the Council on the application of Directive 2009/52/EC of 18 June 2009 providing for minimum standards on sanctions and measures against employers of illegally staying third country nationals COM (2014), 286, final, 22/5/2014.

Communication from the Commission to the European Parliament and the Council. 5th Annual Report on Immigration and Asylum (2013) {SWD (2014) 165 final}. COM (2014), 288 final, 22/5/2014.

Communication form the Commission to the European Parliament, the Council, the European Economic and Social Committee and the Committee of the Regions. A European Agenda on Migration. COM (2015) 240 final, 13/5/2015.

Communication from the Commission to the European Parliament, the Council, the European Economic and Social Committee and the Committee of the Regions. EU Action Plan against migrant smuggling

(2015-2020). COM (2015) 285 final, 27/5/2015.
Communication from the Commission to the European Parliament and the Council Progress Report on the Implementation of the hotspots in Greece COM (2015) 678 final, 15/12/2015.
Communication from the Commission to the European Parliament and the Council Progress Report on the Implementation of the hotspots in Italy. COM (2015) 679 final, 15/12/2015.
Communication from the Commission to the European Parliament and the Council on the State of Play of Implementation of the Priority Actions under the European Agenda on Migration COM (2016) 85 final, 10/2/2016.
Communication from the Commission to the European Parliament and the Council Reporting on the follow-up to the EU Strategy towards the Eradication of trafficking in human beings and identifying further concrete actions. COM (2017) 728 final, 4/12/2017.
Commission Staff Working Document. Mid-term report on the implementation of the EU strategy towards the eradication of trafficking in human beings. SWD (2014) 318 final, 17/10/2014. COM (2014) 635 final, 17/4/2014.
http://www.consilium.europa.eu/en/meetings/international-summit/2015/11/action_plan_en_pdf/
http://www.consilium.europa.eu/en/press/press-releases/2016/03/18-eu-turkey-statement/
Constitutive Act of the African Union adopted on 11/7/2000 available on http://au.int/en/sites/default/files/ConstitutiveAct_EN.pdf.
Convention for the Protection of Human Rights and Fundamental freedoms, securing certain rights and freedoms other than those already included in the Convention and in the first Protocol thereto as amended by protocol no. 11 on http://conventions.coe.int/Treaty/en/Treaties/Html/046.htm.
Council Act of 10 March 1995, adopted on the basis of Article K.3 of the Treaty on European Union, drawing up the Convention on simplified extradition procedure between the Member States of the European Union. On OJ C 78, 30/3/1995
Council Act of 27 September 1996, adopted on the basis of Article K.3 of the Treaty on European Union, drawing up the Convention relating to extradition between the Member States of the European Union. On OJ C 313, 23/6/1996
Council Conclusions on the Sahel Regional Action Plan 2015-2020. Doc 7823/15, 20/4/2015, p. 10.
European Commission- Fact Sheet 'Description of the new measures adopted to tackle the root causes of irregular migration and displaced persons in the Sahel region and Lake Chad Basin, 18/4/2016. On http://europa.eu/rapid/press-release_MEMO-16-1426_en.htm
Council and European Parliament Directive 2011/36/EU of 5 April, on OJ 101/1, 15/4/2011.
Council Conclusions on the Sahel Regional Action Plan 2015-2020. Doc 7823/15, 20/4/2015.

Council Decision of 27 March 2000 authorising the Director of Europol to enter into negotiations on agreements with Third States and non-EU-related bodies, OJ 2000, C 106.

Council Decision of 28 February 2002 setting up Eurojust with a view to reinforcing the fight against serious crime. On OJ L 63/1, 6/3/2002.

Council Decision 2004/496 of 17 May 2004 on the conclusion of an Agreement between the European Community and the United States of America on the processing and transfer of PNR data by Air Carriers to the United States Department of Homeland Security, Bureu of Customs and Border Protection. OJ 2004, L.183/83, 25/5/2004 and corrigendum at OJ 2005 L 255/168, 30/9/2005.

Council Decision of 24 July 2006, 2006/616/EC on OJ L 262/24, 22/9/2006.

Council Decision of 24 July 2006, 2006/617/EC on OJ L 262/34, 22/9/2006.

Council Decision of 24 July 2006, 2006/618/EC on OJ L 262/44, 22/9/2006.

Council Decision of 24 July 2006, 2006/619/EC on OJ L 262/51, 22/9/2006.

Council Decision 2009/371/JHA of 6 April 2009 establishing the European Police Office (Europol) on OJ L121/37, 15/5/2009.

Council Decision 2009/820/CFSP of 23 October 2009. On OJ L 291/40, 7/11/2009

Council Decision 2009/933/CFSP of 30 November 2009. On OJ 325/4, 11/12/2009.

Council Decision 2010/88/CFSP/JHA of 30 November 2009. On OJ L39/19, 12/02/2010.

Council Decision 2014/198/CFSP of 10 March 2014 on OJ L 108/1, 11/4/2014.

Council Decision (CFSP) 2015/778 on L 122/31, 19/5/2015.

Council Decision (EU) 2015/1523 of 14 September 2015. On OJ L239/146, 15/9/2015.

Council Decision (CFSP) 2015/778 of 18 May 2015. OJ L 122/31, 19/5/2015.

Council Decision (CFSP) 2015/972 of 22 June 2015. OJ L. 157/51, 23/6/2015.

Council Decision (CFSP) 2016/993 of 20 June 2016 amending Decision 2015/778 on a European Union Military Operation in the Southern Central Mediterranean (EUNAVFOR MED Operation Sophia). OJ L 162/18, 21 June 2016.

Council Decision (EU) 2015/1601 of 22 September 2015. OJ L 248/80, 24/9/2015.

Council Directive 2001/55/EC of 20 July 2001. On OJ L 212/12, 7/8/2001.

Council Directive 2002/90/EC of 28 November 2002. OJ L 328/17, 5/12/2002.

Council Directive 2003/86/EC of 22 September 2003 on the right to family reunification. OJ 251/12, 3/10/2003.

Council Directive 2003/109/EC of 25 November 2003. OJ L 16/44, 23/1/2004.

Council Directive 2003/109/EC of 25 November 2003. OJ L 16/44, 23/1/2004.

Council Directive 2004/81/EC of 29 April 2004. OJ L 261 p. 19, 6/8/2004.
Council Directive 2009/52/EC on OJ L 168, 30/6/2009.
Council Doc 11528/05, 2 September 2015.
Council Framework Decision 2002/465/JHA of 13 June 2002 on joint investigation teams, on L 162/1, 20/6/2002.
Council Framework Decision 2002/584/JHA on the European Arrest Warrant and the surrender procedures between Member States. On OJ L 190/1, 18/7/2002.
Council Framework Decision 2002/629/JHA of 19 July 2002. OJ L 203/1, 1/8/2002.
Council Framework Decision 2002/946/JHA of 28 November 2002. On OJ L 328/1, 3/12/2002.
Council Framework Decision 2009/299/JHA of 26 February 2009 amending Framework Decisions 2002/584/JHA, 2005/214/JHA, 2006/783/JHA, 2008/909/JHA and 2008/947/JHA, thereby enhancing the procedural rights of persons and fostering the application of the principle of mutual recognition to decisions rendered in the absence of the person concerned at the trial, OJ L 81/24, 27/3/2009.
Council Joint Action 2008/851/CFSP of 10 November 2008 on a European Union military operation to contribute to the deterrence, prevention and repression of acts of piracy and armed robbery off the Somali coast. On OJ L 301/33, 12/11/2008.
Council of European Union The Stockholm Programme-An open and secure Europe serving and protecting the citizens. Doc. 17024/09, 2/12/2009. On C/115/1, 4/5/2010.
Council of European Union ACP-EU Dialogue on Migration and Development, 11/5/2015, ACP-UE 2111/15. On http://data.consilium.europa.eu/doc/document/ST-2111-2015-INIT/en/pdf.
Council of Europe Convention on Action against Trafficking in Human Beings, 2005.
Council Regulation (ECC) No 443/92 of 25 February on financial and technical assistance to, and economic cooperation with, the developing countries in Asia and Latin America as amended by Council Regulation (EC) No 807/2003 of 14 April 2003. L 122/36, 16/5/2003.
Council Regulation (EC) No 2007/2004 of 26 October 2004 establishing a European Agency for the Management of Operational Cooperation at the External Borders of the Member States of the European Union. L 349/1, 25/11/2004.
Craggs. S., and Martens, R. "Rights, Residence, Rehabilitation: A Comparative Study Assessing Residence Options for Traffickers Persons. (2010). Available on http://publications.iom.int/system/files/pdf/iml24.pdf p.55 *at* 56.
'Criminalising solidarity-Cap Anamur trial underway. On http://www.statewatch.org/news/2007/apr/03italy-cape-anamur.htm
Crisp, J., 'Beyond the Nexus: UNHCR's evolving perspective on refugee protection and international migration'. Research paper no. 155, April, 2008.
De Bruycker, P., Di Bartolomeo, A., Fargues, P., 'Migrants smuggled by sea to the EU: facts, laws and policy

options'. Migration Policy Centre (MPC) Report 2013/09 on http://www.migrationpolicycentre.eu/docs/MPC-RR-2013-009.pdf.

Decision taken by Common Agreement between the Representatives of the Member States, meeting at Head of State or Government Level, of 13 December 2003, on the location of the seats of certain offices and agencies of the European Union. OJ L29/15, 3/2/2004.

Declaration of the Ministerial Conference of the Khartoum Process (EU-Horn of Africa Migration Route Initiative) Rome, 28th November 2014. On http://italia2014.eu/media/3785/declaration-of-the-ministerial-conference-of-the-khartoum-process.pdf.

Decreto di Fermo disposto dal P.M.-art 384 c.p.p. *Procura della Repubblica presso il Tribunale di Palermo, Direzione Distrettuale Antimafia*, 30/5/2014, p. 16 (Arrest warrant issued by the Prosecutor's Office at the Court of Palermo, District Antimafia Directorate). Document received by Public Prosecutor Dr Gery Ferrara by e mail on 23/3/2016.

Den Heijer, M., 'Reflections on Refoulement and Collective Expulsion in the Hirsi Case. On *International Journal of Refugee Law* 2013, 25/2, pp. 265-290.

Directive 95/46/EC OJ 1995 L 281/31 as amended by Regulation (EC) No 1882/2003 of 29 September 2003 adapting to Council Decision 1999/468/EC the provisions relating to committees which assist the Commission in the exercise of its implementing powers laid down in instruments subject to the procedure referred to in Article 251 of the EC Treaty. OJ L 284/1, 31/10/2003.

Directive 2008/115/EC of 16/12/2008. On OJ L 348/98, 24/12/2008. (Return Directive).

Directive 2009/50 EC of 29/5/2009, on OJ L 155, 18/6/2009.

Directive 2012/29/EU of 25 October 2012. On OJ L. 315/57, 14 November 2012.

Directive 2013/33/EU of 26 June 2013 (recast). On OJ L 180/96, 29/6/2013.

Doc 14300/15, 1/12/2015. On http://data.consilium.europa.eu/doc/document/ST-14300-2015-INIT/en/pdf

Doc 8366/16, 27/4/2016 available on http://www.consilium.europa.eu/register/en/content/out/?&typ=ENTRY&i=ADV&DOC_ID=ST-8366-2016-INIT and accessed by http://www.statewatch.org/news/2016/apr/eu-council-eu-turkey-standard-operating-procedures-resettlement-8366-16.pdf

Draft Council conclusions on migrants smuggling. Doc, 5481/1/16, 26/1/2016.

Draft Regulation of the European Parliament and of the Council on a European travel document for the return of illegally third-country nationals (first reading). Doc 10638/16, 28 June 2016.

Dwyer, P. Lewis, H., Scullion, L. and Waite, L. (2011) Forced labour and UK immigration policy: Status matters? On https://www.jrf.org.uk/file/41487/download?token=DsgZ8vrL.

https://eeas.europa.eu/diplomatic-network/sahel-region/4094/sahel-region_en

http://eeas.europa.eu/csdp/missions-and-operations/eubam-libya/pdf/factsheet_eubam_libya_en.pdf

http://ec.europa.eu/dgs/home-affairs/e-library/docs/thb-victims-identification/thb_identification_en.pdf
http://eeas.europa.eu/csdp/missions-and-operations/eubam-libya/index_en.htm.
http://ec.europa.eu/anti_fraud/documents/fwk-green-paper-corpus/corpus_juris_en.pdf
ECOWAS Commission Abuja Nigeria. On http://www.ecowas.int/wp-content/uploads/2015/01/Revised-treaty.pdf
http://ec.europa.eu/europeaid/regions/africa/eu-emergency-trust-fund-africa_en.
http://ec.europa.eu/europeaid/countries/sudan_en
http://www.ecowas.int/documentation/ecowas-commission-annuel-report/
http://www.ecowas.int/about-ecowas/basic-information/
http://www.ecowas.int/
http://www.ecowas.int/ecowas-law/treaties/
E mail interview undertaken with Dr Ferrara on 8/4/2016
'EU/Egypt Action Plan' on http://eeas.europa.eu/enp/pdf/pdf/action_plans/egypt_enp_ap_final_en.pdf
'EU Names Anti-Human-Smuggling Mission 'Operation Sophia'. 28/9/2015 available on http://www.wsj.com/articles/eu-names-anti-human-smuggling-mission-operation-sophia-1443471234
EUNAVFOR MED-Operation Sophia. Six Monthly Report: June, 22nd to December 31st 2015. On https://wikileaks.org/eu-military refugees/EEAS/EEAS-2016-126.pdf
https://www.europol.europa.eu/about-europol/european-migrant-smuggling-centre-emsc
http://www.eurojust.europa.eu/doclibrary/Eurojust-framework/agreements/Agreement%20between%20Eurojust%20and%20Europol%20(2010)/Eurojust-Europol-2010-01-01-EN.pdf
http://eurojust.europa.eu/doclibrary/Eurojust-framework/agreements/Memorandum%20of%20Understanding%20between%20Eurojust%20and%20Frontex%20%282013%29/Frontex-Eurojust-2013-12-18_EN.pdf
http://europa.eu/rapid/press-release_IP-16-1206_en.htm.
http://europa.eu/rapid/press-release_IP-16-1444_en.htm
'Europe migrant crisis: doubt cast on identity of 'smuggler' extradited to Italy. On http://www.bbc.co.uk/news/world-europe-36488655
European Commission, DG Migration & Home Affairs 'A Study on Smuggling of Migrants. Characteristics, responses and cooperation with third countries', p. 20, September 2015. Available on http://eucpn.org/sites/default/files/content/download/files/49a._a_study_on_smuggling_of_migrants_characteristics_responses_and_cooperation_with_third_countries_emn_-_full_report.pdf.
European Commission EMN Inform 'Inform on Migrants' Movements through the Mediterranean'. On http://ec.europa.eu/dgs/home-affairs/what-we-do/networks/european_migration_network/reports/docs/emn-informs/emn_policybrief_movementsmediterranean_final.pdf.

European Commission- Fact Sheet 'Description of the new measures adopted to tackle the root causes of irregular migration and displaced persons in the Sahel region and Lake Chad Basin, 18/4/2016. On http://europa.eu/rapid/press-release_MEMO-16-1426_en.htm

European Commission, Member States' Support to Emergency Relocation Mechanism (Communicated as on 9 June 2016), available on http://ec.europa.eu/dgs/home-affairs/what-we-do/policies/european-agenda-migration/press-material/docs/state_of_play_-_relocation_en.pdf.

European Union Committee, 'Operation Sophia, the EU's naval mission in the Mediterranean: an impossible challenge' (14th Report, Session 2015-16, HL Paper 144).

European Union Committee 'Operation Sophia: a failed mission'. (2nd Report, Session 2017-19, HL Paper 5).

'European Union External Action Service Strategy for Security and Development in the Sahel', available on https://eeas.europa.eu/sites/eeas/files/strategy_for_security_and_development_in_the_sahel_en_0.pdf

'European Union External Action Service Strategy for Security and Development in the Sahel', available on https://eeas.europa.eu/sites/eeas/files/strategy_for_security_and_development_in_the_sahel_en_0.pdf

European Union Naval Force-Mediterranean Operation Sophia, Update: 12/2/2016, on http://www.eeas.europa.eu/csdp/missions-and-operations/eunavfor-med/pdf/factsheet_eunavfor_med_en.pdf

Europol Situation Report: Trafficking in human beings in the EU, February 2016, p. 16. Available on https://www.europol.europa.eu/content/trafficking-human-beings-eu, accessed on 8/7/2016.

Eurostat Statistical Working Papers 'Trafficking in Human Beings', 2014 available on http://epp.eurostat.ec.europa.eu/cache/ITY_OFFPUB/KS-TC-14-008/EN/KS-TC-14-008-EN.PDF

Fargues, P., 'Is what we hear about migration really true?'. 2014, available on http://cadmus.eui.eu/bitstream/handle/1814/31731/MPC_2014_FARGUES.pdf?sequence=1.

Fargues, P., and Bonfanti, S.,2014 'When the best option is a leaky boat: why migrants risk their life crossing the Mediterranean and what Europe is doing about it'. European University Institute, Migration policy Centre. Available at http://cadmus.eui.eu/bitstream/handle/1814/33271/MPC_PB_2014-05.pdf?sequence=1.

Fijnaut, C., and Groenhuijsen, M.S., *A European Public Prosecutor: comments on the Green Paper.* P. 10. Available at http://ec.europa.eu/anti_fraud/documents/fwk-green-paper-contributions/gp_fijnaut_nl_en.pdf

Follow-up report on the Green paper on the criminal-law protection of the financial interests of the Community and the establishment of a European Prosecutor. COM (2003) 128 final, 19/3/2003.

Forced Labour in the United Kingdom. On https://www.jrf.org.uk/report/forced-labour-united-kingdom.

Framework Decision 2001/220/JHA. OJ L 82/1, 22 March 2001.

FRAN Quarterly. Quarter 2, April-June 2017 available on http://frontex.europa.eu/assets/Publications/Risk_Analysis/FRAN_Q2_2017.pdf.

http://www.unhcr.org/539809e10.html

Frontex Annual Risk Analysis 2013 available at http://frontex.europa.eu/assets/Publications/Risk_Analysis/Annual_Risk_Analysis_2013.pdf accessed on 1/7/2014.

Frontex Annual Risk Analysis 2014 available at http://frontex.europa.eu/assets/Publications/Risk_Analysis/Annual_Risk_Analysis_2014.pdf.

Frontex Annual Report Quarter 1. January-March 2015, available on http://frontex.europa.eu/assets/Publications/Risk_Analysis/FRAN_Q1_2015.pdf

Frontex Risk Analysis Quarter 2. April-June 2015. On http://frontex.europa.eu/assets/Publications/Risk_Analysis/FRAN_Q2_2015_final.pdf

Frontex Risk Analysis Quarter 3. July September 2015. On http://frontex.europa.eu/assets/Publications/Risk_Analysis/FRAN_Q3_2015.pdf

See Frontex Risk Analysis Quarter 4. October-December 2015, p. 10. On http://frontex.europa.eu/assets/Publications/Risk_Analysis/FRAN_Q4_2015.pdf

Frontex Risk Analysis for 2016, (March 2016). On https://frontex.europa.eu/assets/Publications/Risk_Analysis/Annula_Risk_Analysis_2016.pdf.

Frontex Risk Analysis for 2017, February 2017 on https://frontex.europa.eu/assets/Publications/Risk_Analysis/Annual_Risk_Analysis_2017.pdf

Frontex Risk Analysis for 2018, p. 35. On https://frontex.europa.eu/assets/Publications/Risk_Analysis/Risk_Analysis/Risk_Analysis_for_2018.pdf

Galos, E., Bartolini, L., Cook, H., and Grant, N., *Migrant Vulnerability to Human Trafficking and Exploitation: Evidence from the Central and Eastern Mediterranean Migration Routes.* International Organization for Migration (IOM).

General Assembly Resolution 55/25 of 15 November 2000. Available on https://www.unodc.org/documents/treaties/UNTOC/Publications/TOC%20Convention/TOCebook-e.pdf.

5th General report on GRETA's Activities covering period 1 October 2014 to 31 December 2015, p. 31. Available on https://rm.coe.int/CoERMPublicCommonSearchServices/DisplayDCTMContent?documentId=090000168063093c.

Global Action against Trafficking in Persons and the Smuggling of Migrants (2015-2019) on https://www.unodc.org/unodc/en/human-trafficking/glo_act.html.

Giuffre', M., 'State Responsibility Beyond Borders: What legal basis for Italy's Push-Back to Libya?' On *International Journal of Refugee Law*, 2012 24/4, pp. 692-734.

Green paper on the criminal-law protection of the financial interests of the Community and the establishment of a European Prosecutor. COM (2001) 715 final, 11/12/2001.

Green Paper on the right to family reunification of third-country nationals living in the European Union (Directive 2003/86/EC), COM (2011) 735 final, 15/11.2011.

GRETA's Report on Spain, GRETA (2103), 27 September 2013, p. 31. Available on https://rm.coe.int/CoERMPublicCommonSearchServices/ DisplayDCTMContent?documentId=090000168063c3dc.

Groenendijk, K., and Peers, S., 'Can Member States seize asylum seekers' assets?'. On http://eulawanalysis.blogspot.co.uk/2016/01/can-member-states-seize-asylum-seekers.html.

http://www.bbc.co.uk/news/world-europe-35425735, accessed on 29/1/2016.

Handling of Cap Anamur asylum claims was flawed, says UNHCR. On http://www.unhcr.org/4101252e4.html.

Hartmann, J., and Tan, N.F, 'The Danish Law on Seizing Asylum Seekers' Assets'. On http://www.ejiltalk.org/the-danish-law-on-seizing-asylum-seekers-assets/#more-13995.

Herlin-Karnel, E., 'From mutual trust to the full effectiveness of EU law: 10 years of the European arrest warrant'. On *European Law Review* 2013, 38 /1, pp. 79-91.

House of Commons Foreign Affairs Committee 'Libya: Examination of intervention and collapse and the UK's future policy options'. 3rd Report Session 2016-17, HC 119.

House of Lords Select Committee on European Communities, Ninth Report, *Prosecuting Fraud on the Communities' Finances-The Corpus Juris*, 18/5/1999.

House of Lords European Union Committee *The EU's Global Approach to Migration and Mobility* (8th report, Session 2012-13, HL Paper 91).

House of Lords European Union Committee 'EU action plan against migrant smuggling' 4th Report of Session 2015-16 HL Paper 46.

'How are the war in Syria and the Refugee Crisis affecting Human Trafficking?' *International Centre for Migration Policy Development* on http://www.icmpd.org/news-centre/news-detail/news-detail/new_research_how_are_the_war_in_syria_and_the_refugee_crisis_affecting_human_trafficking/

'Human Rights on the Southern Border'. Editing APDHA Immigration Section, April 2015.

Istanbul Ministerial Declaration on a Silk Routes Partnership for Migration. Available on https://www.icmpd.org/fileadmin/ICMPD-Website/Budapest_Process/November_2013_Update/Istanbul_Ministerial_Declaration_Silk_Routes_Partnership_EN.pdf.

http://www.icmpd.org/news-centre/news-detail/news-detail/new_research_how_are_the_war_in_syria_and_the_refugee_crisis_affecting_human_trafficking/.

https://igad.int/

Ineli-Ciger, M., 'The Missing Piece in the European Agenda on Migration: the Temporary Protection Directive'. On http://eulawanalysis.blogspot.co.uk/2015/07/the-missing-piece-in-european-agenda-on.html.

International Organization for Migration and People Smuggling on http://www.iom.int/jahia/webdav/shared/shared/mainsite/activities/ibm/10-IOM-IBM-FACT-

SHEET-People-smuggling.pdf.

http://www.interpol.int/Crime-areas/Trafficking-in-human-beings/People-smuggling.

Ippolito, F., La 'Tragedia' delle Frontiere Europee. *European Papers,* European Forum, 9/5/2016 p. 3 available on www.europeanpapers.eu.

http://www.ipu.org/idd-E/afr_charter.pdf

International Organization for Migration and People Smuggling available at http://www.iom.int/jahia/webdav/shared/shared/mainsite/activities/ibm/10-IOM-IBM-FACT-SHEET-People-smuggling.pdf.

Issue Paper: A short introduction to migrant smuggling, 2010. On https://www.unodc.org/documents/human-trafficking/Migrant-Smuggling/Issue-Papers/Issue_Paper_-_A_short_introduction_to_migrant_smuggling.pdf

Issue paper: Smuggling of Migrants by Sea', 2011. Available on http://www.unodc.org/documents/human-trafficking/Migrant-Smuggling/Issue-Papers/Issue_Paper_-_Smuggling_of_Migrants_by_Sea.pdf.

Joint Communication to the European Parliament, the European Council and the Council on Migration on the Central Mediterranean route. Managing flows, saving lives. JOIN (2017) 4 final, 25/1/2017.

Landry, R., 'Decriminalising 'Humanitarian Smuggling'. Refugee Studies Centre Research Brief, March 2017, p. 4. On https://www.rsc.ox.ac.uk/publications/research-in-brief-decriminalising-humanitarian-smuggling

"Libya: European governments complicit in horrific abuse of refugees and migrants". 2017. On https://www.amnesty.org/en/latest/news/2017/12/libya-european-governments-complicit-in-horrific-abuse-of-refugees-and-migrants/

Manrique, M., G, Barna J., Pekka Hakala, P., Rey, B., Claros, E., Mediterranean Flows into Europe: Migration and the EU's Foreign Policy, March 2014, p. 4. Available on http://www.europarl.europa.eu/RegData/etudes/briefing_note/join/2014/522330/EXPO-JOIN_SP(2014)522330_EN.pdf accessed on 1/7/2014.

Mercone, I., 'Some notes the relations between UNSC Resolution 2240 (2015) fighting smugglers in Mediterranean and EUNAVFOR Med "Sophia" Operation. On http://free-group.eu/2015/10/19/some-notes-on-the-relations-between-unsc-resolution-2240-2015-fighting-smugglers-in-mediterranean-and-the-eunavfor-med-sophia-operation/

Migrant Vulnerability to Human Trafficking and Exploitation: Evidence from the Central and Eastern Mediterranean Migration Routes. International Organization for Migration 15/3/2017, on https://publications.iom.int/system/files/pdf/migrant_vulnerability_to_human_trafficking_and_exploitation.pdf.

2nd Ministerial Conference of the Prague Process Action Plan 2012-2016' on https://www.pragueprocess.eu/en/documents/category/3-programme-key-documents

http://missingmigrants.iom.int/region/mediterranean.

Mitsilegas, V., 'The Limits of Mutual Trust in Europe's Area of Freedom, Security and Justice: From Automatic Inter-State Cooperation to the Slow

Emergence of the Individual'. On *Yearbook of European Law,* Vol. 31/1, 2012, pp. 319-372.

P8_TA(2016)0300), 13/6/2016 on http://www.europarl.europa.eu/sides/getDoc.do?pubRef=-//EP//NONSGML+TA+P8-TA-2016-0300+0+DOC+PDF+V0//EN

Partnership Agreement between the members of the African, Caribbean and Pacific Group of States of the one part, and the European Community and its Member States, of the other part, signed in Cotonou on 23 June 2000. On OJ L 317/3, 15/12/2000.

http://www.peaceau.org/en/page/27-au-border-programme-aubp

Peers, S., 'Governance and the Third Pillar: The Accountability of Europol'. In Deidre, M., Curtin and Ramsen A. Wessels, *Good Governance and the European Union,* Intersentia, 2005, pp. 253-276.

Peers, S., N. Rogers *EU Immigration and Asylum Law: Text and Commentary.* Martinus Nijhoff, 2006.

Peers, S. EU Justice and Home Affairs Law OUP 2012.

Peers, S., 'The CJEU ensures basic democratic and judicial accountability of the EU's foreign policy'. On http://eulawanalysis.blogspot.co.uk/2014/06/the-cjeu-ensures-basic-democratic-and.html

Peers, S., 'Irregular Migrants: Can human treatment be balanced against efficient removal?' On *European Journal of Migration and Law* 2015, pp. 289-304.

Peers, S., 'Temporary Protection'. On Peers, S., Moreno-Lax, V., Garlick, M., and Guild, E., *EU Immigration and Asylum Law (Text and Commentary): Second Revised Edition,* Volume 3 EU Asylum Law, 2015, pp. 571-598.

Peers, S., "New rules on maritime surveillance: will they stop the deaths and push-backs in the Mediterranean?". On http://eulawanalysis.blogspot.be/2014/06/new-eu-rules-on-maritime-surveillance.html

Peers, S., *EU Justice and Home Affairs Law. Volume II: EU Criminal Law, Policing and Civil law* 2016, OUP.

Perez Cepeda A.I., & Benito Sanchez, D.,*Trafficking in Human Beings. A Comparative Study of the International Legal Documents.* 2014 Europa Law Publishing.

Piotrowicz, R., (2012) "States' Obligations under Human Rights towards Victims of Trafficking in Human Beings: Positive Developments in Positive Obligations'. In *International Journal of Refugee Law,* Vol. 24/2, pp. 181-201.

The Protocol on the Court of Justice of the African Union can be accessed by this website: http://www.au.int/en/sites/default/files/PROTOCOL_COURT_OF_JUSTICE_OF_THE_AFRICAN_UNION.pdf

The Protocol on the Pan-African Parliament can be found on this website http://www.au.int/en/sites/default/files/PROTOCOL_TREATY_ESTABLISHING_THE_AFRICAN_ECONOMIC_COMMUNITY_RELATING_PAN_AFRICAN_PARLIAMENT.pdf

2008 Protocol on the Statute of the African Court of Justice and Human Rights. On https://au.int/en/treaties/protocol-statute-african-court-justice-and-human-rights

Protocol to the African Charter on Human and Peoples' Rights on the Establishment of an African Court on human and Peoples' Rights. On http://www.achpr.org/instruments/court-establishment/

Protocol to Prevent, Suppress and Punish trafficking in Persons, Especially Women and Children, supplementing the United Nations Convention against Transnational Organized Crime. A/RES/55/25, 8.1.2001. Document A/55/383. See Council of Europe Convention on Action against Trafficking in Human Beings, http://conventions.coe.int/Treaty/EN/Treaties/Html/197.htm.

'Rabat Process'. International Centre for Migration Policy Development (ICMPD) on https://www.icmpd.org/our-work/migration-dialogues/rabat-process/

Regulation (EC) No 863/2007 of the European Parliament and of the Council of 11 July 2007 establishing a mechanism for the creation of Rapid Border Intervention Teams and amending Council Regulation (EC) 2007/2004 as regards that mechanism and regulating the tasks and powers of guest officers. L 199/30, 31/7/2007.

Regulation (EU) No 1052/2013 of the European Council and of the Council of 22 October 2013 establishing the European Border Surveillance System (Eurosur). L 295/11, 6/11/2013.

Regulation (EU) no 656/2014 of the European Parliament and the Council of 15 May 2014 establishing rules for the surveillance of the external sea borders in the context of operational cooperation coordinated by the European Agency for the Management of Operational Cooperation at the External Borders of the Member States of the European Union, L 189/93, 27/6/2014.

Regulation (EU) 2016/794 of the European Parliament and of the Council of 11 May 2016 on the European Union Agency for Law Enforcement Cooperation (Europol) and replacing and repealing Council Decisions 2009/371/JHA, 2009/934/JHA, 2009/935/JHA, 2009/936/JHA and 2009/968/JHA. OJ L135/53, 24/5/2016.

Regulation (EU) 2016/1624 of the European Parliament and the Council of 14 September 2016 on the European Border and Coast Guard and amending Regulation (EU) 2016/399 of the European Parliament and of the Council and repealing Regulation (EC) No 863/2007 of the European Parliament and of the Council, Council Regulation (EC) No 2007/2004 and Council Decision 2005/267/EC. OJ L 251/1, 16/9/2016.

http://register.consilium.europa.eu/doc/srv?l=EN&f=ST%2012095%202013%20INIT

Remarks by High Representative/Vice-President Federica Mogherini following the informal meeting of the EU Foreign Ministers, Gymnich, 5/9/2015, available on http://eeas.europa.eu/statements-eeas/2015/150905_01_en.htm.

Report from the Commission to the European Parliament and the Council on the Application of Directive 2003/86/EC on the Right to Family Reunification. COM (2008) 610 final 8/10/2008.

Report from the Commission to the European Parliament and the

Council. Report on the progress made in the fight against trafficking in human beings (2016) as required under Article 20 of Directive 2011/36/EU on preventing and combating trafficking in human beings and protecting its victims {SWD(2016) 159 final} COM (2016) 267 final, 19/5/2016.

Report concerning the implementation of the Council of Europe Convention on Action against Trafficking in Human Beings by Ireland, 26 Sept 2013, GRETA (2013)15. Available on https://rm.coe.int/CoERMPublicCommonSearchServices/DisplayDCTMContent?documentId= 0900001680631cbe.

Report concerning the implementation of the Council of Europe Convention on Action against Trafficking in Human Beings by Sweden, 27 May 2014, GRETA (2014)11. Available on https://rm.coe.int/ CoERMPublicCommonSearchServices/ DisplayDCTMContent? documentId= 090000168063c456.

Reslow, N., ' The Role of Third Countries in EU Migration Policy: The Mobility Partnership'. In *European Journal of Migration and Law*, 14, 2012, pp. 393-415.

Rijken, C., 'Legal and Technical Aspects of Co-operation between Europol, Third States, and Interpol. In *The European Union and the International Legal Order: Discord or Harmony?* Asser Press, 2001, pp. 577-603.

Rules of procedure for evaluating implementation of the Council of Europe Convention on Action against Trafficking in Human Beings by the parties. THB-GRETA (2014)52, November 2014. Available on https://rm.coe.int/CoERMPublicCommonSearchServices/DisplayDCTMContent?documentId= 09000016805a983c.

https://rm.coe.int/CoERMPublicCommonSearchServices/ DisplayDCTMContent? documentId =090000168063c456.

Schengen Border Code, Regulation (EC) No 562/2006 of the European Parliament and of the Council of 15/3/2006. OJ L 105/1, 13/4/2006.

'Smuggled futures: the dangerous path of a migrant from Africa to Europe'. On http://www.globalinitiative.net/smuggled-futures.

'Smuggling of Migrants: the harsh search for a better life'. On http://www.unodc.org/toc/en/crimes/migrant-smuggling.html.

Statement of UNODC Executive Director Yury Fedotov on Italian criminal investigation known as "Glauco 1". On https://www.unodc.org/unodc/en/press/releases/2016/February/statement-of-unodc-executive-director-yury-fedotov-on-italian-criminal-investigation-known-as-glauco-1.html.

Stoyanova, V., 'Complementary Protection for Victims of Human Trafficking under the European Convention on Human Rights'. On *Goettingen Journal of International Law*, 3 (2011) 2, p. 778-817.

Stoyanova, V., 'Victims of Human Trafficking. A Legal Analysis of the Guarantees for 'Vulnerable Persons' under the Second Phase of EU Asylum Legislation'. In *Seeking Asylum in the European Union: Selected Protection Issued Raised by the Second Phase of the Common*

European Asylum System. Martinus Nijhoff Publishers, 2015.

Stoyanova, V., (2017) *Human Trafficking and Slavery Reconsidered* (Cambridge University Press).

Triandafyllidou, A., 'Migrant Smuggling: Novel Insights and Implications for Migration Control Policies' ANNALS, AAPSS, 676, March 2018, Vol. 676, pp. 212-221.

Triandafyllidou, A., and Maroukis, T., *Migrant Smuggling. Irregular Migration from Asia and Africa to Europe,* Palgrave Macmillian, 2012.

Tinti, P., and Reitano, T., *Migrant Refugee Smuggler Saviour.* OUP 2017.

Turkey: EU risks complicity in violations as refugees and asylum seekers locked up and deported. On https://www.amnesty.org/en/latest/news/2015/12/turkey-eu-refugees-detention-deportation/.

Umbriano, P., 'Is it a crime to help people to survive (Cap Anamur and other cases)'. 2013. On http://www.eldh.eu/fileadmin/user_upload/ejdm/publications/2013/Pierluigi_Umbriano_-_Speech.pdf.

'UNHCR: 6 steps towards solving the refugee situation in Europe' 2016. on http://www.unhcr.org/news/briefing/2016/3/56d96de86/unhcr-6-steps-towards-solving-refugee-situation-europe.html.

'UNHCR steps up efforts towards alternatives to detention in Libya and solutions for vulnerable refugees'. 2017. On https://unsmil.unmissions.org/unhcr-steps-efforts-towards-alternatives-detention-libya-and-solutions-vulnerable-refugees

UN High Commissioner for Refugees (UNHCR), UNHCR Note on DNA Testing to Establish Family Relationships in the Refugee Context, June 2008, available at http://www.refworld.org/docid/48620c2d2.html.

https://www.unodc.org/unodc/en/human-trafficking/index.html?ref=menuside

http://www.un.org/en/development/desa/population/publications/pdf/policy/InternationalMigrationPolicies2013/Report%20PDFs/k_Ch_5.pdf.

United Nations Department of Economic and Social Affairs "International Migration Policies: Government Views and Priorities" available on

United Nations Convention against Transnational Organized Crime and the Protocols thereto. Adopted by General Assembly resolution 55/25 of 15 November 2000.

United Nations Security Council Resolution 2240/2015, 9 October 2015.

Valletta Summit on Migration, 11-12 November 2015. On http://www.consilium.europa.eu/en/meetings/international-summit/2015/11/action_plan_en_pdf

Ventrella, M. 'Protecting victims of trafficking in human beings in the UK. The Italian 'Rimini Method' that could influence the British approach'. (2007) 3/2. *The Journal of Migration and Refugee Issues* pages 64-86.

Ventrella, M., *The control of people smuggling and trafficking in the EU: Experiences from the UK and Italy* Routledge, 2010.

Ventrella, M., 'European integration or democracy disintegration in measures concerning police and judicial cooperation?' *New Journal of European Criminal Law* Vol 4. Issue 3, 2013 pp. 290-309.

Ventrella, M., Recognising Effective Legal Protection to People Smuggled at Sea, by Reviewing the EU Legal Framework on Human Trafficking and Solidarity between Member States. *Social Inclusion* Vol 3, 1, 2015, pp. 76-87.

'Vulnerable lives on hold. Refugees are hardly surviving the mass camps in the Athens region'. 2016. On https://www.proasyl.de/wp-content/uploads/2015/12/2016-05-24-Vulnerable-lives-on-Hold-final.pdf

Webber, F., ''Hotspots' for asylum applications: some things we urgently need to know'. On http://eulawanalysis.blogspot.co.uk/2015/09/hotspots-for-asylum-applications-some.html.

Zhang, S.X., Sanchez, G. E., Achilli, L., 'Crimes of Solidarity in Mobility: Alternative Views on Migrant Smuggling'. ANNALS, AAPSS, 676, March 2018, Vol. 676, pp. 6-15.

Zwiers, M., *The European Public Prosecutor's Office* 2011, Intersentia.

www.ingramcontent.com/pod-product-compliance
Lightning Source LLC
LaVergne TN
LVHW052315200926
848481LV00002B/569